THE ROLLERCOASTER TO FORGIVENESS

A Mother's Journey Through

Abuse, Survival, Faith, and Healing

RAQUEL PEREZ

The Rollercoaster to Forgiveness
A Mother's Journey Through Abuse, Survival, Faith, and Healing
by Raquel Perez

For quantity discounts, please contact: Raquel.Perez.Author@gmail.com

ISBN:
Paperback: 979-8-234-01982-0
Hardcover: 979-8-234-02772-6

Editing: A. Thomas Kozubal and Alan Rowland

Illustration: Indra Audipriatna

YOUR GIFT FROM RAQUEL

I am grateful for your company through these pages.
In parting, I offer this gift for the travels that await you.
Please access and enjoy your bookmarks with the QR code below.

DEDICATION

I dedicate these pages to the person still seeking a way out, sharing the raw truth of my own past so you can find the strength to persevere and the courage to begin your journey toward a brighter future.

CONTENTS

Dedication v
From the Author ix
Introduction xix

Chapter 1: One Summer Day 1
Chapter 2: Love Turns Into a Nightmare 9
Chapter 3: Affair and Alone 21
Chapter 4: Beaten and Left for Dead 35
Chapter 5: Second Chance 59
Chapter 6: Friendship 103
Chapter 7: Broken Heart 151
Chapter 8: The Unexpected 175
Chapter 9: Work-Life Balance 187
Chapter 10: The Tide Is Turning 195
Chapter 11: Celebration 205
If You Turn the Page... 211
Chapter 12: Forgiveness 213

References 217
About the Author 221
Let's Connect 223

FROM THE AUTHOR

This book tells my life story, a tale of troubled relationships that included abuse. It tells my journey to forgiveness with God's help.

This memoir was written to give you a glimpse of our lives. During the hard times, we continued to push through. I was a victim of abuse as a teenager. Looking back, it feels like it all happened to the person I used to be. Thankfully, I am no longer a helpless victim. God has renewed me.

You'll see the trauma I experienced and how I was able to see my way through to recovery. If you see some similarities in your situation, you'll know how to survive and get out. If you have already been through an abusive relationship, know that you can recover. Whatever stage you are in, there is something you can do. If you're in the beginning, you can recognize it for what it is, if you're in the middle, you can seek help. If you're at the deep end, you can recover. Whatever stage you find yourself in, keep the faith and seek help.

My purpose in writing is to heal and make others aware of situations like mine. I hope my experience resonates with others who are going through similar situations. I want others to know that they are not alone.

My life experience has taught me that sometimes we want to be with someone for all the wrong reasons, and it's okay. In time, you are able to see that your decision has consequences that impact your mind, body, soul, and spirit. When that happens, you need to get out.

God healed me and showed me my worth. Writing this book has opened my eyes to my failures, strengths, weaknesses, courage, resilience, vulnerability, perseverance, and so much more. I'm so grateful that I was able to share my life with you.

When surviving trauma, it takes time to heal. Life isn't a walk in the park. These memories are forever imprinted. Wounds take time to heal. You'll get through it. There is no set time for the healing to begin or end. Surround yourself with people who promote healing in your life. Look toward a brighter future.

After much reflection, I listed some life lessons I learned along the way. They are in no particular order, but you will find them throughout the chapters as you read the book.

- Put God first.
- We are God's masterpiece.
- You can achieve your goals, but you must create a plan to succeed.
- Trust the process. It's not easy, but don't give up. You've got this.
- In the end, you're only proving it to yourself—not to others.
- Even when you create a plan, things may not go as expected.
- Create short-term and long-term goals. Review them often and revise your course when necessary. Nothing is set in stone; just focus on accomplishing the goal.
- Create a plan and work the plan. No matter how much you stumble, you'll succeed if you push through.
- School, work, and home life can be demanding, but you'll get through it. Create a daily plan of attack.
- If working out is your passion, go for it. Do not let anyone keep you from being physically healthy.
- If you have a goal, create a plan to complete it. There will be obstacles, but one step at a time will lead you to the finish line.
- Time flies quickly. Remember to enjoy the journey. It might not be what you planned, but it will work out. Let go and let God.
- Remember, change is constant. Whether good or bad, try to go with the flow. It gets better.
- Dreams really do come true.
- Never stop living. There is always a new beginning.
- When opportunities present themselves, take a chance. Life is too short to wait.
- If you ever get the chance to volunteer, try it. Giving back is rewarding.
- Go against the grind.
- Lean on family and friends. They will be there if you ask.

- Take a leap of faith when meeting someone new. The opportunity to enjoy a friendship with that specific individual might not come again. Have fun and enjoy the moment.
- Communication is the key to understanding one another.
- Take the time to spend with friends you enjoy hanging out with.
- True friendships bloom when you least expect it. Be open to new friends.
- Separation anxiety from your children is very real. Lean on family and friends to keep you busy.
- Kids, especially teenagers, can be challenging. If you need a different perspective, ask family and friends, or research and read a book to help with decision-making.
- Family is very important, but it doesn't have to be biological. It can be a close friend who, over time, becomes your family.
- Remember, true friends have your back.
- Making daily family decisions isn't easy. Trust yourself. If you've thought it through, consult with supportive friends or family; with their input and your own, you'll make the decision that best fits your family and move forward.
- I am so grateful for the support of my family and friends. When you need them, they truly step up.
- It's okay to cry when you're experiencing joy. Crying helps release stress.
- It's okay to ask for help.
- Report abuse. If the people you report it to do not listen, tell someone else until someone hears and helps you.
- No matter how rough life is, don't give up on yourself. Seek help.
- Your knowledge will help develop your child for the future.
- If you're having problems connecting with your kids, research and find an activity or conversation that can help you move past it.
- In the mist of sadness or turbulence in your life, do something for yourself. Find your passion: volunteer, paint, sing, dance, and more. Do something to help yourself break out of the funk that has you stuck.
- I should have told someone the first day he hit me. Please, confide in someone.

- Co-parenting can be simple sometimes, but in most cases, it isn't. Try to ignore it when the other parent throws tantrums during an adult conversation.
- Being a parent is beautiful and emotional, but it is not a walk in the park. The journey can be colorful (thrilling) and gray (uncertain). A parent's responsibility to see their children through this journey is tough but doable. Embrace the journey.
- Family is sometimes annoying, but they love and care for you. It truly takes a village to raise a family.
- Make memories with your family; the kids grow up quickly. Don't forget to treat yourself and your family, as we all deserve some pampering.
- Remember that the relationships you enter into impact your family. When family meddles in your relationship, try not to get so upset. Listen to them; they may see something in your current relationship that concerns them. They care about you. You don't have to act on their concerns, but "chew" on their words. They may be right or wrong, but it never hurts to hear them out. At the end of the day, you make your own decisions.
- When Mom gives you advice or a recommendation, remember she is looking in from the outside. She is just watching out for you and the family. Listen, even if you don't agree. She could be right; mothers have a unique take on life.
- Try to create memories and traditions that bond your family. When you take steps to complete your goals, find your "why." What motivates you to accomplish the goal? How will your goal impact the future for you and your family?
- Read as often as you can. I have read over 20 books, but life is not always what I read in a book.
- Sometimes a great guy may come along and be ready to sweep you off your feet. Remember, it's okay to decline if you haven't healed from a previous relationship. You can ask him to wait until you heal. Don't force a relationship upon yourself or your kids; sometimes you meet people and it just isn't the right time.

- Kids will challenge a parent's decisions or conversations. It's okay for them to question and challenge us; these are critical skills they will need in the real world. My twins certainly challenged me.
- Educate yourself by reading, returning to school, and listening to advice or podcasts. Knowledge is power. For me, it was always better to have too much information on a topic than none at all.
- There is a lot of pressure in raising children. We aren't perfect, so just do the best you can.
- Simple joys, like a child's handmade cards or gifts, have always brought me happiness and melted my heart.
- If your kids try to prank you, go with the flow and try to flip the prank back on them! However, teach them never to play pranks that scare someone or put their safety in jeopardy.
- Crucial conversations with your kids are vital to their learning. They may not like the talk at the time, but they'll thank you for it later.
- As kids grow, their needs change. They are dependent as infants, but as teenagers, they crave independence. Create new ways to engage with them through activities they enjoy. Remember that one day you'll have to let go so they can begin their own journeys and leave their own imprints on the world.
- Children are true blessings.
- Relationships are complicated. Sometimes you think you know someone, only to realize you truly don't. Always remember: a failed relationship does not define you.
- No one is perfect; we all have our flaws. Even so, go into a relationship with your arms and heart wide open. If it doesn't work out, let go and eventually try again.
- Create boundaries and discuss them with your partner. Respect is essential. Once boundaries are agreed upon, they are already in place whenever you need to utilize them.
- Love vs. Lust: Sometimes what we think is love is actually lust. Once the "clouds" clear, you will see that person for who they truly are. We often ignore signs right in front of us, even when they aren't pretty. To me, a relationship means becoming vulnerable to love in hopes of a blessed future.

- Open your home to those in need. Pay it forward so they can eventually do the same for others.
- The Rope Analogy: Relationships have a bond similar to a rope, with many strands intertwined. The unity of two people is strong, and sometimes that bond remains intact for a lifetime. Other times, if the rope isn't cared for, it can fray. Sometimes, you just have to cut the rope and move on.
- There are good men in the world. Just because one man did you wrong doesn't mean you should blame them all.
- Communication is truly the key to understanding others.
- Be open to experiencing life. You only live once; you might just enjoy it. You'll never know unless you try.
- In life, you sometimes have to accept what was and what you cannot change.
- In life, we have unexpected experiences. It will be hard, but just take one small step forward each day. This too shall pass.
- The passing of a loved one overwhelms you with grief. This road is difficult. Sometimes you have to do your own heavy lifting. One step at a time and one day at a time.
- In life, we will face difficulties, but we need to push through them.
- In life, we make mistakes. We have to learn from them and try not to repeat them.
- There comes a point in your life where you have to put yourself first.
- Remember: people are in your life for a lifetime or only a season.
- Try not to make your life harder by focusing on the drama around you. Focus on yourself first. Once you're okay, you'll be able to lend a hand to others.
- When life gets the best of you, get back up and take one small step forward.
- Refocus your actions and emotions on what matters most.
- It's not always your fault.
- Be accountable for your decisions.
- Sometimes we are too young to understand what is going on.

- People may say mean things about you, but that is not who you are.
- Stop worrying about what other people think of you.
- As a mom, it looked like I had it all together on the outside, but truthfully, I was a hot mess.
- When you least expect it, you'll meet the people you need to lift your spirit.
- Even when you're scared, tell someone if you're being abused. It's not a time to be ashamed.
- Decisions are tough, but they have to be made to change our lives.
- Be thankful for the small wins.
- Unconditional Love.
- Love yourself.
- Don't give up on love.
- When you find love, hang on to it. If it's not love, let it go. Love is blind.
- Seek advice from those you love and trust.
- Open your heart to love again.
- Just because—compliment the kids and show them love.
- I love my twins with all my heart and soul, but sometimes they make it difficult to simply get up in the mornings. You have to find a win for all of you.
- If your kids ask, allow them to join sports, band, or activities that stimulate their agility and mind.
- Love hits you unexpectedly. You'll know when it comes; it will be electric and the chemistry indescribable. Love doesn't always show up, so enjoy the moment.
- You are beautiful inside and out.
- Don't forget to laugh.
- Sometimes in the midst of chaos, you get small breaks that include so much laughter. This keeps you going.
- Laughter is infectious. Do it as often as you can.
- Step out of your shell. It's fun to try something new.

- Have fun! Live life! The stress will always be there; you just have to try to shake it off when you can.
- Enjoy the journey and have fun doing it.
- Find a hobby that releases stress and brings you joy.
- Celebrations don't always have to be large parties. The most intimate gatherings can have the same impact, as long as you have the most important people in your life to celebrate with.
- Don't give up on your dreams. Push through. Life gets in the way, but you've got this. Keep grinding until the day you can celebrate completing your goals.
- When you accomplish your goals, celebrate by giving back to yourself. Only you know what you want. If it took a few months, gift yourself something small. If the goal took years, then go big. Take some time to reflect on your journey.
- When you receive great news, celebrate! No matter what you are going through, take the win. You've worked hard and deserve to celebrate your accomplishments.
- Have hope.
- You can't change what has happened; you just have to look forward to a better tomorrow. The struggle is real!
- I truly believe that when one door closes, another opens.
- Trust in the journey.
- Trust your instincts.
- Allow people to be themselves. If they want to be extra kind, let them. Even though we may not trust anyone at a given point in time, we all deserve to be treated with kindness and respect.
- Honesty is the best policy, but it is not always easy.
- Be honest with yourself and others.
- If you're at a crossroads with a decision, call someone you trust—someone who will be honest and tell you what you may not want to hear.
- When your kids become preteens, be open and honest about what their bodies will be experiencing. Being a teenager isn't easy, and they are already experiencing complex everyday interactions. When their bodies

and feelings begin to change, knowing this is just a phase will help them understand what puberty entails.

- Have patience. It's tough to be patient, but sometimes it is best.
- In your journey, there will always be questions you can't answer. Have patience; the answers will come.
- Don't forget to breathe.
- It's okay to be angry, but don't hurt anyone in the process.
- In your darkest hours, don't give up. Try to push through.
- Don't be apprehensive about seeking assistance from the government. It is only temporary.
- Don't blame yourself for someone else's actions.
- Don't live in denial. Denial leads to cover-ups.
- Don't forget to take care of yourself first. My mom taught me that: if you don't take care of yourself, you won't be well enough to care for others. The rewards of self-care include a sense of peace, relaxation, feeling lighter, less stress, and more energy.
- Surviving day to day isn't a walk in the park.
- Healing takes time.
- Forgiveness isn't easy. It's okay to be angry, but remember that forgiving someone is for yourself. To me, forgiveness is the first step toward healing. Time truly heals-I am a testament to that.

What is the purpose of a woman? This is a question I asked myself as I wrote this. This is a snapshot of what I learned by reading and asking others. I learned so many life skills: greater empathy, life lessons, various viewpoints, and an understanding of the purpose of a woman through many different authors.

As women, we should inspire hope, love, support, patience, gentleness, goodness, and self-control. We should find peace, celebrate life, live for today, and be doers, givers, and people who forgive, trust, and respect. We should strive to be healthy, prosperous, joyful, thankful, blessed, confident, positive, and hardworking.

Be fearless, be courageous, and show up. Know that I am worthy, beautiful, and happy. Have a pure heart, rebuke anxiety, and rebuke fear. Be resilient, persevere, and stay motivated, grateful, reliable, educated, and so much more.

INTRODUCTION

May 27, 2010

As I sit here at work, tears roll down my face. My heart is hurting, and I can't stop the pain. "God, please come and hold me. I hate these moments." I want to be the best parent, yet every time my son acts up, I blame myself. I know it's wrong, but I tell myself it is because I worked two jobs while going to school. Still, he continues to act out. I make excuses for him, even though I know his actions are his own. He is seventeen years old and knows right from wrong. Why do the tears keep falling?

This sadness will pass and my tears will dry, but for now, they keep falling. I continue to type. My colleagues ask, "What is wrong?"

"Nothing," I reply.

They know me as a "happy-go-lucky" person, and most of the time, I am. But then there are these days we must endure as parents. God strengthens, directs, and protects us. It is an honor to parent my twins, and I thank God every day for my breath and theirs. God continues to bless us and move us closer to the Holy Spirit. My twins, who are now in their junior year of high school, believe in God. They are a true miracle.

The tears have stopped now, and my heart feels lighter.

Wow. The first lines of this book just came flowing out, but things happen for a reason. Today was the day to begin healing my heart. I guess I should start at the beginning, so you can get the complete picture of where I am now.

CHAPTER 1

ONE SUMMER DAY

It was the summer of 1986. I was so excited to finally be a freshman in high school! I was looking forward to joining the marching band and meeting new friends. My instrument of choice was the clarinet. I truly loved marching band and was actually pretty good at music. Besides the sporting events I watched on TV with my father, I was never really into them. My sisters were active in sports; one played baseball and the other played basketball. My half-siblings graduated many years ago.

My dad was a carpenter and a blueprint reader for an engineer. My mother was a stay-at-home mom and cared for us. I had five sisters and one brother; I loved my family. Through the good and the bad, we had each other. My dad allowed Mom to have one job for a year, but she had to quit after that year. I also called my dad "Papito". He knew that he couldn't say "no" when I called him that. Dad did great carpentry work for others, but he never finished his home projects. My mom would get upset when he would try to fix things around the house, like the plumbing, the vehicle, or electrical work. Because he never finished things, it would cost my parents more to have projects cleaned up and the work redone by someone else. I remember a time when he was trying to fix the car door because the latch on the inside was getting stuck. My mom mentioned to Dad that she would be calling someone later that day to take a look at it. Dad would grab a beer and try to assess the work. After a few hours, Mom would go outside to see what he was doing, only to find that Dad had pulled out the car door handle and door panel, and had removed the screws. All that was left intact was the shell of the door and the window. My mom was so upset. He would tell her, "Never say that I didn't try to fix stuff". He'd grab his beer, turn around, and walk away. I loved them both so much. Since this was the summer before my freshman year, I wanted to have fun. I was always pretty shy, but I hoped to be more outgoing. Being from a small town, I was lucky to have my best friends live next door to me. Amber was my age and Margo was one year younger than I was. They were both little rebels. I was obedient to my parents and did as I was told. My mom was pretty lenient and trusted me. Their moms were strict with them.

I grew up in a small town in southeastern Texas. At the end of one side of our block, there was a family-owned convenience store. We lived closer to the other side of the block, which was near the Little League baseball fields. We could hear the crowds cheer and smell the popcorn from home. Of course, they had the best pickles and nachos. We also lived near a small park that had a public swimming pool. It was only two blocks away, which was within walking distance. Our parents trusted us to go since they knew the managers who ran the facility. If they wanted us home, they could call the front desk at the recreation facility. The lifeguards would call out our names and let us know we had a call. How embarrassing was that? All your friends knew your parents were calling. It comes with the territory of living in a small town. On Friday and Saturday evenings, you could rent out the recreation facility for private parties. Those were always fun because there were really no rules we had to follow.

During the week, when you entered the facility, you were greeted by a lifeguard and would pay for your admission to the pool. You had the option to rent a locker for your belongings or leave them on the picnic tables. On the left was the ladies' locker room, and to the right was the men's. Each locker room had bathrooms and showers. My friends and I would sometimes arrive dressed in our swimwear or wait to change on-site. If we were already dressed, we would walk directly from the entrance to the pool and leave our belongings on the picnic tables. These were covered areas located on the left and right sides of the grounds.

The pool was L-shaped, and there were three lifeguard stands. Just beyond the double doors was the first stand, located near the shallow end of the pool. This section was always packed with kids yelling, jumping, and running around. The second lifeguard stand was on the left side of the pool, where the water was between five and eight feet deep. The third stand was directly on the opposite side of the entrance; that was where the diving boards were, also known as the deep end of the pool.

CHAPTER 1: ONE SUMMER DAY

On this beautiful sunny day, my life would be changed forever. Summer was coming to an end, and this was the last week for the public swimming pool to be open. Amber and I decided to go one last time. After arriving, we changed in the locker room. As we walked out to the pool, we noticed two nice-looking boys. It was a small town, yet we didn't recognize them. We kept swimming near them, glancing their way while they glanced back at us. We were so giddy, flirting from across the pool. The boys were great swimmers; showing off a bit, they kept diving off the high dive. My best friend begged me to go and ask for one of the boys' names, but I was so shy. She said "you have to go for me, please". She took a liking to him. I was so embarrassed. How could I approach a complete stranger? Amber made it seem so simple but she wouldn't go.

"Just go ask him for his name and tell him I like him," she said.

I replied, "If it's so simple, then you go."

She kept begging me. After a while, I got up the nerve to approach the handsome guy. He had light brown hair, green eyes, and fair skin.

"Hi," I said.

He smiled and said, "Hi."

"My name is Reyna and that's Amber," I said, pointing to her. "She wanted me to come and tell you that she thinks you're hot. She also wanted to know your name."

He replied, "My name is Steven, but I prefer Steve. Where are you from? I am new in town."

I begged him to go and talk to her. "She will be crushed if you don't. Amber would hate me forever."

He hesitated at first, but I continued to beg. I was freaking out. He eventually agreed. "I will be there in a few," he said. I jumped back in the pool. Amber asked, "What took you so long? Give me all the details." I started telling her everything. Steve smiled at us while walking to the diving board. After jumping a few times, he swam toward us. He brought his friend, who was also very hot. Steve introduced his friend Matthew to Amber and me. Matthew had dark, straight, shoulder-length brown hair and brown eyes. He had several moles on his face, but they looked perfect. He also had a beautiful smile. Steve looked at Amber and started up a conversation.

That left Matthew and me alone together. I am extremely nervous and shy when it comes to guys. He asked if I came to the pool often. I replied, "Yes." He mentioned that he was in town visiting his sister and that he lived in another small town with his family. After a while, we looked toward Steve and Amber. They were hugging, kissing, and making out. WOW! That was quick. I turned to Matthew and shook my head "no." That meant don't even try to do that to me. We hung out for the rest of the afternoon. When the pool was closing, we started saying our goodbyes. Steve and Amber locked lips like it was the last time they would ever see each other. It was hilarious.

Steve's parents picked him up while Amber and I walked home. Matthew's sister came to pick him up, but he opted to walk us home instead. That was very unexpected; I was super excited. Amber walked beside us, going on and on about Steve. Matthew took my hand and we locked our fingers tightly. From time to time, Amber would turn to us and say, "Kiss her already!" I responded, "I'm okay." We arrived at the front of my house, and Amber passed us to go next door to hers. He asked if he could call or see me again. "Of course, we can keep in touch," I replied. He memorized my number. We didn't have air conditioning at my house, and we had three windows looking directly into our living room. My dad yelled, "Come inside!" I was so embarrassed. We locked eyes, let go of our hands, and said goodbye.

I strolled into the house, and my dad asked, "Who the heck was that boy?" He then walked to the bedroom where my mom was watching her telenovelas. Telenovelas are a type of limited-run television drama originally produced in Latin America. My mom watched them Monday through Friday from 5:00 p.m. to 10:00 p.m., and she did not like to be disturbed during her stories. My dad told her that some guy had walked me home and that she needed to keep an eye on me; I was fourteen, and he was very protective.

"What dad isn't?" my mom asked. "Who was that boy? You know how your father feels about you hanging out with boys," she said.

I replied, "Just someone I met at the pool. I know, Mom."

She turned back toward the TV and told me to go shower and get ready for bed.

I skipped to my room, feeling super excited, with butterflies in my stomach. I couldn't believe I had met a guy from another town! He was tall and handsome, with several moles on his face. His hair was black, cut short on the sides with a longer style on top. I loved when he ran his fingers through it and let the wind blow it back; it was like a scene from a music video. Did I mention he was a triplet? He was the oldest of the three. So many random questions started playing in my head: "Will he call me? If so, when? Will I ever see him again? Was I too shy? Should I have kissed him? Did I play it too safe?" I ran to the mirror and looked at my hair. "He is definitely never going to call me. Look at these curls!"

My best friend and I got together the next day to chat about the boys we met. Steve and Amber spoke all night on the phone and scheduled their next outing together, but I hadn't heard from Matthew at all. Every time the phone rang, I would run to answer, but my sisters always beat me to it. They laughed because I kept running to a phone that wasn't for me, so eventually, I stopped running.

Then, I heard the phone ring again. I was in my bedroom when my sisters yelled, "Reyna, you have a phone call!" Finally, he had called. My sisters stayed in the living room being nosy, of course. We had a mirror next to the phone, so I checked my hair before picking up to say hello. My sisters started laughing and making fun of me.

"He can't see you! Why are you fixing your hair?" they asked.

I just shrugged my shoulders. I was so excited he called, but I told myself to stay cool. I took a deep breath. He apologized for not calling sooner, explaining he had been with his family. I felt a sigh of relief. We made small talk while my sisters sat through the entire conversation.

"You're our baby sister, and we want to make sure this guy isn't going to take advantage of you," they said.

We spoke for about an hour. We didn't even say much; we just listened to each other breathe. When he asked to see me again, I wanted to jump for joy, but I remembered my audience and promised myself I would play it cool. He was coming back to town in a few days, and we spoke every day that week. Eventually, I had to work up the nerve to ask my parents if he could come over on Saturday. I did extra chores for my mom and dad, but they both suspected something was up because I kept pacing the hallway and passing their room.

"What do you want? You are annoying us," my mom said.

"Well, remember the boy I met this past weekend..." I started to respond.

My dad replied, "What about that shithead?"

"Can he come over this weekend to visit me?" I asked.

Immediately my dad responded, "NO!"

I begged my mom and got down on my knees. She kept shaking her head "no." It took a few hours until my mom agreed to let him visit, saying, "He can only come for one hour, and he has to be here by 8:00 am."

"I'll take it," I said to myself.

Matthew and I spoke on the phone every day. My mom or one of my sisters had to sit next to me while I was on the phone. It was super annoying. I hardly slept the day before he came over. It was Saturday morning, and I woke up very early to make sure I looked my best. My mom always slept in on weekends, but today she and my dad were up by 6:30 am.

Matthew's mom dropped him off on time. He looked so handsome. I couldn't believe he was actually here. As he walked toward the door, I became extremely nervous and excited. Matthew knocked. My dad opened the door and walked right past him. He didn't say one word. Mom was right behind my dad, and I was behind my mom. Matthew introduced himself to my mother. Mom shook his hand and said, "You have one hour, then you have to leave."

What an awkward moment. I came from behind my mom and said hi. We sat on the first step of the porch. My dad made himself comfortable outside, sitting on a chair just 12 feet away from us. We had a screen door, and my mom put a chair next to the door to watch us. Mom said, "I can see you both. Be sure to keep your distance from each other." I was so embarrassed. I apologized to Matthew. My mom interrupted me, "This is our house, and we can sit wherever we want." Matthew didn't bat an eye. I know I was blushing. We tried not to think of my parents being there, but it was very difficult.

Matthew and I started chatting. There were several times during our conversation that my mom interrupted and responded on my behalf. We made the best of our time together. Ten minutes before the hour was up, my mom reminded him that his visit was coming to an end.

"Where is your mom?" she asked Matthew.

Matthew responded, "She went to church and will be back for me."

My mom replied, "If she doesn't get here in ten minutes, you will have to wait outside the fence."

I wanted to hide under a rock. He would definitely never be back. My parents were never rude, but they were so overprotective. Why were they trying to ruin my life? My mom startled us by yelling, "Time's up. You need to go." We both got up really quickly. So did my dad. I was going to give him a hug, but my mom's hand went between us. She was like a ninja boy-blocker. Matthew stepped back and said, "It was nice to meet you, Mr. and Mrs. Mireles. I will call you, Reyna." His mom was five minutes late, so he had to wait outside our fence. He didn't mind; he just stood there and waited until his mom arrived.

I was extremely embarrassed, but I was also very happy to have spent time with him. My parents made sure I came inside the house. I thanked them both for allowing him to come visit, but they just ignored me. I walked to my room and jumped on my bed to relax. My mom started making breakfast and yelled my name from the kitchen. I hopped out of bed. My mom gave me a list of chores to do. "There is no resting; you have plenty to do today," she said. I smiled and started with the chores. You could see me grinning from ear to ear while I cleaned.

Matthew called that afternoon. My dad told him I was busy and hung up, even though I was sitting right next to him watching TV. What! I wasn't busy. I just played it cool and relaxed; I didn't want my dad to think that I was all into him. He called again before dinner. My dad answered, said, "She's eating," and hung up again. Matthew never even had a chance to say goodbye. My sisters looked at me and laughed.

I thought to myself, "Matthew is never calling me again. I can guarantee it. Why would he? They have been rude all day." We weren't able to chat that evening, but the next morning, he called before noon. Dad had left on an errand, so my older sister answered the phone. I was sitting in the living room with her, and the moment she looked at me, I knew it was him. When he asked to speak to me, she responded, "Let me check if she's here." She started yelling, "Chavala, you here?" 'Chavala' in English means 'little girl.' As I walked up to her, she kept yelling even louder, "Chavala, you here? Ohhhh, you're here." Then she said, "It's a chavalo," which means 'male kid.'

I grabbed the phone and she stayed right next to me. "I am not going anywhere," she said. "Dad and mom said we have to listen to all your calls with the chavalo. I do not want to get into trouble." She smiled and just looked at me. What could I say? I tried to ignore her like I did my parents, but like my mother had, she too started responding for me. Matthew was so patient; he didn't mind.

Weeks passed and we spoke on the phone almost every day. My parents allowed him to continue visiting me every weekend, though it was still very awkward. Dad still sat twelve feet away from us, and my mom still watched us through the screen door. Nothing changed for a year. There were plenty of hours when Matthew and I said nothing to each other; we just looked at my parents or smiled at one another.

There were a few weekends that Matthew was unable to visit. I was sad and missed him dearly. He would be upset because his mom wouldn't bring him to see me, so Matthew decided one day to ride his bicycle fourteen miles just to see me. Since it took him most of the day to arrive, we would only have maybe an hour of time to spend together. His mom felt that he was spending too much time with me, but he did not care what she thought. Rain or shine, he would ride his bike to see me. My mom agreed with his mom that he was around too much. My parents were never lenient with us and remained pretty strict when it came to him.

We did not agree with our parents. All we wanted was to spend time together. I was falling for him, and he felt the same way about me.

CHAPTER 2

LOVE TURNS INTO A NIGHTMARE

My freshman year was a blur. I was on "cloud nine" all the time. I started my first job during the fall of that year, working part-time at McDonald's. I also joined the marching band. I spent all my weekdays at band practice; I was basically a geek who loved playing the clarinet. I had been playing since the sixth grade. High school football games were so much fun because I was able to be with my friends and perform during halftime. I loved performing, especially when we didn't make any mistakes. That made all of the practice worth it. Our band director was passionate and always wanted us to have fun; he motivated us to do our best, both on and off the field.

Matthew came to the majority of the games. When he did, we spent a few minutes together after the performance. We would do things like walk to the concession stand to grab a couple of snacks before I had to head back to the stands. When the game was over, the band would get on the bus and head back to our high school. From there, my mom or dad would pick me up, or I'd get a ride home with Amber. Matthew was not able to come by the house after football games because it was past our curfew.

Matthew was my first love. I never dreamed that I would be so lucky to have met such a hot, respectful, soft-spoken, confident, and caring listener who was also a sincere, understanding, and smart guy. He was head over heels for me. I hoped that one day my parents would trust me enough to allow us to go on a real date, as sitting on the porch every weekend was just not cutting it for us.

When Matthew came to visit, my parents would sometimes leave us alone together because Mom had to cook, clean, or do laundry, and Dad would go inside to watch sports. Matthew would look at me and make my heart melt. He would then hold me and passionately kiss me. It gave me goosebumps and took my breath away. We'd sit on the porch for hours and chat about our families and how much we loved them. I still couldn't believe he was a triplet.

Matthew's mom worked in the print shop at my high school. Matthew enjoyed writing letters, and every day I'd go pick up the daily letters he'd written the night before. During or between classes, I would write back. Before the end of the day, I'd go by his mom's office and drop off the note. She was so nice to me. Sometimes I was unable to respond because I had too many projects or ran out of time. In the evening during our phone calls, Matthew would express that he was unhappy that I hadn't responded. Even though I'd try to explain why I didn't have a chance, I could hear the disappointment in his voice. Still, we spoke daily and visited almost every weekend.

One day, I was walking to class when someone whispered my name. The voice sounded familiar. I looked behind a pillar, and there was Matthew. I was completely taken aback; he had come to school with his mother to check on me.

He said to me, "Surprise. I wanted to check out your school and walk you to your classes."

I was happy about this, but I thought it was kind of weird that he skipped school to walk me to class. He did that several times throughout the year. One weekend, we had a serious conversation and Matthew expressed how he felt about me. We had been seeing each other for several months.

He said to me, "I love you."

I thought to myself, "Was I hearing things? He loves me. This hot guy loves me." Having him say those words to me melted my heart. I was in love.

"I love you too," I responded.

I felt like I was floating. Love, love, love, love…

As you already know, I was the youngest of six children. My parents were a bit strict when it came to boys. They allowed me to go anywhere I wanted to—the only caveat being it had to be with a girl. I just had to tell them where I was going and what time I would be home. I loved spending time with both my parents. They were complete opposites: my mom was an extrovert and my dad was an introvert. Whenever I was free and Mom wasn't watching her telenovelas, Mom and I played dominoes or cards, listened to music, and cuddled while chatting or just watching shows that we both enjoyed.

My mom was very blunt with her opinions. I knew when I asked for advice, she would express herself without holding back. Sometimes I regretted asking for her opinion, but I knew she meant well. I loved that about her. My mom's life wasn't a "walk in the park." Her upbringing was very tough. She believed in God and prayed daily. We went to church every Sunday, or any day they needed her. Her words of wisdom gave me comfort. She would always say, "No matter what comes ahead in life, just do your best."

Mom was always there for all of us, no matter what. If my sisters weren't getting along or she could feel the tension brewing amongst us, she would have us come together on a Saturday morning to discuss and express our feelings to each other. Mom never left the room during the discussions. Mom told us to be honest and say what was on our minds. There was always a yelling match between sisters. I would sit there and observe. They were older and I didn't understand all the fuss. Sometimes they would begin to hit and pull each other's hair while screaming at one another. She would give them a minute or two to fight and then she would separate them.

She would say, "STOP! That's enough. I hope you got it out of your system. I don't want to know that you fought about this topic again. Not here or in public. You both sit here until there is a compromise."

My sisters would discuss the topic and never fight about it again. This worked for our family. My dad supported my mom and also agreed that we should work things out at home. Mom and Dad reminded us that in the real world we would face different battles. I later learned what that meant. My sisters also understood.

I had expressed to Matthew that I was not doing well in math. He told me that I was dumb when it came to math. I was pretty shocked. He called me "dumb." I thought he may be right because I couldn't grasp it. My grades proved it. I decided to recruit the best person that could help me excel in math: my mom. Mom was really good at math. I told her about my grades and let her know that Matthew told me that I was dumb because I did not know math. Mom told me that if I wanted her to tutor me, it would take commitment, time, and no complaining with her methods of teaching. She guaranteed that her tutoring would improve my math grades. I shook her hand and I agreed. Dad was our witness. I had no idea what her strategies were, but I trusted her. It was a Sunday evening and my mom told me that at 5:00 p.m. every Monday through Friday, we would meet at the kitchen table. I asked her what I had to bring to prepare, and she replied, "Bring yourself and be ready to work."

It was Monday and I was exhausted from school. I wanted to take a nap, but Mom reminded me that my butt had to be in a chair at 5 o'clock. It was time to begin. My mom handed me 10 sheets of paper.

"I need you to write your multiplications 12 times. Today we will begin with your 2s (e.g., 2 \times 1 = 2 through 2 \times 12 = 24). Once you're done, I will verbally quiz you for 30 minutes," she announced.

"This is pretty simple," I thought to myself.

The next day, we moved on to 3s. I would begin by writing the 2s only one time, then write my 3s. Mom would quiz me on both the 2s and 3s. If I missed one, I would have to write my multiplications an additional time. By the end of the evening, my hand would be exhausted. This went on for several weeks. As I progressed through my multiplication tables, the quizzes grew harder because she would include everything I had already learned. Any mistakes required me to rewrite all of my multiplication tables. I had to write them so many times, but after a while, I wasn't making any mistakes. My mom was impressed. I put a lot of time into memorizing them, and she even gave up some of her telenovelas to tutor me. I have to admit that I did try to fuss, but she was not having it. The tutoring was finally over when she announced, "My job is done."

My math grades in geometry were always over 100% with extra credit. I loved math and felt confident; I had proved to myself that I could do it. My dad was very proud of me. He would tell me, "Hija, you did it. Good job."

I wasn't very close to my dad, but we had a good bond. My dad loved watching sports, drinking beer, reading, and barbecuing for the family. When my dad barbecued while drinking, we had to watch the food; otherwise, it would be charred and we would still have to eat it. He spent most of his evenings and weekends either in the living room or outside. When my dad was reading, I would go and sit by him. We owned two sets of Encyclopedia Britannica. The first set had a red hardcover and was the smaller of the two. The second set of encyclopedias had a brown hardcover, and I remember that this set was double the size of the red one.

My dad would hand me a red encyclopedia and say, "You read with me, Hija. I don't want you to be bored. When you are done reading, I will place a bookmark on your page. Every time you come back to join me, I will give you the same book to continue."

My dad helped me pronounce the words I did not know and explained their meanings, of which there were many. I don't know how long it took me, but I eventually read both sets of encyclopedias. One day, the salesman who sold the first set to my parents stopped by and asked if we were interested in upgrading to the new version.

My mom immediately said, "No. No one reads them." But my dad turned to the salesman and said, "We will take an upgrade. Wabbie has already read them all." Wabbie was my dad's nickname for me. When I was born, I was a very chunky baby, and he called me that all the time.

Some of my dad's favorite sports were boxing, football, soccer, golf, baseball, tennis, and wrestling. He especially enjoyed boxing. My family mentioned that my dad used to box when he was young and that he was very good. He even taught one of my sisters how to box, though none of my other sisters wanted to learn.

During his TV time, Dad did not like to be disturbed while watching sports. Since I was the baby of the family, I got a free pass to sit next to him. Every time we watched a sport together, he would ask if I knew its purpose, and I would always shake my head "no."

He responded, "Well today, you will learn about every sport that we watch together. I'll explain the history, culture, selection of players, rankings, each position, fans, the field, and so much more. Then I expect you to make time on Sundays to sit with me to explain the records."

I had no idea what records meant. When Sunday came around, he would hand me the newspaper and ask me to open the paper to the sports section and say, "Now let's look at each teams' records."

He would begin explaining what the numbers meant next to each sport. He would instruct me, "Become familiar with everything that I am teaching you. I will be quizzing you on it."

If I didn't remember something he taught me, he would just rub my hair and tell me that I needed to concentrate more. He had a lot of patience with me. This went on for several years. I got pretty good at understanding sports and reading the records.

It had been a little over a year, and Matthew and I were still sitting on the front porch, unable to go out on a real date. After much begging and pleading with my parents, they allowed us to go on our first date. I was so excited. Finally, we would enjoy time alone, not having my parents literally breathing down our necks or answering my questions. My parents gave us strict rules. He had to pick me up on time and drop me off on time.

They told Matthew, "You have two hours. If you are late one minute, you'll never see her again."

We had to remain in our small town. We could not travel to the next town. We both nodded in agreement, and we quietly walked out the gate. Matthew had a driver's license and had borrowed his family vehicle. All we wanted was to be alone. We drove around town. At almost every stop light or stop sign we kissed.

I didn't want to go home, but my parents were pretty serious. The time flew by. My dad was waiting outside for us. We arrived ten minutes early. Matthew was trying to build their trust. We both sat back on the porch and for a moment we felt the freedom of relief. I was no longer caged by my parents. As weeks passed, my parents extended our time together. Matthew made it point to always arrived ten minutes early.

We started going to his sister's house when she wasn't home. We would walk to the corner store and pickup burgers to eat. We enjoyed the alone time. Matthew and I were growing closer. It was October of my sophomore year. I lost my virginity to Matthew. I was so in love with him. All I wanted to do was spend time with him. We were sexually active and I did not tell anyone, not even my best friend. Our relationship was going great. He loved me and I loved him. I was a lucky gal.

One day at his sister's house, I was sitting on a dresser. Matthew was standing in front of me. I don't recall the conversation, but I do remember that he slapped my right cheek. I felt like it was an out of body experience.

I held my cheek and said to myself, "What the Fuck just happened? Did he just slap me? Why did he slap me? OMG! He slapped me. My face is stinging."

I thought it was a bad dream, and that at any moment I would wake up. I remember watching him begin to cry and hold me, telling me he was so sorry. He had no idea why he slapped me. He begged for me to forgive him. He leaned on my chest and hugged me. I just held him, still frozen. I couldn't even move or respond to him.

He kept telling me, "I am sorry. Please forgive me."

The tears began to roll down my face and I began to shake. Time passed and we held each other. I was in such disbelief. I could not move.

For the next few weeks, he kept asking me to forgive him. I had never experienced anything like that before. I never told anyone what he did. I thought, "Why would he hurt someone he loves?" I loved him so much. He came to my house more frequently; he wanted to spend time with me, but all I wanted was space. He wanted to console me and reassure me that it would never happen again. I forgave him. I believed him. I told myself, "He'd never hurt me before. He was being sincere, and there was no reason not to trust him." I asked him why he slapped me. He told me that he had no idea why he did it, that it just happened. To keep me closer, we continued to have sex. He kissed me passionately.

On Fridays after my dad arrived home from work, we would pick a restaurant, call in an order, and pick up take-out. During our time together, we would discuss Saturday chores or family outings. Saturday chores were not fun at all. My brother had it pretty easy; all he had to do was gather the trash from each of the rooms and throw it in the trashcan outside, and his chore was complete. My sisters and I would rotate chores. Once a month, the floors in all the bedrooms were waxed. Every two weeks, the curtains were washed, dried, and rotated. Every week we had to mop, sweep, and dust all the frames and items in the house. We also had to wash, dry, and change the sheets on the beds. We would wash the clothes and hang them outside on the clothesline. After they dried, we would fold and place them back in the dressers. We mowed the lawn and weeded the flower beds. Lastly, we washed and vacuumed the vehicles.

Matthew joined us for family dinners from time to time. He would listen to the list of chores my family had to do. The next morning, Matthew would show up really early and begin doing some of the chores for my family—things like mowing the lawn or washing the vehicle, just helping out where he could. My family loved it. He was earning their trust, and they started to like him.

I loved family outings. On Saturday mornings, we would drive to the city for breakfast. The restaurant was small, and the owners knew my parents. The food was great. I always sat next to my dad. We went almost every Saturday. Everyone was so nice. After breakfast, my dad would either take us to the beach, to the park, or to the mall. If we went to the mall, he never went inside. He stayed in the vehicle while he read his paper. My sisters, mom, and I would go shopping. After the mall, we would go to a drive-in to watch a movie. Mom would pack snacks, sandwiches, sodas, pickles, and popcorn. My dad was the only one who would buy himself a soda while he watched the movie.

On weekends, Matthew and I would drive around, go to restaurants, parks, and his sister's house. I truly enjoyed our time together. We never discussed the slap on the cheek again. I still wondered to myself, "Why did it happen? What did I do wrong to deserve that?"

We were inseparable on weekends or when he was visiting. Everywhere we went, we would hold hands; he would put his finger on my belt loop, hold my waist, or hug me throughout the store. He would kiss me, bring me in closer, and squeeze me. Once, we came home from an outing together and he wasn't himself. As soon as we arrived back at his sister's, he started yelling at me that guys were looking at me.

"Did you like it? Were you looking for attention?" he screamed.

He began to shake me. I had no idea that anyone was looking at me. My eyes were locked on him. In my heart, he was all I wanted and needed in life. He began shoving me. I kept pleading with him to calm down.

He continued to scream, "You wanted attention? Didn't you?"

Tears started rolling down my face. I thought, "What is happening?" I had no idea. We had never fought like this before. Then he shoved me to the ground. When I stood up, he grabbed my arms and pushed me again. I stood up again. He grabbed my hair and pushed me again to the ground. He began to hit me, but not on my face. I tried to block his punches. I began to cry and yell at him. I couldn't stop him. Then, he just stopped.

He knelt on the ground next to me and said, "What have I done? I am so sorry. I love you. Don't leave me." Matthew began to cry. He apologized to me, saying, "I thought I was about to lose you to those guys that were looking at you."

I had no idea what guys he was talking about.

Matthew then said, "You know what guys. You looked their way."

I was in utter shock and disbelief; I was shaking. Matthew just held me while he cried. We stayed on the floor for a while. As time passed, he began to kiss me and tell me how much he loved me. He then told me, "I am never going to lose you to anyone."

I kept telling him that I wasn't going anywhere; he was the love of my life. We continued to kiss and then we made love. I was going through the motions, but I was truly scared. I was dismayed, thinking, Where did my Matthew go? Who was the guy who just hit me? It was getting late, and I had to head home. When we arrived at my house, he begged me not to leave him. I assured him that I wouldn't.

He told me, "I'll call you when I get home. Please answer." That night, we talked on the phone until I fell asleep.

The next morning, he showed up at my house. He brought me tacos. The family hadn't planned for him to come over that early. He mentioned that he felt so bad he couldn't sleep; he just wanted to apologize and make it right. My stomach was in knots, but I still ate the tacos. We sat outside. I had nothing to say. I couldn't even look at him; I kept replaying what had happened to me. Matthew apologized over and over until I forgave him. I had to say it several times, as if I were convincing him that I was not upset.

We came inside and sat in the living room with my family. My sisters noticed the bruises on my arms and legs. They asked what happened.

"Clumsy me... I fell."

Matthew agreed that I was a bit clumsy. "Are you sure he didn't hurt you?" they asked.

"No, he wouldn't hurt me," I responded.

I wanted to protect him. He had just apologized, and we had made up. Matthew asked if there were any chores he could do while he was there. My sisters looked at each other. "There are several chores you could help us with." Matthew and my sisters walked outside to discuss the chores.

My parents then took me aside and asked me in private, "What really happened?"

"I truly fell," I answered.

My dad looked at me and asked, "Did he hit you?"

"No, Dad. I fell," I repeated.

He responded, "Be careful, hija. Those are big bruises."

I told them that I would do my best not to hurt myself and walked out of the living room to my bedroom. I lay on my bed and the tears started rolling down my face. The weekend was a blur.

One day after school, I wanted to go and play with the neighbor who lived behind our house. Before getting to her house, I had to cross the alley made of white rocks. Her dad was outside on the driveway. He let me know that his daughter was not home. They lived in a one-story, red-brick house.

I asked her dad, "How does someone own a house like this?"

"You have to get a college education," he responded.

I had never heard the word "college." I asked him, "What is a college education?"

He replied, "After high school, you go to either a two-year college, known as a community college, or a four-year college, known as a university. Find a relative who has a degree and ask them to guide you through the process."

I ran home to tell my mom that I was going to college so I could buy a brick home. She replied, "You're crazy. You need to focus on a high school education."

The houses on that block were very nice. I remember asking my mom why we didn't live on that block. She would reply, "You should be happy we live on this block." My mom and sister later earned their Associate's degrees in Computer Science, though they never got jobs in that field. Their diplomas hung on the wall in our living room.

The abuse with Matthew continued. He started going with me to pick out new outfits. He felt that the ones I owned were too revealing. I remember we went to the mall to purchase a dress for a celebration that would be held at a dance hall. He said that he would be selecting the dress; I could select the shoes and accessories. Matthew selected a two-piece olive green dress. It was a turtleneck, long-sleeved top with gold buttons in the front. The skirt was floor-length. It was pretty. With the dress, I selected red closed-toe flat shoes with a gold tip and gold jewelry.

Before entering the hall, he looked at me and announced, "If anyone gives you a compliment, we will turn around and leave. Then you will suffer the consequences."

I was frightened. We walked through the double doors. His cousin stopped us and said hi; then he complimented my look. Matthew put his hand around my waist. We turned around and left the hall. He gripped my hand and began yelling, "You know what this means. You're going to suffer the consequences for his compliment. I have a surprise for you when we get home."

We arrived back at his sister's, and he had purchased a pair of camel steel-toe boots. He took them out of the box and put them on. He started attacking me. I hit him back. I was able to get to one of the bedrooms and lock the door. He used his body to push the door and frame off. I tried to escape through a window. I had had enough. My body was halfway out, but I never made it outside. He grabbed my legs and pulled me back into the house.

The next morning, I decided to call an emergency family meeting. Some of my sisters were not happy because they had made plans that morning, but my mom made it mandatory. I was so scared, but I knew the only way out was to tell my family.

I started by saying, "I've been lying to everyone. The bruises you saw months ago were from Matthew. I am not clumsy. He did this to me." I then showed them all the bruises on my body.

They all looked at me and told me, "You're lying. Matthew is a sweet guy. He wouldn't hurt a fly. We trust him. Why are you making this up? Not cool. We do not believe you. You made us come here and waste our time to tell us that he hurt you. You should be ashamed of yourself. He's a great guy. What you are telling us is messed up."

I was upset. I thought, "What is going on? I cannot believe what I am hearing. I showed my bruises, and they are defending him. My parents even took up for him."

They wouldn't listen to me. They were disgusted with me and my accusations. Everyone got up and left me sitting alone on the living room couch. I thought, "This is a bad dream. I will be waking up in a few minutes."

Matthew kept calling all day. I refused to speak to him. My family was very apologetic to him. My sisters would come to my room and tell me how mean I was being to a guy who cared for and loved me. He showed up again, and they let him into the house. I could not believe what was happening. He was in the living room, and I refused to go and see him. After all the unwelcome verbal crap my sisters gave me, I went to the living room to talk to him.

He told me, "You weren't taking my calls and I wanted to see you."

I told him that the relationship was over.

He exclaimed, "No! It is not over. We'll get through this."

I kept quiet. I could see his mouth moving, but I didn't listen.

It was my junior year and the abuse continued. None of my family listened. I was all alone with a guy I thought I knew. I was scared. I was becoming exhausted and felt isolated. I decided to turn to my cousin Antonio. He was my age and like a brother to me. He was a football player; also, he was very protective. One day after school, I told him everything. I showed him my bruises. He was extremely upset. My cousin believed me. We met up with his friends later that evening. He told them everything. They wanted to beat him up. I told them that they could not touch him. All I wanted was protection. I finally felt that I could breathe. During school hours, football games, and parties, I was watched like a hawk. If Matthew came around me, they would hover over us. Matthew knew I told my cousin.

Matthew would whisper in my ear, "He can't protect you all the time."

I decided to join my cousin at a party they had after a football game. Matthew showed up at my house and I wasn't home. He drove all through the small town and found the party. He got out of his vehicle and demanded that I come outside and leave with him. My cousin and half the team came outside to meet him. They told him that if he ever hit me again, they would hurt him. Matthew left the party without me. He showed up at my house early the next morning and was extremely upset. I avoided going anywhere with him. Once, I let my guard down and trusted that he wouldn't hurt me. Within a few minutes of leaving to run a quick errand, he began yelling at me and hurting me.

It was my junior year, and I still worked part-time at McDonald's. Amber's mom wanted her to get a part-time job where she worked. My best friend, Amber, asked me to work with her at Dairy Queen (DQ). She told her mom if I didn't work at DQ with her, she wouldn't take the position. Her mom agreed. I had no idea how I was going to manage working two part-time jobs, band, a boyfriend, and school. I managed for a few months. They increased my hours at DQ. DQ was also closer to my house. Amber and I worked the same shifts. That made it easier to catch a ride and have fun with my best friend. Since her mom was the assistant manager, she worked with our school schedule. DQ was located right across the street from our high school. In the evenings, our friends would come by and visit us. Matthew was there frequently. He would show up unexpectedly. Amber was aware of the abuse. If Matthew walked into the DQ, she would have a snarky comment.

Finally, I was a senior! My last year of high school. I was so excited. Amber and I were looking forward to going to college. I tried to break up with Matthew. He wasn't having it. He was still my boyfriend. There were so many times that I would remember the kind, loving, caring, and honest Matthew. I thought, "What happened? He has to be in there somewhere." I loved him, but I was so tired and worried—continuously watching my back.

As much as I tried to avoid Matthew, there was even more abuse. My family had fully accepted him. He could come over whenever he wanted. I was trapped in my own home. Enough was enough. My body was always covered in bruises. I started to believe my own lies—that I was clumsy—even though I knew the truth. One of my friends lived down the street. I decided to go and visit with her. She had no idea that I felt alone, depressed, sad, unhappy, lifeless, and beat down. I walked in the house and she was watching TV. I told her that I had a headache. She mentioned that there was some medicine in the bathroom cabinet. "Don't take the wrong ones," she mentioned, referring to one medication in particular.

I found the pills she mentioned and grabbed a handful of them. She had no idea I did. I told her that I had to go home—that I needed to go home and sleep. We had a mutual friend who lived across the street, so I stopped by to say hi. I told him exactly how I was feeling, but I never mentioned why. I told him goodbye. He looked at me in a strange way.

I went home and walked past my parents in the living room. I took all the pills.

My dad told me later that he found me on the floor next to my bed. He said that he called my name and I did not respond. He picked up my hand and let it go; he knew something was wrong. He yelled for my mom to call the ambulance. He carried me to the shower. My mom turned on the water and tried to wake me up.

They asked what I had done. I told them that I didn't want to live because no one believed me about the abuse. I took the pills hoping not to wake up. My mother stuck her finger in my mouth to make me throw up. The ambulance showed up. The next thing I remembered was waking up at the hospital. All my family was there, including Matthew. They said that the doctors had lost me for six seconds.

I was released from the hospital a few days later. The counselors came, and they made me feel like I was the crazy one. I thought, "Still… why didn't anyone believe me?"

The abuse stopped for a few months. That year, I graduated from high school as a member of the National Honor Society. Amber and I enrolled for fall classes at our local community college. A new beginning was emerging.

CHAPTER 3

AFFAIR AND ALONE

Matthew and I broke up for a few months. The breakup was filled with torment, fear, stalking, and abuse. No matter where I went, he found me. We eventually got back together. Going to college and working full-time kept me pretty busy. Amber and I would carpool to school, but parking was really bad. We had to arrive an hour or two before class just to find a spot and walk the long distance to the building. Sometimes we would get lucky and find parking near one of our classes. I wasn't prepared for college and had no idea what to expect; all I wanted was to earn a degree and begin a new career.

The campus was so big. We rarely interacted with people while walking to class because everyone looked so focused. Students either carried their textbooks or wore backpacks—some on both shoulders, others with one strap. The students in my classes, however, were very friendly. The invitation to study together was something you heard in every class, and I exchanged numbers with quite a few people. A syllabus was handed out in each class, which helped me plan my homework and exam preparation. I sought out study groups when I knew a class would be difficult. Between classes, we would finish our homework. If we were caught up or didn't feel like working, we would head to the mall or the beach. I really enjoyed the beach; it felt so calm. We would sit on the pier and put our feet in the water. I loved walking on the sand and feeling my feet sink in with every step.

I decided to quit my job at McDonald's because it was tough having two jobs. In the evenings, I worked at DQ, though I sometimes worked the day shift. My sister was seeking a new job, so I recommended she apply for an available full-time position. She was hired and really enjoyed working in the restaurant industry. During the night shift, Matthew would come by to visit. He would go through the drive-thru just to chat. One day, he mentioned he was invited to a party near his city. He asked if I minded if he went and told me I could join him if I wanted. I told him he should go out and have some fun.

"Would you like me to call you when I get home?" Matthew asked. "Nope. You have fun," I responded.

It was a relief to have some time away from him. Every weekend after that, he started asking if he could go to these parties. I encouraged him to go and make some friends.

On a Saturday evening in January 1992, my cousin Antonio asked if I wanted to join him and his friends at a club. I called my best friend, Amber, and she was in. I wondered what I was going to tell Matthew, but he actually didn't come by DQ that evening. Instead, he called and asked if he could go to his friend's house for one of their weekly parties. I was so excited that he canceled our plans. Since we weren't 21, the club wouldn't let us in until 2:00 a.m. I knew Matthew wouldn't call because he never did, and my parents would have been extremely upset if someone called that late.

I drove Amber and myself to the club. My cousin and his friends were already in line. While we were waiting, I noticed Matthew's truck driving around looking for a parking spot at the very same club. His windows were rolled down, and you could hear the music blaring. I was shocked. He wasn't alone; there were two other girls with him. I couldn't believe what I was witnessing. I started running toward his truck, with my cousin, Amber, and their friends running behind me. I reached the truck and started yelling. He looked dumbstruck. I told him to get out of the vehicle. When he did, I jumped into the driver's seat and asked the girls who they were. The girl sitting in the middle said she was Matthew's date. I pulled back my right hand to punch her, but someone jerked my arm, grabbed me by the waist, and pulled me out of the truck.

"He's not worth it," I heard someone say. It was an officer. He kept holding me, then he turned me around and looked into my eyes.

The officer continued, "He's truly not worth it. You and your friends go back to the club and have fun. This guy and his friends will be leaving the property."

Matthew refused to get into the truck. He told his date that she could take the truck back to her place and he would be there in the morning to pick it up. The officer looked at him and repeated, "Get in your vehicle and leave the premises. Now. I don't want to arrest you."

Matthew's date was upset. He finally got back into the vehicle and they left. I was furious. My cousin and friends grabbed me by the hand, and one of them said, "Let's go inside and have fun."

It took a few minutes for me to snap out of it. I tried to play it cool, just going through the motions, but then I finally snapped out of it. We had a blast. We danced so much my feet were hurting, which took my mind off what had just happened. I couldn't believe that he was so possessive over me when he had another girl—he was dating someone else. I felt so stupid.

We left the club when it closed, which was around 4:00 AM. When Amber and I walked to my vehicle, Matthew jumped out of the backseat. I forgot he had a spare key. We were startled.

I yelled, "Where is your date?"

He replied, "I took them home and drove back to see you."

Amber asked what I wanted to do. Matthew said he just wanted to talk. He continued, "I'm not upset with you. I should be the one apologizing."

Amber said I shouldn't trust him, but I gave in to Matthew. Amber went home with one of our other friends, and we both got into the vehicle and left the club parking lot. Once we got on the road, he started yelling at me.

He screamed, "You didn't tell me you were coming to a club! Who did you come with? Did you have a date? I hope you had fun dancing because you're going to pay for embarrassing me."

I started yelling back, letting him know that he was the one who embarrassed me with his date. I asked him who the girl was.

He answered, "I've been seeing her for a while. She is the girl who has been having the parties."

I began to yell louder, "Are you kidding me? Why should you be mad? You have been going behind my back and you still think you can tell me what to do!"

He grabbed the back of my neck and took a handful of hair. He kept pulling my hair and banging my head against the window. We didn't go back to my house; he took me to his parents' house in the rural part of the city and snuck me inside.

I was alone with the boyfriend I thought I knew. He was still upset with me, making threats about how he was going to harm me. I was so scared. I knew if I yelled there would be more repercussions. We went into his bedroom before I even had a chance to run. He grabbed my neck, pushed me down, and pulled my hair. He began to hit me. After a while, I stopped fighting back.

It went on for a bit. Then, he just grabbed me and pulled me onto his bed. He lay behind me, holding me with his hands wrapped around my waist. He whispered into my ear and told me that he was sorry for hurting me. I lay there, frightened and still. Time passed. He started kissing my neck and we had sex. I couldn't even call it making love anymore. My stomach ached.

Afterward, we started talking about everything. I told him that our relationship wasn't working. I told him that if he cared for her, he should stay with her. He told me he had feelings for her but that he still loved me. We just held each other. I kept telling him that I would not be mad about it and that I completely understood that relationships end. I told him we would always have memories to cherish.

Finally, he agreed to break up. I was crushed but also relieved. We had met when I was fourteen, and now I was twenty. He was my first love and my first everything. I kept quiet for a while, then I grabbed my stuff and drove home. Emotions washed over me and I just wept. I was free at last from the torment and abuse.

Even though our relationship did not work out, I still loved and cared for him deeply. It was a tough time emotionally, but I was also relieved because someone else could take him off my hands. The abuse was too much. I missed him because we spent almost every day together. It felt weird not having him around—not having him call me several times a day or show up at my house unexpectedly. I experienced so many emotions after our breakup. I cried a lot for him. I knew I was safe, but I still had emotions I needed to express.

I didn't realize I had trauma from our relationship. I remember when my family or friends would raise their hands in the air while speaking; I would duck my head under my arms, thinking they were going to attack me. Every time they raised their voice, it would make me jump. My family and friends reacted by holding me. It was something I had to work through.

A little over a month passed, and Matthew and I reconnected. He called to tell me that he missed me and wanted to see me. As much as I missed him, I couldn't bring myself to see him at first. Matthew continued to call and beg me for a meeting. He told me, "She doesn't mean anything to me. I love and miss you." He promised not to hurt me and said that he wanted to make it up to me. Every time my parents or siblings answered the phone and knew it was him, they would simply hang up. The only time I spoke to him was when I picked up.

After a few weeks, I agreed to meet him. I truly missed him. He sounded like the Matthew I met when I was fourteen. Was it really him? Had he changed, or was I creating a story? He sounded so sweet and sincere. I drove to his parents' house to meet him; I was excited but also cautious. I had seen him be nice one minute and angry the next. When I arrived at his parents' home, he was waiting outside for me. Matthew was so handsome; his beautiful smile could light up a room. I grabbed my bag from my vehicle and walked toward him. We held each other and didn't say a word. For that split moment, I truly felt he was the Matthew I first met.

He took my hand, and we entered through the garage carport side door. As soon as we walked in, we entered the laundry room. Passing the laundry room, the first door on the left was Matthew's bedroom. On the right side of the bedroom, he had a couch facing the television. On the left side was his bed. His room was quite large; you could fit three full-sized beds and a matching dresser inside. When he was younger, this was the room his brothers had shared with him.

The evening passed, and all we did was watch TV and make love. We didn't talk much. I think we both needed this moment to say goodbye. He kept telling me we would be a part of each other's lives forever. I was a bit confused; I didn't understand what he meant. I reassured him that I wasn't going anywhere. We hardly spoke about the other girl or any of the bad moments we had. It was nice. We both just enjoyed our time together.

The days and evenings passed. I spent several days with him. Finally, I packed my bag, said goodbye, and went home. The drive home felt longer than usual. I knew our relationship was finally over. A flash of memories went through my mind. My heart sank, and I cried.

In March of 1992, I started getting back into the routine of finding who I was. In the back of my mind, I still had the fear of seeing him. I just had to get through the day without thinking of my past—one step at a time, one day at a time. I enjoyed going to college; I focused on my courses and meeting other students. One of the classes I registered for was dance. It included country, waltz, ballroom, and line dancing. I had no idea what I was signing up for, but I needed a fresh start. It was so much fun to learn the history and the moves for each style of dance. There were several of us who were beginners, while others could have become dance instructors. The class flew by, and as the semester was coming to an end, I realized we had learned so much in a short amount of time.

A couple of months passed, and I hadn't heard from Matthew. One day while I was at school, Matthew called me unexpectedly. He asked if I was pregnant.

I replied, "No, I am not pregnant. Why would you call and ask me that question?"

He began to explain that he had been sick for the last two weeks. During his visit with the doctor, he was asked if the person he was dating was pregnant, or if anyone else he knew could be. The doctor explained the meaning of sympathy pains (couvade)—sometimes men experience morning sickness or cravings that their significant other is experiencing. I reassured him that I was not pregnant. To confirm this, I agreed to go during my class break to the nearest hospital for a pregnancy blood test. I was informed that the results would be ready in an hour. That gave me enough time to have lunch before heading back to class.

The hour went by quickly, and I was feeling a little anxious. As I walked into the lab, they handed me my results. I read them: I was pregnant. So many emotions surged through my body. I walked out of the lab in shock, yet I was happy and excited. After I passed through the hospital's double doors, I jumped into the air with joy. Matthew and I were going to have a baby. I remembered him telling me we were going to be together forever. I called him immediately. The results were positive; we were going to have a baby. I skipped all the way to my vehicle and went back to school to finish the day.

While driving home, I wondered how I would break the news to my family. I was 20 years old and weighed 98 pounds. How much weight would I gain? Would I get stretch marks? Would my breasts grow? The news started sinking in. Matthew and I were not getting back together; he was already seeing someone else. I would be a single mom. Oh no... this was great news, but also terrifying. I walked inside and went into my parents' bedroom. Mom was watching her telenovelas. She did not like to be interrupted, so I sat next to her, waiting for the right moment to tell her. She could tell something was wrong and immediately muted the television. I took a deep breath.

"I'm pregnant," I said.

Mom gazed at me. I knew I was in trouble.

"¡Qué! ¿Qué? (What! What!)"

"I'm pregnant," I said.

"How many months along are you?" she asked.

"I don't know. I just found out today," I replied.

She opened her arms to hug me. It felt so good to fall into her arms.

"Go tell your father," she said as she grabbed me by my hand. We walked into the living room and stood next to the TV. My dad was reading the paper and watching TV; he loved reading while watching television.

"Your baby has something to tell you. Dile (tell him)," she said.

I was extremely nervous. My dad began to raise his voice, repeatedly asking what had happened.

"I'm pregnant," I replied.

He rolled up the newspaper he had in his hand and began to shake his head. The news spread like wildfire.

I woke up one morning and was spotting blood. My mom told me that it wasn't good news and that we should go to the hospital. Matthew's mom recommended their family doctor because he knew their family very well. I called to make an appointment, but the earliest availability was June 26th—my doctor's appointment was still a few weeks out. We prayed on the way to the hospital. I was extremely nervous, but Mom calmed me down. Once we arrived, I checked in and began to fill out the paperwork. We sat until they called my name; it felt like forever.

Finally, my name was called. The technician told me that we were going to do a sonogram. We would be able to see the baby and produce images for the doctor to review. I asked him if it would hurt. He grinned and said, "No." The tech asked me to raise my shirt and let me know that he would be applying a gel. When he began to apply it, it felt cold. He found the baby and began to take images. I was so excited to see the baby.

"Wow, that is so cool! You can see the front and the back of the baby. Can you always see the back and front of the baby?" I asked.

He began to laugh uncontrollably. "Give me a minute," he replied. "I have to go get another tech."

The two guys walked back into the room. He told me to ask the question again.

"Can you always see the back and front of the baby?" I repeated.

They both laughed uncontrollably. I began to get a little nervous. That is when the doctor walked in, and one of the techs left the room.

I asked, "Doctor, is everything okay? These guys are laughing because I asked if you can always see the back and front of the baby."

The doctor held my hand and said, "No, you can't see the front and back of the baby. Do you see the two sacs? They look like two circles."

I answered, "Yes, I do."

The doctor continued, "The reason you can see the 'front and back' of the baby is because you are going to have twins."

I started crying. I was going to have twins! He asked if there was anyone waiting for me in the lobby. I told him that my mom had come with me. The doctor left the room to break the news to her. I was in utter shock. He walked back into the room with a big grin.

The doctor announced, "When I walked into the waiting area and called your mom's name, she immediately ran up to me. I told her that I had some news. She bowed her head, and then I said, 'Your daughter is going to have twins.' Your mom jumped on me! She is so excited."

He looked over the images and assured me that nothing was wrong. The doctor told me to make sure I let my primary doctor know what happened. Mom and I left the hospital excited. When we walked into the house, Mom started yelling, "Reyna is going to have twins!" My dad's face turned pale. It was a priceless expression.

I reached out to Matthew and broke the news. He was really excited that I was going to have twins. He immediately spread the news to his family, and they asked if they could see the sonogram. Matthew picked up the images while I was at work. I had to create a financial plan for myself and the twins; the goal was to save enough money not to work for the first two years. Since I lived with my parents, that would be doable.

On June 26, Mom and I headed to see the doctor, sonogram images in hand. We checked in when we arrived, and the receptionist gave me a clipboard with several forms to fill out. When the nurse called my name, I took my mom's hand and we walked back to the patient rooms. The nurse asked me to stand on the scale. I was three months pregnant and weighed 101 pounds.

She then walked us to a room where we waited for the doctor. He walked in and greeted us. We spoke for a bit, and I showed him the images. The doctor did an ultrasound and took new images. I was able to hear both heartbeats. Mom held my hand, and we both started smiling from ear to ear; my heart melted. The appointment went smoothly. We thanked him and walked to the receptionist's area to schedule my next appointment.

When I arrived home, I called Matthew to give him an update. After my appointment, it felt like my body was going through some weird changes. I was definitely hungrier than before and never really felt full. From one day to the next, my belly "popped." You could tell that I had a bump, and I had to request a size up on my uniform pants. I was working full-time at DQ, but nothing else had changed; I wasn't tired at all.

On July 22, Mom and I headed to my second appointment. We checked in, and within a few minutes, they called my name. I was four months pregnant and weighed 109 pounds. The doctor asked me about the types of foods I was eating. He was concerned and told me that I had to eat food that would help the twins grow. I didn't understand what he meant, so he explained that fatty and sugary foods did not nourish the twins—they only helped me grow. His goal was for the twins to weigh over five pounds. For that to happen, I would have to follow his nutritional diet and exercise plan. He handed me some papers to read and follow.

Then, he asked if he could speak to my mom alone. I stepped out and waited right outside the door. A few minutes passed before he called me back in. They both looked at me and began to express their concerns about me being a single mother of two children. They said that having two kids is a "perfect number" for someone to raise and expressed that my journey raising twins would be very tough.

After a few minutes, the conversation changed, and they both recommended that it would be best if I had my tubes tied once I had the twins. This would prevent future pregnancies. They mentioned that the procedure could be reversed.

The doctor then told me, "Don't think about it now. We just want you to consider the option." I shrugged my shoulders and nodded. I didn't really understand what they were asking of me. Mom and I left the office, but we didn't discuss it at all.

It had been a few months since I learned that I was pregnant. Not only did I have to worry about my finances, but no one in our family had ever raised twins. I didn't want to seek advice from my ex, Matthew, who was consumed with his new girlfriend. I hardly spoke to him, though he would call from time to time to check in on me. I missed him. Our family knew how to raise children, but not twins. I went to our local library to check out books on how to raise twins and how to be a single mom. I also purchased some additional books.

Since I was on a budget, I decided to put all the important items I needed for the twins on layaway. I went to Weiner's and a local downtown store. I spoke to each store manager and let them know that I chose their layaway plan to select merchandise for the twins I would be giving birth to in a few months. I also let them know that I was paying the majority in full and leaving a balance of $5 on each layaway because we had nowhere to store the items at home. I promised to pay off the balance a couple of weeks before their birth. They both agreed.

During my pregnancy, I spent a lot of time with Margo. She was my best friend and lived two doors down from my house. Margo was also pregnant, and her due date was one month before mine. Our bellies looked the same. None of our clothes fit us anymore. We loved to eat and shop for bargain clothes; we didn't want to spend money on items we weren't going to use again.

Our favorite place to invite people for dinner was an all-you-can-eat buffet. We would invite her brother at around 5:30 p.m. and her mom at 8:00 p.m. Her mom always tried to put us on a diet, so when we had dinner with her brother, we ate whatever we wanted. When her mom showed up, we had salads, chicken, vegetables, and dessert. We never had more than one serving in front of her mom because she wanted us to watch our weight.

On August 19, I was five months pregnant, and it was time to see my doctor again. Mom and I went together, but she decided not to join me when they called my name, choosing instead to wait in the lobby. The nurse had me step on the scale; I had gained six pounds and weighed 115 pounds. The doctor reminded me that I needed to eat nutritional food for the babies, not for me. I did not listen and ate whatever I wanted—which was everything. I was always hungry. Before my appointment ended, he again recommended that I tie my tubes after delivery. The doctor let me know that the procedure was quick and could take place six weeks after the delivery of the twins.

On the way home, I discussed it with my mom. She told me it was my decision, but she agreed with the doctor. Being pregnant with twins was great; they kicked all the time. I was always taking naps or eating. One day, my cousin Antonio called me. He was in a bind and needed to borrow money for rent, promising to pay me back. Antonio was like a brother to me. I wasn't feeling well that day and had no energy to go to the bank to withdraw cash. Antonio asked if our mutual friend could come to my mom's house and pick up the debit card. My cousin lived out of town, and our friend was heading north to visit him. Antonio promised that he'd withdraw the exact funds and have our friend return the card to me once he arrived back in town. I agreed to the plan. I called my cousin a few days later to ask about my card. He mentioned that he had forgotten to give it back, but it was safe with him. I wasn't worried about the card because I only wanted to put money into the account to save; if I needed cash, I could just go to the bank.

I couldn't believe that I was already six months pregnant. I truly loved being pregnant. It was time for my next doctor's visit on September 21, and I weighed 122 pounds. The doctor mentioned some concerns regarding my pregnancy. He felt I needed more rest because I had been having contractions every day since my first sonogram. He asked me about my daily activities. I told him that I worked 40 hours a week and was always on the go with my best friend. He let me know that rest was what I needed. I didn't agree with him, but I wasn't going to tell him that. After my daily naps, I always had enough energy to hang out with my friends.

The doctor asked me where I worked. "I work at Dairy Queen as the assistant manager. It's the only one in town," I replied. He also asked if I had been thinking about the procedure. I told him I had, but I hadn't made up my mind. I left the office and went home to rest for the evening.

I showed up to work the next day, but my manager informed me that I was unable to clock in. She explained that my doctor had called to let her know I had been put on bed rest and was unable to work until after I delivered my twins. I was dumbfounded. My manager said she was sorry and gave me a hug.

I walked out of the restaurant and was extremely upset. I worked only a few minutes away from home. Mom was in the kitchen when I walked in, and I started telling her what had happened. Mom shrugged her shoulders and told me that the doctor had told me to rest and I did not listen. She said that he was just watching out for my twins. What was I going to do? I had to continue to save money, and now I had no job. But the doctor was right; I had not rested enough.

Due to my contractions, the doctor recommended I come into the office every week to have a sonogram to monitor the twins. On October 3rd, my mom went to my next appointment with me. She walked with me to the room. I was not looking forward to seeing the doctor; I was still upset because I had to quit my job. When the doctor completed my sonogram, he was disappointed because the twins were underweight. He left the room for a few minutes. When he walked back into the room, he informed me that I needed to report to the hospital immediately. I was a bit confused.

The doctor then told me, "You did not follow the diet I recommended or rest when I asked you. I'm truly concerned with the twins' weight. Since I cannot trust that you will rest and eat food that helps the twins grow, starting today, I'm admitting you into the hospital. They have a room ready for you. You do not need to bring anything with you. For the next four weeks, you will be restricted to complete bed rest. I'm doing this for your babies."

He handed me some paperwork and I left the room. The hospital was nearby. I couldn't believe what was happening. My mom kept telling me that the doctor was right. I was always on the go and I never ate what he wanted me to. Mom and I walked into the hospital. I went to the front desk and checked in. The doctor himself had called them; they were really expecting me.

After filling out all the documents, I was escorted to my own private room. My mom went home to gather some clothes for herself. She wanted to be with me at the hospital, and I didn't want to be alone. I changed into the gown and waited for dinner to arrive. The doctor had a nutritionist select my meal plan. The food was bland. The nurses informed me that I had to eat all of my food or they would call the doctor. It was his orders. I did what I was told because I knew it wasn't about me anymore; it was about the twins. I wasn't able to get out of bed to shower or go to the bathroom. Everything was done in the bed. Mom tolerated my mood swings. Mom had to watch her telenovelas, so she was able to find a room that had a TV to watch them every day.

The doctor came to visit me twice a week. Those four weeks went by pretty slowly. On the day of my release, I was waiting for my paperwork. I decided to get out of bed and go to the bathroom. The nurse caught me and immediately told the doctor. When he came in that morning, he denied my release. Since I had not learned my lesson, I had to remain at the hospital for a few more days. I was so upset. Mom shrugged her shoulders and walked out of the room. The doctor was serious. I knew I had messed up. When it was finally time for my release, I did not get out of bed. I was so ready for a long shower. I was told that I had to report to the doctor's office the day after my release. On October 29th, the nurse weighed me in at 125 pounds. I was seven months along. He did another sonogram and was pleased with their weight.

October had almost passed. Reflecting on my stay at the hospital, I was not happy that I had been on complete bed rest. Hospitals are extremely boring. The food was horrible, though the staff was very nice. The twins both weighed over five pounds. I was happy with the results. Before I checked into the hospital, they were both weighing a little over three pounds. I'm glad I ate all the food and listened to the nurses.

November came, and I knew I had to pick up both layaways. I had to set up my bedroom with the crib and all the merchandise I had purchased, so I decided to check my account balance. My checking was depleted; I had no money in my account. I didn't even have enough to take out the two layaways I had for the twins, which totaled $10. I was devastated and felt betrayed. I called my cousin, but he avoided me. After a few weeks of calling his home, he finally answered. He told me that he didn't mean to spend all the money. He was so sorry and said he was going to pay me back, he just didn't know when. I was extremely upset. What could I do? The money was gone. The damage had been done. I called the bank to cancel the credit card and cried for days. He had stolen from me and my twins.

Then there was the dreaded call. I hated that I had to reach out to Matthew and ask him for $10. I received a lecture before he came over and dropped it off; it was like a drive-by.

I woke up on November 22nd, and the twins weren't moving. This was the first time I couldn't feel them move, and they were always active. I was extremely scared. I called the doctor, and the nurse told me I should head to the hospital immediately. She informed me that my doctor was on vacation, but she would let the on-call doctor know I was coming. I went to my mom's bedroom and woke her up. I told her the twins weren't moving and that I needed her to take me to the hospital. I wasn't able to drive anymore; my belly was so big it didn't fit between the steering wheel and the seat. Even with the seat moved all the way back, I still couldn't fit.

We arrived at the hospital, and my mom was complaining about us having to come back. I checked in and waited to be called. When they called me in, Mom decided to stay in the waiting room to pray. The technician did a sonogram and was able to hear both heartbeats. What a relief! I took a deep breath and gave thanks. On the way home, we stopped by the church to pray.

When Mom and I arrived home, Dad had invited our family over for a barbecue. We walked in the front door to find my aunts and cousins chatting in the kitchen. We hugged everyone, and they started asking questions about the morning hospital visit. A few hours passed and the food was ready. My mom had just sat down to eat when I noticed the dishes were piling up. I decided to start washing them so I could continue my conversation with the family. While standing next to the sink, I felt something wet on my pants. I turned my body to face the kitchen table, and at that moment, my water burst. My aunt and mom both yelled at me not to move, fearing I would fall. As I stood there holding onto the counter, they each grabbed an arm and walked me to the bathroom. I showered and changed into dry clothes, then immediately told my mom we had to head back to the hospital.

She replied, "Hija, I am hungry. Let me eat and relax. You will be in labor for at least ten hours."

I begged and pleaded with her. "Mom, let's go. Please."

She looked at me and grabbed her purse. Once we arrived at the hospital, they immediately walked me to a room. The nurse walked in and asked me to change, letting me know I would likely be in labor for several hours.

The nurse said, "You're not in much pain compared to the other ladies in labor and delivery. I'll come back and check on you in a few."

Since the beginning of my pregnancy, my contractions were always two to three minutes apart. Pain was a constant for me; I had just gotten used to it. But today, the pain had increased.

The nurse opened the door and said, "Do you hear the ladies in the other rooms yelling? They are ready to have their babies. I do not think you are ready to have yours."

She began to check my cervix. Suddenly, the nurse started yelling.

"Your baby is coming out! I have to get a doctor now!" she exclaimed.

She really scared me. However, the doctor walked in very calmly and greeted us both. He checked my cervix and let me know that I was dilated over 8 cm. He then said, "We have to do an emergency C-section. One of your babies is coming out breech. You're going to have your twins in the next 30 minutes."

At 7:00 pm, my daughter was born. She was 5 lbs, 3 ounces, and measured 18 inches. My son was born at 7:01 pm; he weighed 6 lbs, 2 ounces, and measured 20 inches. That night, five sets of twins were born. While I was in surgery, my mom called both families. When I woke up, I was surrounded by family. Matthew was happy. My miracle angels were beautiful; they both were light-complected and had full heads of jet-black hair.

Four days had passed, and Matthew had not been to the hospital since the twins were born. We were finally being released. It was Thanksgiving Day, and Matthew showed up around 7:00 am. He stopped by for only ten minutes, claiming he couldn't stay long. He let me know that he was leaving town with his girlfriend and her family. I was very hurt and sad when he left. "I'm a single mom with twins," I said to myself.

My family's support meant so much to me. I was excited to be going home and beginning our new lives. When we arrived home, all my family members were waiting to greet us. A couple of weeks passed. I was near the phone when it rang; it was Matthew's girlfriend. I asked if everything was okay, and she told me the news: she and Matthew were pregnant. I wished her all the best and hung up. I was devastated.

CHAPTER 4

BEATEN AND LEFT FOR DEAD

As I reflect on that year, I can say that it was fast and furious. I felt as if one day I got the results that I was pregnant, and the next thing I knew, I was in labor with twins. I had to create a plan; I read over 40 books on how to raise twins. I felt all sorts of hormonal changes. I was jobless, broke, and single. I was truly grateful for the support of my family and friends. The news of Matthew having an affair was heartbreaking. Catching him in the act was even worse. After the ordeal, I was blamed for his actions.

You may be wondering, "Could it get any worse?" Yes, it could—and it did. I received a call from his girlfriend saying that she was pregnant. That truly upset me. The nerve of her to call my home! I couldn't believe that happened, but it did. I thought, "Why didn't he call and give me the news?" I broke down and cried. My mom comforted me. I loved her so much; she always held me and made things better. Her words were so comforting. I remember telling my mom the news about Matthew. I didn't find out until after high school that Matthew had attended a minor seminary school during his freshman year. The purpose of the school was to train boys who had expressed interest in becoming Catholic priests. Doesn't that just knock you off your chair?

After everything I had been through, he was considering being a priest. He mentioned that he liked the school because he was in love with God. He served as an altar boy for many years. Once he finished his freshman year, he transferred back to public school. Matthew was no longer the man I had met over seven years earlier.

I was now 21 years old, and I wasn't able to celebrate a huge milestone. I turned 21 and gave birth to the twins just 11 days later. I am blessed to have had two beautiful, healthy babies—a boy and a girl. In my wildest dreams, I never would have thought that I'd have twins. Being a single mom of twins took a toll on me. I felt like my days were a blur. I was always on the go—either feeding the twins, changing their diapers, washing them, cleaning, preparing their milk, bathing them, burping them, and everything else you do because you have to. On some days, I don't even recall if I showered. There were several occasions when I decided to nap while the twins were sleeping. I had no idea that I would sleep through their cries. My family wouldn't wake me; they just called my relatives and watched them while I slept for hours. I would suddenly wake up frantically. It would be dark, and the twins were still sleeping. Mom would come into my bedroom and let me know that the twins hadn't woken up at all. She didn't want me to panic or feel stressed. They did that for several months without my knowledge.

After having the twins, I never went out with friends. My life was dedicated to being the best mommy I could be. Many of my friends came to visit. It was nice to see them, but I really didn't have time for myself. My social life was nonexistent.

To celebrate the birth of my beautiful twins, we had a baby shower. I invited family and friends. Matthew and I both had large families. We had so much fun. I was so excited to see everyone and introduce the twins. Since my financial situation had changed, I felt blessed to have received everything we needed. However, the supplies I purchased and the gifts I received only carried me so far. My tax return was a big help, but it wouldn't be enough to allow me to stay home. I had to go back to work. My parents tried to watch the twins, but it was too much for them; they were also taking care of nieces and nephews while my sisters worked.

I applied for government assistance and qualified for free daycare. On the first day, I took the day off. I parked my vehicle across the street from the center—just in case they called because the twins needed me. But the call never came. My twins were nurtured by people I trusted; I truly believe God had His hand in selecting their care. I had read that the first years of life are critical, and they were so loved by those beautiful women. We were truly blessed.

I eventually went back to work at Dairy Queen. Matthew started visiting the twins and me more frequently. In the beginning, his visits were short, but after a while, he stayed for hours. On several occasions, he even slept on my bedroom floor to help me through the night. We would go out for lunch or dinner. I never asked about his girlfriend; I didn't care. All I wanted was for him to spend time with us.

But spending time with him came at a price. He became aggressive, calling at all hours to make sure I was home—even when he was with her. We started going to his sister's house to have our alone time. It wasn't long before he started hitting me again. I recall the twins sleeping while I was pushing him off me. When he put on his steel-toe boots, I knew what was coming. He would start hitting me for no reason. I would return home tormented, thinking to myself, "Why do I continue to go back? Why? I don't understand. He is supposed to protect me, not hurt me."

But I loved him. This went on for several months. He never hit my face, only my body. One day, though, things were different. He told me he had a surprise for me: a new pair of boots. Matthew put them on, but his demeanor was different this time. He lifted his hand and slapped me so hard it dropped me to the ground. I just curled into a ball until he was done.

I went back to work that Monday morning, feeling like I was just going through the motions. My sister was working the afternoon shift. She greeted me with her beautiful smile and asked, "Hi little sis. What happened to your face?"

I looked at her and replied, "He hit me. Nothing new."

She completely freaked out and started crying. "I am so sorry that I did not believe you," she said as she hugged me. She immediately picked up the phone to call my parents and sisters to tell them about the bruise on my cheek. After the call, she told me, "Go home now. Everyone is waiting for you. I love you. I am sorry, little sis, that we didn't believe you. We know the truth now, and we are going to protect you."

I walked out of work and shrugged my shoulders. I thought, It's too late. The damage has been done for a while. As I approached home, I saw my parents and siblings waiting outside. They ran to the vehicle, looked at my face, and started hugging me. They were crying and asking for forgiveness. My sister started cursing, vowing that he was going to pay. Mom and Dad were furious, telling me this would never happen to me again.

I began to cry. My sister asked me to go inside and change my clothes. "Hurry up," she said, "because we're leaving."

I wondered where we were going. She took me to the police station. We entered the building and walked up to the window. "How can I help you ladies?" the officer asked.

My sister moved away from the window and gestured for me to speak. She told the officer that I was there to press charges against my ex-boyfriend and file a protective order. She then tilted my face to show him my cheek and pointed out the bruises on my body. The officer got up, opened the side door, and asked us to come in. Before I entered the room, I excused myself to make a call. I didn't want to press charges; I loved him so much. I called Matthew just to ask him why he hit me.

"Because I wanted to," he stated. I responded, "I want you to apologize to me. Please say you are sorry." "I'm not sorry," he said. I hung up the phone and returned to the office. Soon after, a temporary restraining order was put in place. Matthew was served papers and summoned to court. We went to court a couple of weeks after they served him. My family was with me. After the proceedings, I walked out of the courthouse and felt like I was truly free of him.

We stayed away from each other for a few weeks. He called several times a day. We would stay on the phone for hours. He never apologized. I cared for him deeply. I wanted us to be together. I wanted a chance for us to become a family, to have kids together. Matthew and I began to see each other again. I didn't dare tell my parents. He asked me to drop the assault charges. I agreed. I went to the police station and filled out the paperwork. Once I was done, it was submitted. All we could do was wait and see if the documents were accepted. I also didn't mention this to my family.

It was the summer of 1993. Our families came together to have the twins baptized. It was beautiful and I felt overjoyed. A few weeks passed. Matthew and his parents stopped by my house. This visit was unexpected. They knocked on the door and asked to speak to my parents. I was in my bedroom when I heard them. I walked toward the living room. I peeked and leaned in a bit to hear the conversation. Luckily, the twins were asleep.

My father was very upset. My parents greeted them. They walked toward the couches. Mom and Dad sat on the loveseat. Matthew's mom sat between his dad and him. They were sitting across from each other. His mom thanked them for their time.

She then announced, "I am here to apologize for Matthew's behavior toward your daughter. He is very sorry." Matthew agreed by nodding his head. She also said that the affair was a mistake. She continued, "Matthew and Reyna have a long history together. They now have a family and deserve a chance to see if their relationship could work. I am asking for your approval to have Reyna and the twins move in with our family. Matthew and Reyna have a responsibility to raise the twins together as a family."

My dad stood up, and with a raised voice said, "No, I do not approve. But the decision is not mine. It's my daughter's choice. I will not give you my blessing."

With that, he stormed out of the room. I ran back into my room and jumped on my bed. My dad walked in and told me everything. He told me, "I don't like him. I do not approve. This is your home. You do not have to leave."

At that time, my mom walked in and asked me to join her in the living room. I was so nervous. We walked into the living room and sat across from them. They said hi. His mom asked me if I loved Matthew. I said I did. She began to explain the reasons why they were there. She told me, "Matthew loves you too. We don't condone Matthew's behavior and his affair. He is sorry." Matthew agreed by nodding his head.

His mother continued, "You've been together for over seven years. You both deserve a chance to make this relationship work for the twins. We would like you and the twins to move in with us. We'll buy everything you and the twins need." I was overwhelmed with emotion. I thought, 'This must be a dream. I can't believe they are in our home asking us to move in together.' I asked if I could think about it. She said I could. "We will be here waiting until you decide," she said.

My mom and I stood up and walked back to my bedroom. My dad had been listening to the conversation. He told me, "Hija, you don't have to go with them. You don't need them."

He then walked out of the room. My mom sat next to me. "Reyna, this isn't my decision; it's yours. Your father is right—you don't need them. We are here for you," she said. Mom put her arms around me and hugged me. After a few minutes, I raised my head and held her hand.

I finally said, "Mom, if I don't give us a chance, I'll always wonder what could have been. I'll never forgive myself if I don't try. This is our last chance to see if we were meant to be together. I will never be able to let go of this dream to be a family. I love him so much. His family supports our relationship and they are here asking for another chance. I want to be able to tell my twins that Mommy tried again—that I didn't give up hope."

My dad was listening to our conversation again. He walked back into the bedroom and said, "You can come home anytime. I love you. Don't forget that. We're family. This door is always open for the three of you."

My mom and I walked back into the living room and sat down. I said, "We'll go live with you. We can move in tomorrow."

She asked, "Why tomorrow?"

I told her that I had to pack and wash all the dirty clothes. She said that I could wash at their home, but I responded that I preferred to wash here.

She replied, "Well, we don't have any plans today. We will stay until you are ready. Matthew will help you pack and wash clothes." She stood up and asked my mom if she could help her in the kitchen.

My mom added, "We should eat since we will be here for a few hours."

I had to wash several loads. Once each load was washed, we both hung the clothes outside on a clothesline. We were finally packed and ready to head out. I didn't take all of our belongings; the majority stayed at home. I hugged my parents and let them know that I loved them so much and that we would be coming home to visit.

A month passed and the relationship was going well. Matthew was different; he was a great father and a good boyfriend. His family was so nice to me. One day, his sisters approached me. They told me that I should marry Matthew. They said the wedding could be planned in a month, I could pick out my wedding ring, and I could select a live band or DJ. They told me I could have anything I wanted and that they would make it happen. They even said my parents didn't have to spend any money. I let them know that it was too soon to think about marriage. I thanked them, and they told me that if I changed my mind, I should let them know.

One day, his family got a call to head to the hospital. There had been an emergency. They asked if I could watch their kids, and I said I would. They all got into their vehicles and drove away. When they arrived home later, no one really discussed what happened; all I heard was that everything was okay.

A few weeks passed. One day, we were in the living room watching a movie with the family. The twins were asleep in our bedroom. We had a voice monitor, but I decided to go check on them. I found them sound asleep. As I turned and started walking out of the room, I heard Matthew's pager go off. I checked the number and did not recognize it. It kept beeping, so I decided to call.

Guess who it was? It was the other girl. I asked her if everything was alright. She told me that I was dumb. She also let me know that she had her baby boy a couple of weeks ago.

I hung up. The emergency had been about her baby. I was fuming. I thought, What the fuck? While they were in the other room, I packed our bags and put the kids in their car seats. I walked back into the living room and started yelling.

"Why didn't you tell me that the emergency was the birth of your baby boy? I had to hear it from your other baby momma! We're leaving, and it's over for good!" I screamed.

I turned around and walked swiftly to the bedroom. I could hear Matthew coming behind me. He got upset because he noticed that the bags were packed and the kids were asleep in their car seats.

"You're not leaving," he announced.

Like hell I wasn't, I thought. He reached out to grab my hair, but his brothers held him back. They let him know that he should have told me and that this was his fault. His brothers helped me carry the twins to the vehicle and buckled them in. They also put my bags in the vehicle. Matthew stayed inside.

I cried and cursed all the way home. I couldn't believe that this happened to us. I truly tried to make it work. My heart was yanked out again. I decided I was never going back—that I was done and wanted nothing to do with him. We would never become a family. I drove up to the house. My dad was sitting outside. Dad could tell that I had been crying. He walked up to the vehicle and didn't say a word. He hugged me and helped bring the twins inside. My mom just held me. She listened to me while I cried and told her what had happened.

It took a few days before I calmed down. Matthew tried to call, but I refused to speak to him. He came over to visit with the twins; I just stayed in my bedroom. After a few weeks passed, my mom mentioned that I looked stressed and that I needed to relax. She said that I was always "on edge" and that I needed to have fun. I told her that I had no social life and I liked it that way. I was a mother now, and that is all I wanted to be.

Late one Saturday afternoon, my mom asked me to get dressed as if I were going to a club. I didn't want to get all dolled up. I hesitated, but she insisted. The twins were napping, so I complied. I tried on several outfits. The last outfit I put on was a coral two-piece with an open back. I looked super cute. My mom asked me to go and get something out of her vehicle. After I walked out of the house, she threw my purse and keys outside.

She then locked the front door and yelled through the window, "Go have fun and don't come home until 2:00 a.m. Your dad filled up your gas tank. I also put $50 in your purse. You're too stressed out and we can't handle it anymore."

I started yelling for her to let me in.

She responded with, "Be here by 2:00 a.m. and don't be late."

I pushed my head against the front window screen. I noticed my dad was in the living room and asked him to open the door. He told me that he was reading the paper and I should listen to my mother.

I replied, "Dad, the paper is upside down."

He turned it around, gave me his back, and stated, "I'm going to get into trouble if I let you in. Go do what your mother said."

I had no friends that I knew who went to clubs. I also had no idea where I was going to go. I sat in my vehicle and started to cry. I then decided to call one of my friends. Once she answered, I told her what happened. She told me that this was a good thing and that I should drive to the nearest city and go have some fun. She kept me company while I drove into the city.

During the drive, my cell phone fell on the floor of the passenger side. I bent down to get my phone, and my vehicle swerved to the right. I looked up into my rearview mirror and saw that a police officer was pulling me over. What luck.

I put the phone down on the passenger seat. I was still crying when the officer approached my vehicle. He asked me if I knew why I was being pulled over. I responded that I did. The police officer noticed that I was crying and asked if I was okay. I began to tell him what happened. The officer smiled and asked me to step out of the vehicle. He started to tell me that maybe my mom was right, and that going out would be a good thing to relieve some stress.

He asked to look at my outfit. I did a spin. The officer complimented my outfit. I also let him know that I didn't have any friends because I'm a full-time mom. I told him I had no idea where to go. He excused himself for a minute. A moment later, he walked back toward me and told me that he knew an officer at a club in the city. He contacted him and let him know what I was going through. Since it was early, the officer at that club was able to place a cone in a parking space right in front of the club. I was then told that he was the only officer on duty and that the rest of the team would arrive later. He also told me that he gave the other officer my name and that he would take care of me. I told him that I was very appreciative and thanked him.

I arrived at the club and saw a line of people waiting to go in. I drove toward the front entrance where an officer was standing and gave him my name. He pointed to a parking space right in front. After I parked, I walked toward him and thanked him for the spot. The officer then escorted me to the entry door and told me I did not have to wait in line; he told me to just go inside and have a good time. WOW! Within the span of a couple of hours, I had been tricked by my mom, got all dolled up, and now found myself inside a club all alone.

As I walked into the club, I found a large, open space. To the right, they were playing hip-hop. To the left, they were playing Tejano and country music. I opted for the left side. When I entered the dance hall, I saw a dance floor in the center and a bar in every corner of the room. The DJ booth was located in the back left. I decided to stop at the first bar on the left. Once I purchased a beer, I walked toward the back of the room. The music was great. In my opinion, there were more people in line outside than there were inside. I stood there all alone, still unable to believe I was at a bar on a Saturday night. I guess I was going to be a people watcher.

While I was watching people walk into the room, I noticed two girls enter. They passed the first bar, and someone handed them each a beer. They passed the second and third bars and then stood in front of the fourth bar. By then, they each had three drinks in their hands. I knew these were the girls I needed to meet; they were clearly very popular, as even the DJ gave them a shout-out. After a while, the girls headed to the restroom. I thought to myself that this would be a good time to meet them.

While washing our hands, I complimented one of the girls' belt buckles. She complimented my outfit. They asked who I was with, and I lied, telling them my friends had stood me up. I felt bad about lying, but I didn't want to let them know my mom had kicked me out because I needed to release some stress. They invited me to hang out with them, and we had a blast. Time flew by, and soon I had to head home. I thanked the police officer on duty at the club. On the drive home, I was pulled over by that same officer; he was just checking on me. I was very grateful and let him know I'd had a wonderful time.

I was home before 2:00 a.m. As soon as I walked in, I had just enough time to change, thank my mom, and feed the twins. In the morning, I thanked my mom profusely. She always looked out for my best interests, even if I didn't always agree with her tactics.

While raising twins and working full-time, I still made time to go to church and read books about parenting as a single mom. Most of the books I read were very inspirational and gave me hope. Every paycheck, I would go on an outing with just the twins and myself. During the week, we would head to the mall to look for bargains. My favorite stores were The Children's Place, Dillard's, Old Navy, JCPenney, and Montgomery Ward. I made friends with the employees, and they would let me know the best days to shop for sales or clearance items. I gave them my phone number and asked them to call me if they found matching clothes for the twins.

I enjoyed getting the twins all dressed up, especially when I had them wear similar outfits. Everyone thought I paid a lot of money for the clothes, but the truth was I couldn't afford full price. I was on a budget. After shopping, I would have lunch at the food court while they enjoyed a bottle of milk. Once we were done, we'd head to a dollar movie. I wanted them to get used to listening to a movie without crying. We would stay for about an hour until they had enough of the loud noise. After several attempts, they learned to sleep right through the movie. I still made time for family outings; my mom, nieces, nephew, twins, and I would pack ourselves into my vehicle and head to dinner and a movie. Other times, we would have lunch and head to the park.

Mom allowed me to continue going out dancing. She said that I was happier and didn't look so stressed out. It also kept my mind off Matthew. He hardly made time for us because he had another family. The twins were growing so fast, sitting up on their own and eating solid foods. They always had smiles on their faces. My dad came into my room every morning; he'd carry one of the twins to the living room to watch TV, then he would bring the baby back for me to change their diaper. He would then take the other twin with him to finish watching his show. My mom and sisters spent time with the twins, too. They truly helped me out.

One Saturday evening, I decided to head to the city to meet my friends at the Tejano club. I arrived and was immediately asked to dance. He danced so well I thought he was a dance instructor. Once we were done, he asked if we could have a conversation. He walked me to a table where a lady was sitting. They both began to explain to me that they were professional dancers. They had a competition coming up in a few months and needed someone to finally get them to the championship. The dance competition included Tejano and Country dance. The lady let me know that she was going to have surgery on her ankle. She would not be able to compete, but she hoped to be able to dance on the last day of competition. They had been competing for years and had won several championships.

I was a bit confused. I let them know that I had no idea how to dance professionally in either genre. They were aware that I was not ready, but because I was a good follower, I could be trained. They mentioned that they had been scoping me out for some time. If I was interested, they would be able to teach me to dance. It sounded nice, but I had no confidence in my skills. They gave me their business card and let me know that they would like to begin the following day. They said that if I wanted to move forward, I should meet them at the address on the card. They thanked me and left the club. I walked away shocked.

The next morning, I discussed it with my mom. She looked at me and responded, "What's the problem? Go learn to dance and help them get to the championship round." My mom always believed that when opportunities present themselves, you have to take a chance. She believed that life is too short and that we should enjoy the journey and have fun. So, I drove to the address on the card. They were both waiting for me under a gazebo.

They greeted me by saying, "We didn't think you would show. Thank you for coming."

They didn't waste any time; we danced for a few hours. She was scheduled for surgery that Monday morning. He let me know that our new meeting point would be at the club. We would meet at 8:00 pm sharp. They let me know there was one rule: no drinking while in training. The training was rigorous. The female dancer also joined us at the club, coaching from the edge of the dance floor. I was always very sore. I used muscles that I did not know I had. I didn't stay long at the club after our rehearsals.

We spent a few weeks practicing for the dance competition. Our first competition was coming up soon. It was nerve-wracking to know that I had to help them get to the championship round. I wasn't very good at dancing, and they had more confidence in me than I did in myself. After a few weeks, the moves came so naturally, and I felt more confident. They were both tough on me, but I understood; dancing is what they loved to do, and it meant so much to them.

On the day of the competition, I was so nervous. The female dancer hugged me and let me know that I would be fine. She told me to trust him and that he would guide me. She also told me to go out and show them what we had learned in the last few weeks.

Numbers were placed on our backs. Once our numbers were called, we would go to the dance floor. The DJ would begin the music, and we'd start dancing. We advanced to the next round. Every week we practiced and competed, and we kept advancing. Eventually, we made it to the final competition. I could not believe we had made it. The female dancer was so excited when they announced our number—they had won the competition. I was so happy to have been selected and to be part of this great memory.

Life with Matthew and the Twins Sometime after that, I reached out to Matthew to discuss the twins' first birthday celebration. I was a planner and knew that we were either celebrating the party together or apart. Matthew wanted to celebrate together as a family. He started coming around again, spending time with the twins while I was at work. I loved him, but I was in a different place in my life. I knew our breakup was still recent. It had taken all of me to pick myself up again and continue to look forward rather than behind me. It took time to realize that I could not change the past, but I could hope for a better future. I was determined not to tolerate his bullshit.

Goals and Transitions While planning for the party, I decided to seek a new job. I was grateful for my job at Dairy Queen, but I needed a change. DQ paid the bills, but up to that point, I wasn't able to finish college. I knew my goal was to return and finish; my college degree would secure a good job and enable me to purchase my dream brick home. My only focus was my twins. Finding a job that paid more would allow me to move out of my parents' home. My parents didn't want me to move, but Mom was a full-time babysitter. My sister dropped off her kids in the morning and picked them up late at night. We always had a full house.

The Party Planning We decided that the twins' first birthday party would be at Peter Piper Pizza. Matthew would pay for all the food, and I'd pay for the drinks.

We split the cost in half for the twins' gifts. Matthew and I took a count of family members that would be attending the party; we had a count of 75. This did not include any of our friends or all of the family. I had a couple of months to save.

Matthew and I started hanging out a little more frequently. His demeanor wasn't very positive—maybe because now he had two "baby mommas" to spend time with. When we were alone, his temper started flaring up. I was happy that the protective order was still in place. When he started yelling at me, I reminded him about it.

The Law Firm Opportunity During this time, my cousin who lived in the city reached out to me and informed me of an opportunity to work as a filing clerk at a law firm. It paid more than I was earning. The hours were 8:00 am to 5:00 pm, Monday through Friday. I immediately agreed to interview for the position. What a turn of events! When I walked into the office, everyone was dressed so professionally. Men wore suits and women wore dresses. My current attire at DQ was a head visor, red polo shirt, grey slacks, and black tennis shoes. The interview went great; I was hired.

The attorney who interviewed me asked if I could start immediately. I let him know that I accepted the position but that I would like to give DQ a two-week notice. We negotiated and agreed to a one-week notice. I left the office wanting to jump and touch the sky. No more working late nights, cleaning, stocking, cooking, and leaving home with grease or ice cream all over my clothes. I drove straight to my job and gave my notice. When I arrived home, I ran inside and started shouting the great news. Luckily, my twins were awake. When Matthew came over, I let him know that I was hired at a law firm as a file clerk. He wasn't happy about the news.

The following Monday morning, I was off to work. I dropped the twins off at daycare and drove into the city. It was nice to work at a job where I could dress professionally. My first day went well, and everyone was very kind. They informed me that if I needed time off, I just had to call; they were aware that I had twins.

A couple of weeks passed, and everything was going great. However, one day after I dropped off the twins, I noticed Matthew's vehicle behind me. He signaled for me to pull over. I called him from my mobile phone to tell him I was heading to work, explaining that I had just started a new job and did not want to be late. He began yelling for me to pull over. When I didn't, he started hitting the back of my vehicle with his front bumper. When he hit my car again, I thought to myself, this guy is going crazy.

He called again, demanding I pull over. I hung up and kept driving, immediately dialing 911. I told the dispatcher that my ex-boyfriend was hitting my car with his bumper and informed them that I had a restraining order against him. An officer took over the call and asked for my location. He told me I would have to trust him and follow his instructions exactly.

During the call, Matthew continued to ram my vehicle, nearly making me crash into parked cars. I remained on the phone with the officer, who told me to focus on his voice. He directed me to turn onto specific streets with stop signs—streets I had been trying to avoid. The officer explained they were securing a four-way stop to intercept him. Fearful for my life, I began to yell.

"What if you're not there? What if he catches me?" I screamed.

The officer managed to calm me down enough to listen. He reassured me they were ready and that they already had eyes on us as we came down the street. He instructed me to pass the next four-way stop, but at the following one, I was to stop and not move.

I arrived at the four-way stop and stayed put. Matthew jumped out of his car and lunged onto the hood of mine. To my right, his car continued to roll because he had jumped out without putting it in park. He started yelling and banging on my windshield. Suddenly, from both the right and left, officers swarmed the scene. They grabbed him and tackled him to the ground. Matthew's unoccupied vehicle eventually hit another car and a fence.

I was shaking and couldn't stop crying. Once I calmed down, I called the office to let them know I would be late. I arrived at work feeling frazzled. My colleagues didn't ask why I was late, and I didn't tell them; I was simply too embarrassed.

When I arrived home, I let my family know what had happened. They were extremely upset and disappointed by his behavior. They asked if I was okay and why I hadn't called them when it occurred. I reassured my parents that I was unharmed, explaining that I wasn't going to allow anything to ruin this new opportunity. Matthew had been calling the house all afternoon. We finally spoke later that evening, and he apologized for his behavior. I was still upset and let him know he could have hurt me; I also told him I didn't know how I could continue our friendship. The twins' birthday celebration was only a week away, and our dynamic just wasn't working. He continued to apologize, explaining that he couldn't lose "us." In his mind, I would always be his—but there was no "us." We were simply going to co-parent the twins.

I was so frustrated and couldn't understand his behavior. After a few hours, however, I calmed down and accepted his apology. He also agreed to repair my vehicle if there was any damage. I owned a four-door, gray Buick Century. After checking the car, I didn't see any dents on the bumper, but it did have plenty of scratches. I ultimately decided there was no point in repairing it since I was already planning on purchasing a new vehicle.

The following Saturday morning, my family and I were up early getting ready for the twins' first birthday celebration. I had booked the party at Peter Piper Pizza, which meant we had to drive into the city. My babies were turning one year old; I felt like I had blinked and they were suddenly a year older. I felt so blessed to have those two beautiful babies.

We arrived at the party with gifts, party bags, favors, and a cake. Matthew and his family arrived around the same time; he came over to say "hi" and helped us carry the party supplies. I had reserved the space for 75 people. I don't think anyone believed that many would show up, but they did. We hadn't even invited all of our family or friends! Since it was our first big party, I was a bit overwhelmed by how to host so many attendees.

During the party, I barely held my twins until it was time for the cake and gifts. Every time I looked up, they were being held by a different family member. This gave me a chance to mingle and personally thank everyone. Matthew was being very nice, walking around to chat with the guests. I had worried that the day wouldn't be perfect, but it all worked out. Everyone had fun and thanked us for the invitation. The twins received so many presents, for which I was very grateful. By the end, we were exhausted. When we got back to the house, the twins were already asleep. We brought them inside and they didn't even wake up, allowing us to bring in the gifts, shower, and take a much-needed nap.

After a while, I established a steady routine. I would pack the twins' bags and my lunch the night before, and I also laid out our clothes. In the morning, I'd get the twins fed and dressed first. Then, I would quickly eat, do my makeup, and get dressed myself. I'd gather our things and place them in the vehicle before coming back inside to carry the twins to the car one at a time. Once they were buckled into their car seats, it was only a ten-minute drive to daycare. Dropping them off was easy, as someone was always there to help me bring them inside.

My drive to the city was less than 30 minutes, and I truly enjoyed my job. Work was going well; I liked being a file clerk, and they even trained me to relieve the receptionist during her lunch break. Being an extrovert helped—I was always cheerful and enjoyed interacting with the clients.

Matthew kept coming over on the weekends, often without calling first. He would just drop by and expect me to be home. Consequently, my family and I started taking weekend trips to the city, volunteering at the church, and attending Mass. Matthew began to get irritated because I wasn't around, but I didn't care. I was with my family. I felt he shouldn't get so bent out of shape. The weekends flew by, and it was nice to have some extra cash. I didn't miss my old job, but I did miss the ice cream.

I remember one beautiful morning during this time that I woke up in a great mood. The twins were all smiles. Since I was full of joy, I decided to change the outfit I had laid out the day before. I went to my closet and selected a two-piece maroon top and skirt. The top was sleeveless and fitted; it had a long V-neck, black buttons down the front, and two front pockets. I wore the matching long pencil skirt and black closed-toe heels. I felt festive.

I dropped the twins off at daycare, then decided to drive a different route to work. While I was driving, I noticed Matthew behind me. He was following my vehicle quite closely. He started raising his hand and motioning for me to pull over. I was not going to pull over and be late to work. He kept motioning, but I wouldn't pull over. He then began to hit the bumper of my car. I reached to grab my phone to call 911, but it slid onto the passenger-side floorboard. I couldn't reach it. I was afraid to stop; I remembered what happened the last time I stopped my car. The route I had selected did not have many businesses that were open.

Matthew began to hit the right side of my bumper, forcing me to make a left turn onto a gravel road. He used his vehicle to force mine to turn. He was not letting off the gas. I started driving down this gravel road with no houses in sight. I was crying and scared for my life. I started yelling and looking around my vehicle for items I could use to defend myself. I tried reaching for my phone several times, but I still couldn't reach it.

There was a road coming up that went right. Matthew pushed my vehicle that way; it was a dead-end road. I stayed in my vehicle. Matthew parked behind me, leaving about a car's space between our vehicles. He walked up to the driver-side window and started banging on the glass, demanding that I open the door. I refused. He kept banging on the window and windshield, yelling for me to open up. I couldn't find anything in the vehicle to use as a weapon. I was so scared that I couldn't move. I finally cracked open the window. His voice got calmer.

He then announced, "When I get you out of the vehicle, you are going to get it. Open the door now. Do you think you can run from me? You think you can do what you want? Who are you all dressed up for? You're not home when I come over. You're making me do this to you. You think you have freedom. Do not keep my twins away from me."

He pried his fingers through the gap where I had cracked the window and started trying to bend the glass toward him. I knew eventually the window would bust, so I unlocked the vehicle. He immediately reached in to grab my hair. It was waist-length. He yanked me, but the seatbelt kept me in. He unbuckled my seatbelt and jerked me out of the car. He dragged me to the passenger side of his car. While he was dragging me, so many thoughts were going through my head. I had to fight back at all costs. I was not going to let him intimidate me. He was holding my chin, yelling and cursing at me. I could feel his spit all over my face.

He then told me, "Guess what? It's your lucky day. I just bought a brand-new pair of steel-toed boots. You know what that means. Do you know why I hit you? Because you make me hit you. No one can save you now."

He pushed my face down toward his boots. He slapped me and began to punch me. I started to fight back, but he was too strong. I could feel every punch. I lost my footing and fell. He picked me up and kept punching. I wasn't going to stop fighting, even though I was getting the air knocked out of me. I fought back until I couldn't. I started using my hands to block the punches to my ribs and stomach. I leaned on the vehicle and ducked down. I fell, my body facing his front tire. He started kicking me everywhere, from my head to my feet. I tried to get up several times, but I wasn't able to balance myself. I stayed on the ground. He kicked me so hard that my body would rise a few inches off the ground. Every time I attempted to get up, he would kick me harder. I don't know how long it lasted because I blacked out. When I regained consciousness, he was still kicking me.

I said a prayer and told God that I was ready to go. I could no longer sustain the pain I was feeling. I closed my eyes and stopped moving; I was dead weight. Matthew noticed that I was neither moving nor yelling at him. He kept on for a bit, but after a few more kicks, he stopped when he didn't get a reaction from me. I didn't move. I heard him turn on his vehicle. When I opened my eyes to see where he was, my face was towards the tire—I was only a few inches away. He put the vehicle in drive and started to pull away. Before closing my eyes again, I watched the tire pass right in front of my face.

I was in so much pain. I lay there for a while just to make sure he was gone. I couldn't believe this was happening to me. I thought to myself, "Why did he want to hurt me? What did I do wrong?" He had left me there to die. He never even checked to see if I was alright or still breathing. I then wondered why I had continued to have a personal relationship with him.

I just lay there and cried. When I finally decided to get up, my body was in such shock that I could hardly move. I prayed and prayed. I forced myself up and dusted myself off as best I could. Every part of my body ached. Using all my remaining energy, I drove myself to work. I grabbed my phone and called the office because I was already running late. I should have gone home or called 911, but I didn't do either; I couldn't lose this job. I had to survive to save myself and my twins.

Once I arrived, I did my best to ensure all the dust was off me. I met with the attorney and told him everything, asking him to keep our conversation confidential. I also let him know that I intended to stay at work. He wanted me to go to the police station, but I refused. He told me I could leave whenever I was ready. I didn't want to think about what had just happened. I had no energy and felt so weak. I knew I had to go home. After staying a couple of hours, I left. I didn't pick up the twins from daycare yet; I needed to rest. When I arrived home, I went straight to the shower, and once I got out, I took some medicine.

I never told my family or reported the incident. I was fearful that he might retaliate and do it all over again.

For the next few weeks, I felt like a zombie, constantly replaying the incident in my mind. To release my emotions, I cried in the shower, but I continued to go out with my friends. No one noticed my bruises because I made sure to cover them up. I was in constant pain, which I felt even more whenever I carried the twins. They gave me hope. I decided then that I had to create a plan to move out of town and into the city—moving so far away that he wouldn't be able to bother me.

I truly loved being a mom. I felt a sense of purpose and wanted to protect my kids at all costs. However, I was having mechanical problems with my Buick. It didn't feel safe enough for my family. I had purchased it used and it had served its purpose, but it was time to look for a new vehicle. One day after work, I stopped by a Dodge dealership and found a cute small car: a 1993 Plymouth Colt four-door sedan. It was purple. They ran a credit check to see if I qualified, and I was prepared to give a down payment. However, the bank denied me because I hadn't been at my current job long enough to establish a steady income. They requested a cosigner.

I went home disappointed but remained hopeful that I could find someone to cosign for me. I called everyone I knew, but they were unable to help for various reasons. There was only one person I knew who would qualify: Matthew. After what happened, I didn't want to call him. A few days passed before I finally decided to make the call. He was willing and ready. The following afternoon, he met me at the dealership and cosigned—with a few conditions, of course. He told me he would not help with the down payment or the monthly payments. I never asked him to do those things, but he wanted to make it known. I was so happy to drive home in a safe, new vehicle. The only thing I didn't like was that he held onto the spare key. I didn't care; I just needed the car. The salesman mentioned that after a year, I could reapply at the bank to be the sole owner. For a while, Matthew kept his distance.

Work was going well; it occupied my mind. Since it was Christmas, they gave us a bonus. I was so happy, as I'd never experienced getting a bonus from a job before. I felt so blessed. The twins spent Christmas with me and one day with

Matthew. I didn't like it when holidays came around and he wanted to keep them, but since I was receiving child support, it was court-ordered.

My family and friends would console me. Living with my parents was nice, but we needed our own space. I'd been saving the majority of my money because my goal was to purchase a home of our own. My parents didn't want me to leave; they told me that we could stay as long as we wanted. However, my mom had too many kids she had to take care of already, and I didn't want to burden them.

The twins were heading to their dad's for New Year's Eve. I begged him to let me have them, but he said, "NO!" I think he took them on purpose just to hurt my feelings. I had found out that when he picked up the twins for his weekends, he would spend the majority of the time at his girlfriend's house and leave them with his mom. His family loved my twins, but Matthew didn't have to take them if he wasn't actually going to see them. That really upset me, but I couldn't do anything about it. I just had to stay busy.

I joined my friends at the club to celebrate New Year's Eve, and we had a blast. Before the night was over, I met a guy named Marcus. Everyone kept telling me that he was shy. We danced for the majority of the night; he was a good dancer. We exchanged numbers, but I didn't expect to ever see him again. I wasn't interested in a relationship; my focus was on my twins, my family, and my work.

A week after we met, Marcus called the house. I was pretty shocked. He asked to take me out. I let him know that I wasn't ready for a relationship, but he insisted. I met him at the club where my friends and I hung out. We had fun and danced all night. I still wasn't interested in hanging out with him alone, and I didn't mind meeting him at the club, but he was persistent and asked if he could take me out to dinner before we went to the club. I agreed—a girl has to eat. We had a good conversation, but something was off. I couldn't pinpoint it; it was just a gut instinct. I let him know that, at that time, we could only be friends.

Once he agreed, I started meeting him for lunch or dinner. I felt more comfortable because he knew the boundaries. He was living with his parents, but I wasn't judging because I lived with mine, too. One day, I went over to his house to have lunch. The phone rang while he was outside, and he asked if I could answer it. I picked up the phone, and it was his ex-girlfriend. She knew my name, which left me stunned. She told me that she and Marcus were still trying to work on their relationship. I apologized; I didn't need or want any more drama than I already had. I hung up the phone, walked outside, and told Marcus about the call. I was so disappointed. I asked him never to approach me at the club or call me ever again. He kept trying to stop me to explain what happened, but I just got into my vehicle and didn't look back. No more drama.

The days flew by. I focused on my twins, my family, and my friends. I was saving up for a down payment on a home and was happy that I was able to save so much. As often as I could, I went to church with my mom to give thanks. She was always at church; she was our family's glue. She always supported us when things didn't go as planned and always knew what to say. She knew that sometimes a hug, a caress of our faces, or someone playing with our hair was all that we needed. She was bold and honest. My mom always looked toward the future and what God had in store for us; she looked for His plan and His timing.

The twins were growing up so quickly, and the daycare staff adored them. I trusted them. Marcus kept calling, but I wasn't having it. One night at the club, my girlfriends approached me. Marcus had spoken to them about what happened and provided his side of the story. Since my friends wouldn't stop harassing me about it and because I trusted them, they convinced me to hear him out. He was sitting at a table all alone and looked sad. I decided to listen.

Marcus began by apologizing and explaining his side of the story. He said he and his ex-girlfriend were over, and he had told her that he was seeing me. He explained that she was upset and had lied to me. I let him know that I did not want any more drama in my life. He begged me to give him a chance. I told him that we could take it one day at a time, but for that night, we would just dance and celebrate life. Marcus was so sweet; he tried really hard even though I had been so mean to him.

After a while, I finally gave in. I introduced him and his family to the twins, and they fell in love with my little angels. I started going over to his family's house almost every weekend. The twins' father was so upset when he found out about Marcus; he called and cursed me out, telling me, "If I can't have you, no one else can." But I didn't care what he said, and it didn't bother Marcus. He told me he would protect me.

Sometime later, I reached out to a realtor to begin the process of purchasing a home. I had saved enough money for a down payment and was so excited when I qualified for a $55K mortgage. I couldn't believe it; my dreams of owning a home were about to become a reality. My parents were excited for me, but also very sad to see me go.

I found the perfect home on the outskirts of the city next to a bay. The bay was fed by a freshwater creek and saltwater from the gulf. So, at the age of 24, I purchased my "mini-mansion." The house was on a corner lot and was 900 square feet with two bedrooms, one bathroom, and a detached garage. It needed a lot of work, but I fell in love with it. I could see the beauty of the home, even though the walls were three different colors: "Pepto Bismol" pink, blue, and cream. This color scheme continued throughout the house, including pink cabinets. It had original hardwood floors, but the exterior of the home desperately needed paint.

I was on a budget and knew the remodel would take several months before we could move in. My parents were happy I had purchased a home and were glad I planned on staying with them until the work was complete. Marcus had a cousin who owned a door company that also sold trim, flooring, paint, and windows. Marcus's cousin mentioned they had a pile of doors and trim they were about to throw out. He told us we could have them for free as long as we picked them up, noting they were slightly damaged but salvageable.

Marcus gave his cousin a tour of the house. His cousin joked that he was about to get sick looking at the wall colors, saying it looked like someone had thrown up paint without caring where it landed. As a gift, he offered to paint the interior for free using several extra cans of white glossy paint he had in stock. I was so touched by his offer.

It took three months to complete the house. During that time, the twins and I moved in with Marcus and his parents. The transformation was incredible. The inside of the house was painted white with brand-new trim. We chose a cherry wood finish for the trim to match the freshly sanded cherry wood floors. We replaced all the doors in the home, and the cabinets were sanded and repainted burgundy. Finally, we installed new full-length mirrored closet doors, which gave the rooms the illusion of being much larger.

My friend worked at Lacks furniture store and offered me her discount, which allowed me to purchase all my furniture there. I made a down payment and took advantage of their zero-percent interest rate for the balance. While my dad painted the garage, I hired a painter to repair the home's exterior and apply a fresh coat of paint. Marcus, the twins, and I moved in after three months of hard work. We hosted a housewarming party with over 80 guests. Since it was a corner lot, I had a very large backyard. This was my second chance for a brighter future, and I believed the twins and I deserved it.

I felt safer living outside of my hometown. I decided not to move the twins to a daycare in the city, which allowed me to visit my family after work; it also meant my family could pick up the twins if I was running late. My commute was an hour in both the morning and the evening.

Raising the twins without my family's daily help was a lot of work. I was up at 5:30 every morning to feed them. Once they were fed, I would get dressed for work. I didn't wear much makeup or have time to get all "dolled up." I had long, black, curly hair that reached down to my waist, and I would style my bangs. I packed the twins' bags the night before. Each morning, I would buckle the twins into their car seats, grab the diaper bag, and take the babies to the car one at a time. Then, I would drive back to my hometown, drop them off at daycare, stop at the Mexican restaurant to grab a taco, and head to work.

In the evenings, I would pick up the twins, visit my family, or head straight home. I would feed the twins, make dinner for us, repack the diaper bag, bathe them, feed them again, shower, breathe, and go to bed. Weekends were a little more relaxed. I still had chores to do, but I wasn't in a rush, and I was able to spend quality time with my family.

Matthew didn't know where I lived, though he had my home phone number. I still didn't feel safe enough to give him my address. He knew when I picked up the twins from daycare or when I dropped in to see my parents. Every time I looked at him, I remembered the last beating. I felt scared, but I played it off in front of my parents. Matthew would show up and be nice when my parents were around, but once they left, he would make comments under his breath. I didn't know how long that would last. My parents always walked me to my vehicle and entertained Matthew until I left. It was as if they knew something didn't feel right between Matthew and me.

As I avoided Matthew, he started being nicer. When we spoke on the phone, he was polite. We met up every other weekend because his visitation with the twins was court-ordered. He made it a point to always be on time. I was never on time; he eventually got used to it and realized he had no choice.

Matthew did not like that Marcus was living with me, but I didn't care—it was not my problem. He kept his comments to himself. Marcus and his family were a big help, watching the twins when I wanted to hang out with my friends or just have some alone time.

Work was going well, and I was settled in at home. I felt blessed to have a vehicle, a house, and a boyfriend who really loved me. As summer approached, Matthew asked if the twins and I would join him and his family at Garner State Park. He told me they were going to camp there for a week and that they would provide me with my own tent, blanket, sleeping bag, pillows, flashlights, and chair. I discussed it with Marcus. He was aware of Matthew's temper but told me I could go if I wanted to and that he would support my decision. I wanted to create family memories for my twins and their father's family.

After much thought, I packed our bags and went on the trip. It felt a bit awkward being around the family, but after a couple of days, I was fine. Matthew was extremely nice, yet I kept my guard up; my gut instinct told me something was going on with him. I focused on my twins and family, living for the moment.

The park was beautiful and peaceful. Along with swimming and hiking, Garner State Park is well known for its large outdoor pavilion, which holds dances throughout the summer. The twins and I had a wonderful time. When I arrived home, I was happy to reunite with Marcus. As I lay in bed, I reflected on the past few months. I thought, "Being a single mother is tough." People often asked how I managed to raise twins all alone, and my reply was always the same: "I just do."

Before the twins, I had never had children, so learning to care for two at once felt like my only "normal." I hardly slept, ate, or even thought about myself. My twins were my life, my purpose, and my entire being. It was a whirlwind, but I felt blessed with the opportunities God had bestowed upon my family: my "angels," a new job, a home, a car, and a relationship. It seemed like everything was coming together—my second chance at a new beginning.

As fall approached, I couldn't believe the twins were already turning two. Unfortunately, my job at the law firm was not going well. I had been hired as a file clerk, but after a few months, they moved me into a new role. The position turned out to be different than I expected. It was difficult, and though I tried to keep up with the firm's fast pace, I struggled. A few months later, the firm let me go. I was devastated; I had bills to pay.

With the twins' birthday party at the end of the month, Marcus told me not to worry and offered to help with the bills. I applied for several jobs but didn't receive any immediate replies. Sometimes, things just don't work out the way we plan.

After applying at several retail stores, I visited my cousin's girlfriend at a men's clothing store. I mentioned I was looking for work, and she told me she and my cousin were moving to San Antonio. The store needed someone to replace her. She introduced me to the Assistant Manager, and we spoke for a few minutes. He was impressed and told me he would recommend me to the General Manager. I met with the manager three days later; he interviewed me and offered me a full-time position as a Sales Associate. I left feeling so excited—when one door closes, another opens. I called my mom with the great news, relieved that I had been unemployed for less than a month.

We celebrated the twins' second birthday at Peter Piper Pizza with over 100 guests. Since many people were disappointed they weren't invited to the first birthday, we extended the invitation to all our extended family and friends. To our surprise, everyone came! I was so glad I had started saving for the party back in January.

Matthew was again very polite and helpful; I just hoped it would last. We have a large family, and even if we don't see each other as often as we'd like, they show up when it matters. My twins were surrounded by people who loved them. Once again, I hardly held them because everyone else wanted to; I only stepped in to sing "Happy Birthday" and help open gifts. I was so grateful for the support. After the party, we were exhausted—we went home, showered, and napped.

A few days later, we gathered for Thanksgiving. I spent half the day with my mom and the rest with Matthew and his family. They invited me to join them for Christmas as well, and I told them I would think about it. I loved that Marcus was so understanding and supported all of my decisions.

My job at the retail store was fun; there was no stress, and the employees were nice. As a Sales Associate, I acted as a cashier, assisted the sales team with accessorizing customers' suits, received shipments, stocked new merchandise, and maintained a clean, organized store. I no longer had a Monday-Friday schedule. In retail, one works five to six days a week, but our managers were pretty flexible with our schedules. That really helped me out when picking up the twins from daycare. If I worked weekends, I would drop them off at my mom's or Matthew's parents' home. During the holidays, we had to work six days a week. I was grateful to be employed and to have someone to care for the twins while I was at work. On weekends when the twins were with Matthew, Marcus and I would meet up with our friends and head to the club to dance. We both enjoyed dancing.

Christmas came around, and I agreed to go to Matthew's for a few hours. As I drove to his house, I was happy that we were getting along. I was also hesitant because so much had happened over the past year, but I pushed through my emotions. When we arrived, he was waiting outside for us. He helped bring the twins inside, and we went into the living room where his two older brothers were watching a movie. Matthew brought me all the gifts his family had for the twins. They received so many gifts, and I received some as well. It was very thoughtful of them to think of me.

During the visit, while we were all in the living room, Matthew's phone rang. It was his significant other. He was sitting right next to me. I picked up his cell phone and said, "Hi." She had no idea I was at Matthew's mother's house. She then told me, "You have no clue that last month, Matthew and I had our second child together."

I congratulated her and gave the phone back to him. I had no idea she had been pregnant again. I thought, "What the fuck?" Of course, no one had shared that information with me. No wonder he had been so nice to me the last few months; I felt so dumb. He grabbed the phone and mumbled something to her.

I got up from the couch and walked toward the front door. He slammed the phone down, and I could hear his footsteps racing toward me. I started running. When I reached the door, I turned around to face him. He put his face right in front of mine, his hand raised to punch me. His brothers were right behind him; they each grabbed one of his arms so he wasn't able to move. In a split second, I began scratching and punching his face. I became enraged, remembering everything he had done to me.

I kept punching and hitting him. His brothers began to pull him away from me, but I kept going, punching and kicking. Matthew tried to get his hands free, yelling at me. I didn't care. All I wanted to do was hit him. This was my chance to get him back for what he had done to me. For many years, I had told his family that Matthew was abusive, but they never believed me. Today, they witnessed first-hand that he was the one who had laid hands on me.

CHAPTER 5

SECOND CHANCE

In less than a week, it would be a New Year: 1994. With all of the events that had transpired over the past year, I felt very blessed to have survived—to have lived to see my twins another day. They inspired me to look forward and have hope for a brighter future. The past year had brought sadness, tears, joy, laughter, hope, love, and continued blessings.

However, rearing my beautiful twins wasn't a walk in the park. I was scared for our future. I kept asking myself if I was enough. I thought, "What could a single mom give them? Would they hold it against me because they wouldn't experience waking up with both their parents in the same household, having both parents day in and day out? When they get older and begin to reflect, will they question their upbringing? Would they blame me for rearing them alone?" But God saved us. I hoped they understood that I was doing what was best for us.

Being sleep-deprived, I couldn't remember if I had eaten—I was burping one kid while still feeding the other, carrying them at the same time, bathing both, preparing bottles, doing loads of laundry, changing diapers, buckling and unbuckling their car seats, carrying them to the vehicle, and dropping them off and picking them up from daycare. Every time I was tired, I kept telling myself that I would sleep when I died. My daily motivation was their beautiful smiles, the cuddling, the kisses, touching their chubby cheeks, hugging them, dancing with them, hearing the baby talk, and so much more.

It seemed like yesterday that I gave birth. I remembered waking up in the recovery room with my twins lying on each of my arms. I remembered the newborn baby smell and their soft skin, seeing the most adorable fingers, toes, perfect noses, ears, soft lips, and full heads of jet-black hair. I also remembered the next morning when they rolled the twins into my room in their own bassinets. The bassinets were clear and mounted on a silver cart that held all their essential items. Each had its own white banner on the crib that read "It's a Girl" in pink lettering on one and "It's a Boy" in blue lettering on the other. In addition, each had a paper that had their weight and height listed on it. They were wearing newborn white tank tops. My princess had on a striped pink and white beanie, and my prince had a striped blue and white beanie.

I remembered that when we left the hospital, I changed them into matching "Minnie and Mickey" blue striped onesies. She wore pink socks with a pink crochet beanie and matching crochet booties, and he wore blue socks with a blue crochet beanie and matching blue crochet booties. I know they will not remember, but almost every day for the next two years, I took a photo of them. I also remembered going to take portraits at Sears for several holidays.

These were just the beginning of the long-lasting memories that I will keep in my mind and heart forever. From the time they were born, I continued to read books. Some of the topics were how to be a single mom, how to be a single dad, best parenting practices, and how to raise twins. I read over 40 books. I wanted to make sure that I was prepared. I also needed all the help I could get; no one in our family had ever raised twins.

My goal for next year was to enroll part-time in community college. I truly missed school. If I earned my education, I thought more job opportunities would become available to me. I thought I could then purchase my own brick home.

I wasn't happy spending this New Year's Eve celebration without my twins. It was their father's holiday. It tore at my heart every time they had to leave me to go with him. I cried a bit because I missed my little angels. Marcus and I brought in the new year with friends, and we also celebrated our one-year anniversary. I couldn't believe we had met only a year ago; he was really good to us. I was looking forward to what the future had in store for us.

Going from a standard work week to retail hours was tough. I missed out on a lot. Retail hours varied from 9:00 am to 9:00 pm, and I worked five days a week. Everyone worked on Saturdays and rotated Sundays. I would stand for the majority of the day. The hours were very long, and I would leave work exhausted. When I'd get home, I would spend time with the twins before they went to bed; other times, they were already asleep before I arrived. Many nights I had lukewarm dinners. Don't get me wrong, I enjoyed my job, but it was a sacrifice. I wasn't able to be home as often as I wanted to be.

The twins stayed at my mom's while I worked. One day, I received a call from my family. When I picked up the phone, I could hear my sister's voice. She was so excited.

"Reyna, did you hear that? Look! Did you see that?" she asked.

"Sis, I didn't hear anything. And I definitely couldn't see because we are on the phone," I replied.

She started to laugh and then yelled, "The twins are taking their first steps! They are wearing their cute white shoes!"

I cried because I had missed a special moment in their lives.

She continued, "We just called to tell you."

In that moment, I realized that with this job, I would be missing several special moments.

It was the new year, and it was time to invest money to save for the twins' third birthday party and Christmas gifts. Last year, the investment had really come in handy. I had been able to pay for the twins' party and Christmas gifts and still have money left over. I also met with a college advisor. After a discussion, I registered for the Medical Assistant, Phlebotomy, and EKG programs. A medical assistant performs a variety of administrative duties, including taking medical histories, recording vital signs, explaining treatment procedures to patients, preparing patients for examination, and collecting and preparing lab specimens. In the Phlebotomy and EKG programs, students are trained in the use of phlebotomy equipment, asepsis, venipuncture, and electrocardiography procedures.

I was interested in being a nurse. The advisor suggested that I enroll in workforce programs. Enrolling in a workforce program would allow me to earn a certificate and enter the workforce soon after. Once I completed the programs, I would then register for academic courses. My plan was to attend classes part-time until I earned my undergraduate degree.

Matthew had kept his distance from me. I truly enjoyed the peace that came with his absence. He only reached out to discuss the twins and the logistics of picking them up for his visitation. However, this visitation day was different. I had worked a long day and had some errands to run before picking up the twins from daycare. I walked outside that afternoon and discovered my vehicle was gone. I started to freak out. I walked back inside the store to ask one of my colleagues to help find my vehicle, just to double-check and make sure I was not panicking without a good reason. After looking, we agreed that the vehicle was gone. At that very moment, my manager called me back into the store. He said I had a phone call, that it was Matthew, and that it was important I take the call immediately.

I picked up the phone and Matthew asked how my day was going. I wasn't going to tell him that my vehicle had been stolen. Matthew asked if I had been outside yet.

"No, why?" I asked.

He replied, "I took your vehicle and parked it somewhere else."

"What is wrong with you? I have to do some errands and pick up the twins. If I am late to daycare, they will be charging me a late fee!" I exclaimed.

He then told me that he would give me a hint and announced, "I parked it at a grocery store."

I screamed, "Why are you doing this to me?!"

"Because I can. It is my vehicle, too," he replied.

I hung up and started to cry from being so angry. All of my colleagues were around me when I was on the call. I let them know what Matthew had done. What a jerk! My manager allowed one of my colleagues to take me to find my vehicle. I worked in a shopping center, and there was a grocery store located behind our building. We got into a vehicle and headed in that direction. Sure enough, my vehicle was parked at the end of the parking lot. I was so embarrassed because he had humiliated me in front of my co-workers. I apologized for the drama. They said it wasn't my fault and that they were glad to help. Meanwhile, Matthew kept calling my mobile phone. I ignored his calls. I left work and went directly to pick up the twins.

Being back in school and working long hours was tough to juggle. In the end, I knew that all my sacrifices would pay off for us. Marcus was a huge help during this time. Every time I looked at the twins, my heart melted. They filled my heart with so much joy. I would run to hug them just to let them know Mommy missed them and loved them so much.

I also told them every day that they were beautiful. I would say, "Mommy loves you and you're beautiful. Never forget that." I wanted them to know that they were loved and meant the world to me. The time I spent with family was very valuable. I made it a point to create special memories. We didn't have much time to travel; so instead, we would go to the beach, fishing, movies, restaurants, or barbeque at home with family and friends. We truly enjoyed going to restaurants, and when we did, the twins did well. They didn't act up.

Around this time, Marcus and I headed out to meet up with the twins' father on his weekend. we met at a gas station halfway between our houses. Matthew didn't know that Marcus would be joining me at the meetup point. Marcus had never gone with me to drop off or pick up the twins. We pulled into the gas station and parked. As soon as Matthew noticed that Marcus was with me, he started making negative comments to antagonize him. Marcus would not budge until Matthew walked up to him. Matthew put his face directly in front of Marcus. I immediately put the twins in the vehicle.

Marcus asked Matthew if he had a problem with him. Matthew began to yell in his face and they began to fight. All I could do was yell and stay near the vehicle with the twins. No one walked in or out of the store; there was no one around to help. After a while, Marcus and Matthew stopped fighting and walked away from each other. We were so scared. I couldn't believe they just fought. Matthew sped off in his vehicle.

Marcus got in my vehicle. I began to apologize and checked to see if he was okay. He grabbed my hand and said, "I am okay. How are you and the twins? Let's go home." As we drove home, tears started rolling down my cheeks. We didn't say much. I apologized again for Matthew's actions. I was shaking, sad, and furious. My emotions were high. The only drama in my life was Matthew. Marcus was upset, but he kept his cool. When we arrived home, we had dinner. I got the twins showered and ready for bed while Marcus went outside.

Once the twins fell asleep, I packed their bags for daycare. I made my lunch for work and started finishing my homework. Marcus came inside, and we talked about what had happened; he was disappointed in Matthew's behavior.

For the next few months, Matthew kept taking my vehicle and hiding it at different grocery stores. I called the police, but there was nothing I could do because he co-signed for the vehicle. I purchased a steering wheel lock, but it didn't work. Matthew was able to remove the lock and take my vehicle anyway. It was so annoying that he would hide the car; he didn't care if I had plans after work. He would just call and give me a hint as to where my vehicle was. I had to do something. I went back to the dealership to see if I qualified for my own vehicle. I explained my situation to the salesman, but he informed me that I had not possessed the vehicle for long enough and that I should try again in a few months. I completely understood. The extra time would give me time to save for a down payment on a new vehicle.

That same afternoon, when I picked up the twins from daycare, I was reminded that picture day was the following week. I had completely forgotten. Luckily, I had purchased matching outfits which I still had in the closet. We hadn't taken our family photos yet, but the outfits were perfect. They wore matching sailor outfits for the photos. My prince wore a solid navy-blue sweater with white stripes around the collar and down the buttons. The outfit also had a white striped pocket on the lower right and left sides of the sweater, with a white anchor on the top right side. Lastly, he had striped white and navy-blue shorts with white socks and shoes. My princess wore a matching sailor navy-blue and white striped dress with a white star on her sailor-collared necktie. The outfit also had matching white socks and shoes. The outfits were adorable.

The daycare they attended had an amazing staff. They were so caring and loving toward my twins. On one occasion, I recall that when I picked up the twins from daycare, they had made me Mother's Day cards. On the outside of the card was a yellow flower. The words 'Happy Mother's Day' were written on it. I started tearing up. When I opened the cards, there was a hand trace of my little angels. The words on the inside of the card read, 'Thank God for Moms and Grandmothers.' My eyes teared up. I hugged the ladies; the cards touched my heart. I felt so much joy. I was happy that the twins were around people who truly cared. That weekend, we went to my mom's house for Mother's Day. We had a great weekend with the family. I love my mom so much. I was so grateful for her enormous love and support for us. My mom was beautiful inside and out, and she was my world.

I enjoyed working but dreaded walking outside after my shift. I didn't know if my vehicle would be there or not. I tried to park it in different areas, but he would still find it. My family was upset because he kept taking my vehicle. Our hands were tied, but I knew they would not be for long. I had a plan and was in the process of executing it.

One day, I received a call from Matthew. His voice was shaky, and I was concerned. He began telling me that the assault charges I had pressed and then dropped a couple of years prior had been picked up by the state. He was charged with assault, given probation, and mandated to take anger management classes effective immediately. I kept quiet; he had only called to let me know. I didn't show any emotion, but inside, I felt that the classes might help him. There was hope.

A few weeks passed. I met the twins' dad on Father's Day. He seemed a bit different; his tone was calm, and he didn't seem so wound up. I helped him get the twins settled in his truck, and then we both drove away. As I left, I thought, "Maybe the classes are helping." We had been at this place in our relationship before—one day he is nice, and the next he is upset. Only time would tell if things were truly different. I headed to my parents' house to spend time with my dad and family. I loved my dad so much, and we had an amazing time cooking for him and enjoying the afternoon.

Matthew had stopped hiding my vehicle, but my mind hadn't changed. I wanted a car that I could call my own. After work, I asked my mom if she could pick up the twins from daycare. Since a few months had passed, I decided to go back to the car dealership. When I arrived, the salesman recognized me, and we chatted for a bit.

After our conversation, he said, "I have a plan and I think it might work. This might take a few hours. Do you have time to wait?"

I nodded and replied, "Yes."

He stood up and asked me to walk around the lot to look at the cars. He wanted me to point out the vehicle I wanted just in case I qualified for a loan. He then walked into the office in the center of the dealership. I didn't go to the lot; I just sat there. This was out of my control, and all I could do was wait. After a while, he walked back into the room and said his manager agreed with the plan. Since I had been paying for my Plymouth Colt for over a year, they were going to tell the bank everything Matthew had been putting me through. They were also going to verify that Matthew did not make the payments—that I was making them on my own. They told me that if they could prove the payments were made on time, I might qualify for my own vehicle. They added that if the bank approved, they would remove my name from his vehicle title. If all of this was approved, I would be able to purchase my own car.

I informed them that I had money for a down payment, which was a plus. They had never done this before, but they felt confident it might work. I was happy, but I was also scared. In the end, I thought, "What the heck! Let's do this."

We all walked out of the room. They went back into the office, and I walked out to the lot. If this plan worked, I would be leaving with my own vehicle. I started to pray. I didn't care what car I got as long as his name wasn't on the title. As I walked down one of the rows, I stopped at an emerald green, four-door 1995 Dodge Neon. This was my car. I turned around and walked back to the office.

After a few hours, they informed me, "The bank approved you for a loan. Are you ready to purchase your vehicle?"

I couldn't believe it. I started to cry and hugged them both. The salesman asked if I had found my vehicle, and I replied, "Yes, I did." We walked back out to the car I had selected.

The salesman then stated, "You know that you could go with something a little more expensive. The bank approved you for a higher amount of credit.

I thanked him again for all that he had done, but this was the one. My boyfriend was later dropped off at the dealership. After all the paperwork was completed, I drove off in my brand-new vehicle. I thought, 'God is great. All the time.'

My boyfriend drove the Plymouth Colt on our way back to my hometown. We stopped by my parents' house, and they were so excited for me. My sister and I then drove to Matthew's sister's house to drop off his vehicle. What a surprise!

Matthew was outside. He definitely was not expecting me. I drove up in my new car, and my sister pulled up behind me. She tossed him the keys and walked toward my vehicle.

I rolled down my car window and yelled, "I don't need your vehicle anymore. Thank you! I removed my name from the title. It's all yours."

He didn't say a word. He was pretty shocked. My sister and I laughed and then drove away. It was the best feeling to be free from him.

The next few days felt amazing. I wasn't as stressed as I had been in past months. One evening after work, I was combing the twins' hair. As I brushed my little princess's hair, I remembered that before she was born, I had purchased a mannequin head to help me train. I practiced and learned to do several braiding styles, like the French braid, fishtail braid, pull-through braid, pigtail braids, herringbone braid, halo braid, reverse braid, and diagonal braid. I trained because I wanted to be prepared for whatever braid my princess would request. My little princess had adorable dimples and straight, jet-black hair that went below her mid-back. She really didn't like her hair in a ponytail or pigtails; she preferred a bow in her hair or nothing at all. My son also had cute dimples, and his hair was also jet-black. His hair went past his shoulders. I was planning on cutting his hair when he turned three years old, which was just around the corner.

As I looked back at our journey, I realized it had many windy roads. But I also realized we were blessed to experience another day; it was just the beginning. With much prayer, perseverance, and support from my family, we were in such a great place. They were extremely supportive, always trying to help when they could. After all, rearing twins isn't a walk in the park. At times it can be physically exhausting, and a second set of hands was always welcome.

The twins' laughter was infectious and had everyone laughing with joy. I have to give praise to my niece, who is the oldest. I never had to ask for help from her. She was there for us, offering to bathe the twins, wash their dishes, wash their clothes, feed them, change them, and watch them while I was at work or wanted "Mom Time." She loved my twins like they were her own children.

Even though I had a full schedule, I made time to take the family out to eat, to the movies, to the park, or to theme parks in other cities. My vehicle was small, but we managed to squeeze all of us in. It was certainly a bit tight! My mom would sit in the front and the kids would be in the back. We loved it. I once had a dear friend mention to me that when you have kids, your social and personal life ends. I completely disagreed with her. Life with my kids was just the beginning. I realized that we have to enjoy the new journey that God has given us and that He never wanted us to stop living. God wanted us to embrace these moments and experience life. I truly appreciated all the time we spent together.

My mom, the twins, my sister, my aunt, my niece, and I all shared the same birthday month. We loved celebrating birthdays. Mom and Dad told me that when children are born, parents begin to celebrate early on. A few weeks before a baby is born, family and friends have a baby shower for the expecting mom. There are always food and games, and guests bring gifts for the coming child. After the baby is born, the men celebrate with cigars and drinks. My parents told me that the birth of a child should be celebrated every year because when a couple falls in love and marries, they conceive children out of love.

Mom wanted her birthday gatherings to be at her home with family and friends. Dad would always barbecue; we would have chicken, fajitas, sausage, hot dogs, and burgers for the kids. Some of the sides we ate were rice, beans, corn, potato salad, guacamole, salsa, and tortilla chips. We especially loved the homemade cake my sisters would make. They would rotate who was responsible for the cake for family celebrations. We would all gather together to sing "Happy Birthday" in English and in Spanish. "Las Mañanitas" is a traditional Mexican birthday song. The parties always started early and ended late. As the sun set, everyone would begin to dance, play games, and laugh for hours. The kids were always allowed to stay up late, play games, and stay outside with the adults. It was so much fun. The next day, we would wake up and clean together.

Growing up with my family was fun, though sometimes it wasn't. My parents taught us to take life one day at a time and explained that many of life's problems can't be solved in a single day. They taught us to just live in the moment, be grateful, be thankful, and have fun. Even when we weren't smiling and hit our rough patches—some of which were pretty tough—Mom reminded us that after the dust settles, everything is going to be okay. She said that we just have to continue to have faith.

I loved being a mom and having a purpose. My mom reminded me that I had to celebrate my own life; she reminded me that I had an identity before I was a mother whenever I needed to hear it. The twins were two years old and were soon turning three. They were adorable and so much fun, but they had incredible energy. You had to watch their every move. One moment they were walking, the next they were running, and then they were jumping on the couch or bed. We would turn around and they would be on the kitchen table. They would get into drawers and cabinets, eat what was on the floor, try to put their fingers in the wall sockets, and so much more.

I was so happy that the twins loved to nap. When they napped, I would either join them or do laundry, clean, cook, or read. The best part of their nap was watching them as they slept. It was an honor to be their mom. They were a miracle, and I was blessed to be part of their lives. I was always happy when my family would join me to run errands with them, though the majority of the time it was just the three of us. I liked going out and shopping with the twins. They were always looking around; I bet they wondered, "Where is Mom taking us today?" I wanted them to see the outdoors and always experience life.

My birthday celebrations were not as grand as my mom's. When I was growing up, my parents would invite family and friends to a party where Dad would barbecue. We'd have cake, games, and a piñata. As I grew older, smaller parties became perfect for me. It was more about the twins. Birthdays for me became a time for reflection and being grateful for the blessings and love we received from everyone.

The twins' birthday was approaching quickly, and I was on a budget. Planning for their party always started at the beginning of the year after I filed my taxes and received my refund. I would set aside money to invest and then pull the funds out a month before their celebration. Between both immediate families, the guest list would start at 75 people. Matthew and I would split the cost of food in half, and we would each buy our own gifts for the twins. I would select the theme and the location. This particular year, I decided to celebrate the twins' 3rd and 4th birthdays at Peter Piper Pizza. We had a good experience there the previous two years. They offered handcrafted pizza, new and classic games, and a dedicated party host. I especially loved their chocolate and vanilla ice-cream swirl. We only had to bring the cake. The twins received a lot of attention; every time I looked up, a different family member or friend was carrying them, running after them, or playing games with them. The twins enjoyed the rides and the arcade section of the venue. The parties were scheduled for two hours, but time would fly by because everyone was enjoying themselves. Luckily, the host kept us on schedule. After the party, we would head home, ready for a nap. I was always so grateful and blessed for all the love that surrounded our family.

It felt like I had napped. I woke up and the Thanksgiving celebration was upon us. We would spend part of the day at my parents' and part of the day with his family. Even though Matthew and I were not together, we celebrated the occasion as a family.

November and December were pretty busy months for our family. I was rearing twins, going to doctor's appointments, working full-time, and purchasing Christmas gifts with the money I had invested. The doctor's appointments were quite frequent. My daughter was often sick with a cold, and she would then pass it along to her brother. I felt that my daughter's immune system differed from her brother's; she seemed to catch whatever illness the daycare kids had before he did. The doctor's office and the hospital staff remembered the twins and me. One day, I would bring my daughter in, then a few days later, I would bring my son in to see the doctor. After a few months, they told me to just fill the prescription for my son if he had the same symptoms as my daughter. They told me there was no need to make a second trip. Apparently, after they read the twins' charts, they realized there was a pattern.

During the Christmas holiday, I worked six days a week. The Christmas season was our peak time. It was hard to have a personal life when I felt that I spent more time at work than at home. I enjoyed my job, but our busy season was pretty hectic. When I had a long, exhausting day at work, opening the front door and seeing the twins run toward me changed my mindset. The hugs and kisses they gave energized me.

Matthew and I spent Christmas separately. He had the twins on Christmas Eve, and I would have them on Christmas Day. It worked out perfectly. Our family had a tradition of gathering and opening gifts on Christmas Eve. We would wait for the twins to come home and begin the celebration when they arrived. I loved witnessing the twins' sweet moments. If one of them was having trouble unwrapping a gift, the other would put their gift down to help. It was so adorable. Hearing them say "thank you" just melted my heart. I loved my twins and told them so every day. I would tell them, "I love you, and you are beautiful."

Christmas Days were relaxing. We would eat and then attend church with my mom. When we got back home, the family would relax, and the kids would play outside. My twins would run to join in the fun.

I forgot to mention that since the twins were potty trained, I saved a lot of money. Diapers were a huge expense; they went through so many! I was lucky to have a village of people to help me potty train them. I purchased a potty-training toilet before the twins were two years old. We started teaching the kids to just sit on the toilet at a young age.

As they got older, I purchased their favorite character-based underwear. Many may not agree with this tactic, but it worked for my twins. I told them that they could not pee on their characters, that the characters would know if they did, and that the characters would not like it. Every time the twins accidentally wet themselves, they would come to me immediately and ask me to change them because they did not want their characters to be sad. I would hug and thank them for letting me know. I would then clean and change them immediately. They tried their best not to go in their underwear. Their daycare, however, had a different tactic: the kids were taken to the bathroom every two hours. With the help of the daycare staff and my family, it wasn't long before they were fully potty-trained.

The daycare staff was part of the "village" that helped raise my twins, and I am still grateful for them. It is not easy raising children, so having a good support system is a significant plus. The staff not only assisted with potty training but also organized various activities to help the children develop their motor skills. They taught them group activities, colors, puzzles, and games, as well as arts and crafts.

I recall the twins each bringing home a 10" x 13" piece of paper. In the center of the page, the artwork looked like an anchor. While a typical anchor is made of metal with a ring at the top, a pair of curved flukes at the other end, and a rope used to secure a boat, this version was special. As I looked closer, I saw that the top of the anchor consisted of imprints of their hands in yellow. The rod leading toward the curved flukes was aqua, and the pair of curves were imprints of their left and right feet. The top left side of the paper featured their first names and an inscription that read, "I love my mom because I want to." It was perfect. I was their anchor. They brought home many different forms of art, and I saved most of their projects. The staff also reinforced the importance of washing hands before breakfast, lunch, and snack time. At the end of the day, the kids cleaned up and had free time before we picked them up. I was truly blessed to have that extended family.

New Year's Day was approaching. It had been a couple of years since Matthew and I ended our relationship, but I felt like he couldn't let go. He continued to be verbally aggressive whenever he felt he was right or didn't get his way. It upset me deeply when he got in my face and reminded me what could happen to me if I didn't listen. I reminded him that he could go to jail if he did anything to me.

But the threats kept coming. He couldn't stand seeing me happy or with someone else. I had moved on. I understood that it was hard for him to let go, but I was over it. He will always be in our lives because God blessed us with beautiful angels. I hoped that, in the coming year, our parenting relationship would be easier; but for the time being, I still walked on eggshells when he was around. I took it one step and one day at a time.

Before the new year began, I looked back to see how far we had come. I reviewed my current goals and assessed whether I had gone off track. If I had, I redirected my efforts to ensure I accomplished them. I tried to let go of what I could not control. It wasn't easy, but I tried. I had to let go and let God guide my way. I began by setting goals and creating a plan to achieve them. Some were short-term—perhaps a week long—while others were longer, spanning months or years. The goals I explored had to involve passion, serve our collective interests, and contribute to the continuous development of who I am and where I want to be. I wanted to look and feel better on the outside, but I realized that progress always begins on the inside by feeding my mind with books and nurturing my heart.

My main goal was to be the best mom possible and build memories that showed the twins how much I loved them. I set goals that put them first in all my decisions. I always believed that the plans I made for our future would impact our family positively. I couldn't fail or give up on them. Sometimes the decisions were tough, but they had to be made to change our lives for the better. I acknowledged that the twins might not understand the decisions affecting their lives now, but I hoped that one day they would.

My mom was tough on my siblings and me. We all knew she meant well. When it came to her grandchildren, Mom showed them so much love. In her eyes, they could do no wrong. When it came to the grandchildren, Mom was all about forgiveness and teaching them life lessons. She was patient, a good listener, comforting, and a shoulder to cry on. She caressed their faces and played with their hair; she encouraged them, offered emotional support, and hugged and kissed them often. Mom wanted them to have fun and to be safe, but she was still a tough cookie when it came to disciplining them. When she did, it was in a manner that they understood. At times, she brought out the "big guns": my dad. He would get out of his chair, raise his voice, point at them with his newspaper, and then walk away. His tone settled the kids pretty quickly. Every time family or friends left the house, Mom would say, "Que Dios te bendiga (May God bless you)."

My mother was also the voice of her grandchildren. Whenever any of them felt that their voices weren't being heard by my siblings or myself, she would approach us alone and do her best to speak on the children's behalf. She tried to create an understanding between both parent and child. Sometimes we, as parents, didn't take her advice, mainly because we believed that our way was right. Being a first-time mom wasn't easy, and I wasn't even close to being perfect. I grew up in a household where Mom expected everything to be clean. As I grew older, I was the same way. I didn't like it when the twins had a stain or dirt on their clothes. I knew that kids get dirty, but I just didn't like my kids to be in clothes that were stained; so, I'd change their clothes several times a day. I also had them washing their hands constantly. I didn't know that this was affecting them emotionally. Mom kept telling me to let them be kids and get dirty, but I didn't listen.

One day after work, I drove to my mom's house to pick up the twins. I had had a long day. When I walked inside, I went straight to the bathroom. When I walked out, I heard the twins and Mom laughing. I walked down the hallway and into the kitchen. From the kitchen, we had a back door that led outside. I peeked out, and my jaw dropped. The twins and my mom then noticed I was at the door.

The twins immediately stopped laughing and hid behind my mom. Before I could say one word, my mom interrupted and announced, "What you're teaching these kids is wrong. They are so scared of getting dirty. They can't live in fear of living and enjoying life. Now, you go get changed and come outside and play with us. If you don't come outside, I will go in and get you."

When Mom gives you that sort of look and tone, you listen. What I didn't mention is that when you walk out the back door, there is a large patch where grass doesn't grow. It's pure dirt. The three of them were in their swimsuits. Mom had the water hose turned on, and all three of them were rolling around and playing in the mud. I turned around, found some clothes to change into, and walked outside to join them. In the beginning, I felt so dirty, but it was so much fun playing with them. The laughter that came out of them was pure joy. I loved it. I did not love the dirt, but I cried because I was truly happy. Mom looked at me and winked. From then on, I let them be kids. If they got dirty, I didn't say one word. My mom had her unique tactics; I was grateful that she had the best interests of our family at heart.

It was the new year, and one of my goals was to join a gym. I needed to relieve some stress and focus on myself. I had never joined a gym before, but I had heard that a membership would be a game-changer. I decided it was time to change my life. I hired a trainer for six weeks and learned so much. I immediately fell in love with working out. The energy I felt afterward was awesome. Leaving the gym, my body was relaxed and less stressed. The gym kept me going. I was attending college part-time, working over 40 hours a week, navigating a relationship, and being a full-time mom. It was tough to make time for it, but the gym gave me the energy to accomplish my day-to-day tasks and obligations.

With a new year beginning, a great opportunity presented itself. I knew that my schedule would be shifting. It was hard to believe that I had completed my studies in the Medical Assistant, Phlebotomy, and EKG Technician fields. I cried with joy when the certificates were awarded. I learned that an executive medical company in the area was hiring part-time. I was curious to know if healthcare was a good career to pursue, so I applied and was hired.

What a kickoff to the new year. I celebrated the weekend before I started my new part-time job. The workday at the medical company began at 6:00 a.m. and ended at 8:00 a.m. The office scheduled us to meet at different high school locations throughout the week. The schools provided the tables and chairs for us to set up in the cafeteria or gymnasium. The teachers and staff would line up to complete their patient chart paperwork for their free physical assessments. They had the option to begin their assessment by receiving a flu shot or having their vital signs administered. Patients' vital signs included measurement of body temperature, pulse rate, respiration rate (rate of breathing), and blood pressure. We also did blood draws to send to the laboratory for testing, in addition to operating EKG equipment to perform diagnostic tests to assess the patients' heart rhythms and rates. I enjoyed interacting with the patients. I knew I was burning the candle at both ends, but I kept going. Before I knew it, summer was over.

I left both part-time jobs. Seven months flew by fast. I felt that all I did was work, work, and work. My twins still recognized who I was when I walked in the door in the evenings. After my summer experience, I have come to the conclusion that healthcare is not a career that I would like to pursue long-term. I will be registering for courses to continue my academic degree. I will be registering as an undeclared major and will focus on completing my basics.

At the beginning of the year, I filed my taxes in order to save the return for the annual family fall festivities. The daily commute to Mom's and back into the city was long. I knew that if I was working or running late—and I was often running late—my family would help by picking up the twins from daycare. I couldn't help feeling guilty that I wasn't spending enough time with the twins, but I had to stay focused on my goals for our family. I knew that in due time, it would pay off.

I hardly had time to rest. I kept telling myself that I could rest when I was dead. Matthew would pick up the twins once or twice a month. When I would call to check on the kids, he would sometimes tell me to call his mom, explaining that he had plans and had dropped them off for the weekend at her house. Sometimes he wouldn't pick them up at all. He would tell me that they were my responsibility and that I had no business being out with friends on the weekends. He would say that my place was at home watching the twins. He was annoying, so I didn't listen.

If I needed time to unwind, my family would watch the twins for the evening. Matthew would be so upset when I had a date night with my boyfriend. He knew that the twins were at my parents' house, and he would call to yell and curse at me. In response, all I did was hang up the phone. He was a jerk, and he wasn't changing anytime soon.

During the beginning of the year, Matthew reached out and wanted to discuss enrolling the twins in pre-kindergarten in the coming fall. I was shocked that he approached me about it. I hadn't put too much thought into researching an elementary school yet. I had several months to find a school in the city or enroll them in my hometown. He had a good idea: his mom volunteered at a Catholic church that was affiliated with a private school. She worked in their print shop creating the weekly bulletins for Mass. In return, the church offered her family the opportunity to attend their private school at a huge discount. Because we were family, it was a no-brainer.

The school had an excellent curriculum and received great reviews. The uniforms were very expensive, so we agreed to split the cost for uniforms and school supplies. I had a few months to save before the fall semester. Sending them to a private school meant we would have to pay monthly tuition, but it would also reduce the expense of daycare. It was definitely doable because the money saved on daycare would go toward the tuition. I was excited that my babies would be attending school in the fall; it tugged at my heart with tears of joy.

Due to my already tight schedule, I had no clue how it was all going to work out, but I decided I had to make it work. Spending long hours at work was exhausting. Sometimes we stood around for hours waiting for customers; at other times, we hardly had time to eat lunch or take a break. During our downtime, we would all stand around and talk with each other. I gravitated toward a fellow employee named Mont. We worked the same shift. Mont and his wife had been married for over ten years and had lived in the city for several years.

One day he told me, "Reyna, when you meet the one, it's like the universe gives you a sensitive connection with someone. It's magical. You can see something between the two of you before it happens."

Mont was a retired minor league baseball player and the popular guy of the group. He had a unique look; every time he stepped through the double doors at work, he looked like he had just walked out of GQ magazine. Mont was frugal when it came to spending money on his suits. As employees, we received a nice discount, and Mont would tell me that it wasn't about how much you spent on your clothes, but the confidence you had while wearing the garments.

Mont's friendship and mentoring made a significant impact on my family's life. He mentioned that money should be spent on giving back to yourself and your family. Our conversations about life were deep. His outlook was simple: have fun, travel, live in the moment, learn from your mistakes, and don't look back. Mont also passed along his father's advice to me.

Mont described his father's advice and its effect like this: "The best advice I have for you, before or soon after you're married, is to make sure that you open up three accounts: one for your wife, a general account, and an account for yourself. In the general account, the two of you will deposit the majority of your earnings to pay all the household bills. In the other two accounts, both of you should decide on an agreeable amount—between $50 to $100—that will go into your own separate accounts. The money will be automatically deposited when you receive your individual paychecks. No one dips into the general account to buy personal items or utilize the funds for anything other than household bills (e.g., no purchasing shoes, going out with friends, clothes, or dinner). That is why you have your own accounts. As the man, you pay for all the outings when you have date night with your wife. The woman will always have more money, but the men typically get the most expensive gifts. The wife won't be dipping into her account as often as you are. This reduces arguments in the relationship. We don't question each other about money or what we buy with our own funds. If we didn't have our own accounts, we would be questioning why the other took money out of the general account. We also open accounts to deposit funds for vacations and Christmas. Since the household bills are always being paid, it's worked for us."

On another occasion, he commented to me, "Do you know that every hour you work, you give a cut of your pay to someone else?" I didn't understand his comment. He began to explain that we were all laborers and that no one was watching out for us; we had to watch out for ourselves. He noted that the government takes a cut of every paycheck.

He would say, "Life is too short. You have to live and enjoy life. Vacations are trips that you plan specifically for your family. Do you go on vacations with your family or with friends?"

I would go out of town to visit relatives, but I had never planned a vacation specifically for my family. He recommended that I plan family vacations in addition to planning vacations for myself. Mont would say, "Creating special memories with the family is important. Going on vacations with your significant other or friends reenergizes your spirit. Read a book, relax, enjoy the outdoors, and be adventurous. You can work for others and treat yourself at the same time. Remember, keep life simple. Research your travel destinations. From every paycheck, save money to go into a separate account. Once you reach the goal, travel and enjoy the journey."

So, I immediately opened a vacation account. I focused on my family and what they needed. His words resonated within me; it all made sense. Sometimes I made my life harder by concentrating on the noise—the drama—around me. That moment changed my life. Anytime I needed advice, I would reach out to Mont to get his perspective on the matter. At the retail shop, there were also two male tailors who had a lot of life experience and were able to give me solid advice. I learned a lot from these "three wise men." I was grateful they were there to guide me through some of my life experiences.

Spending time with my family gave me so much joy. Time would go by so fast that I constantly reminded myself to slow down and live in the moment. The twins had so much energy. To entertain them, my nieces would join me in the mission of getting the twins tired; sometimes their cousins would join us as well.

We would load up adult lawn chairs, four plastic toy baskets, traffic cones, soccer balls, basketballs, maracas, full-size colorful vinyl balls, mini colorful vinyl balls, frisbees, and footballs.

Once the family was loaded into the vehicle, we would head to the dollar store for them to select another toy. Then, I would drive us to the nearest park. We would set up the baskets on a small hill that had an incline, arranging them to create the shape of a square. The toys were divided into the four baskets. My nieces and I placed the lawn chairs next to the baskets. With the traffic cones, we created obstacle courses utilizing the toys we brought with us. We would each have a maraca to root for the twins and their cousins while they ran around. They had so much fun running up and down the hill. When we left the park, the kids were tired. Once we got home, I would bathe them, we would eat, and they would fall asleep for a few hours. The adults weren't exhausted; all we did was sit in the chairs and watch them run. If we weren't at a park, we'd be fishing, at the beach, at the movies, or at indoor gaming arcades. We loved the outdoors.

When the days were filled with work, family, and activities, I would often forget to meet my own needs. My mom tells me that I worry too much. As a mother, I truly feel that there is a lot of pressure in rearing kids. I wanted everything to be perfect. Sometimes I felt emotional, overwhelmed, or constantly worried. I would think, "How will the twins be when they grow up? Will I be able to prepare them for life? I wonder if the life skills I teach them will be enough? Will people judge me every time they see us?"

I understand that worrying about the future can never help me control it. I also understand how difficult it is to control the thoughts that run through my head. I tried not to let the twins see me cry. I recall many times when I did cry, but my crying usually ended once I was in the shower.

Crying tears of joy felt like an overwhelming release of positive emotions. At other times, the tears came because of exhaustion or sadness. I consider myself to be a happy person with a positive outlook on life, but I can't always hold back the tears. Sometimes life got the best of me; when it did, my response was to just get back up and take one step forward.

The twins' first day of school was that fall. I had tears of joy running down my face. They were growing so quickly that I didn't want to blink and miss it. Planning for our future was thrilling. I just knew that releasing these emotions would make me feel better.

Co-parenting with the twins' father wasn't easy. When he was in a good mood, everything went well. If he wasn't, I had to watch out for his attitude. Planning for holidays gave me a headache; we would plan something, and a few days later, it would change. If I wanted peace, I had to go with the flow. If I didn't, all I would hear was him yelling and getting upset because things didn't go his way. One thing we both agreed upon was that no matter which parent they were spending time with, the twins would be our first priority. We also agreed that we would always make sure they had a good time. Mother's Day and Father's Day were special for the two of us. He would pick up the twins early and drop them off late in the evening. Usually, the day would work out well for us.

The twins attended their first day of Pre-Kindergarten at a private school. I was in total disbelief that my babies had grown up to be little kids. In a few hours, they would be meeting their teachers and classmates. Walking into their bedroom with tears in my eyes, I stood at their door to watch them sleep, knowing that today they would begin their new journey. While waking them up for school, I was an emotional wreck. I couldn't stop the tears from rolling down my cheeks. We were all nervous, excited, and happy at the same time. Their uniforms were so adorable. My prince was sporting a white polo with dark blue shorts. My princess was also in a white polo with a dark blue jumper dress.

The twins' father met us at the school for their first day of class. The school recommended that the twins be enrolled in separate classrooms, and I agreed that they should have their own individuality. I requested the day off from work and stayed in town just in case the school called me. They never did. I picked up the twins from school, and they were so excited to see me. They couldn't stop raving about the great day they had. I felt a sigh of relief knowing that they were filled with joy. They were both looking forward to the next day of school.

The daycare staff picked up the twins from school for the next few weeks. If I was working late, my family would pick them up from daycare and take them back to my mom's. Mom would change them out of their uniforms and feed them. The twins would play with their cousins until I arrived from work. On the drive home, the twins would talk about their day, telling me what they learned, who their best friends were, their favorite subjects, and the food they ate. They both had a folder with the work they had completed—basic number and letter worksheets, coloring sheets, glitter drawings, handcrafted construction paper projects, books they designed, and various other projects. I kept every piece of their work; my little angels were my mini-artists.

When the twins' father learned my schedule for drop-off and pick-up, he started meeting us at the school to harass me. The kids would be so excited to see their father. I would smile, but inside I still feared him harming me, sensing that he was only there to get on my nerves. He joined us to walk the kids to their classroom and would whisper in my ear, "Remember, I am never going to leave you alone. You will always be mine." I could feel the hairs rise on the back of my neck. He was out to make my life miserable. He reminded me often that the twins were getting a discount because of his mom; he always had something negative to say. Ignoring him was so hard, but I did my best. I knew that this was only temporary. If his behavior continued, I would have to come up with a new plan to be near the twins during the day. On my days off or the times when I worked the late shift, I opted to volunteer at their school. I loved seeing the twins walk in a straight line with their classmates to the cafeteria, PE, and Mass. They all looked so adorable. It is an honor to rear them and be their mom.

That year, we celebrated the twins' fifth birthday at Chuck E. Cheese. I wanted to change the venue. Chuck E. Cheese featured arcade games, amusement rides, crawl tubes, and a character stage show for the kids to enjoy. They served pizza, salads, and other food items. The twins invited their classmates, and we all had a blast. There was so much entertainment for the kids and adults that time flew by quickly. The twins' father and I split the cost; he didn't give me a headache, which was nice for a change. My sisters had mentioned to me that they had spotted him out on a date, and I was so happy to hear that. I thought, "I hope she keeps him occupied and out of my hair."

We didn't have time to open gifts at the party, so the twins' father and I packed all their wrapped gifts into my vehicle. When we arrived home, the twins opened them and immediately started playing with their toys. Marcus and I decided to relax and watch them play. Every day, I could see the twins grow and change; I was so grateful to be part of those moments. For the past few years, to keep the peace between the twins' father and him, Marcus hadn't attended the twins' birthday celebrations. Marcus's family attended, but he felt that the event was about the kids, so he opted out. Matthew always told me that if Marcus attended, he would cause a scene. Matthew and I had our challenges, but we worked through them. My relationship with Marcus was special; he was thoughtful, kind, and patient. He loved us, and he showed it.

Not long after the party, we celebrated Thanksgiving. The twins went to their dad's house for half of the day. I joined Marcus and his family, and we later joined my family. Mom still kept that extra chair for the guest she invited. My mom and I would sit right beside them, and we wouldn't eat until they arrived. My dad would sometimes get grumpy because we were all hungry. The person she invited was always someone she had met in our small town; they could be homeless or perhaps the paperboy who distributed the newspapers in the neighborhood. Mom always reminded us that we had to give back to others. When the guest arrived, he would get cleaned up and join us at the kitchen table. Mom would pray and give thanks, and we would enjoy a wonderful meal. After we ate, we'd watch the football game and play games. Mom and I would then head to the church to pray and drop off food. The twins' father would drop off the kids at Mom's house; he always came inside to say "hi" to everyone, and he would even greet Marcus. After a long day of enjoying good food and great company, we'd head home. I knew that the weekend at work would be extremely busy.

The company I worked for held parties and events during the year. For four years, I had been attending our annual Christmas party for the surrounding cities. The holiday party was about a two-hour drive away. Our company rented limos and party buses to take us to and from the event. We were allowed to invite one guest. The men wore suits or tuxedos, and the women wore formal gowns; everyone looked amazing. The owner flew in on a private jet, accompanied by some of the best DJs. The reserved party room had large centerpieces on round tables with white linens and chairs. The dinners were exquisite, and there was always an open bar. After dinner, they gave out awards and party favors, such as top hats, glow necklaces, sunglasses, foil horns, colorful feather boas, free T-shirts, and so much more.

Once the award ceremony was complete, they would dim the lights and the DJ would begin to play a set of dance music. During the DJ set, balloons and confetti would fall from the net above us. There was a photographer taking photos all night long. I think that the law firm I worked for and this job changed my palate; it opened my eyes to excellent food and a whole new way of celebrating.

School was going well for the twins, and I was looking forward to my spring semester college classes. One day, my mom called my workplace. She told me that I had received a certified letter from the Department of the Treasury, Internal Revenue Audit Department. I thought that was odd. I told her that I'd be there later to pick up the twins and open the letter. When I arrived home, I was greeted by my mom at the door. She handed me the letter. As I opened it, I could feel my anxiety rising. My jaw dropped as I read the contents. "What the heck?" I thought. I was being audited because the twins' father had claimed the kids on his tax return. I was so furious. I called him, but he stayed quiet while I yelled and cursed at him. He didn't say one word before hanging up. What a piece of work.

In the letter, the IRS required me to respond to the request with proof within ten days. I had to prove that I was their parent. In addition, I had to provide notarized documentation that the twins lived with me. The letter stated that after I submitted my information, I would receive one of the following responses: a request for further information, the total amount I owed, or a notice that the explanation was accepted and I was cleared. I was steaming mad. Mom held me as

I cried, feeling the anger inside of me. I thought, "Hadn't he done enough to try to ruin my life?"

For the next ten days, I gathered documentation. I reached out to the twins' school, daycare, and doctor's office, asking if they could please provide a notarized letter on behalf of each organization confirming that I was the twins' parent. Once I received the completed documents from all parties, I submitted the information to the IRS. In the meantime, I had to go about my day and try not to worry about it. Waiting for the response was stressful, but what else could I do?

The holidays were in full swing. With the season in full effect, we were slammed at work and didn't have much time for breaks. When we did, we walked outside to get away from the chaos. To the right of our store, there was a restaurant that had the best-tasting chocolate and banana shakes. To the left, there was a retail store that sold office furniture, supplies, and electronics, and provided print services. Next to that was a mattress store. I'd been in that store before; they sold mattresses, box springs, bedding, and other furnishings.

One day, I ran into the owner of the mattress company. We started a conversation, and he asked if I wanted a part-time job. I thanked him for the opportunity but told him that I wasn't seeking part-time work.

He replied, "After your shift, come by the store."

I decided to go and chat with the owner. The job opportunity intrigued me; the extra money would allow me to save and travel with the family. I wouldn't have to worry about using money from my full-time job. I thought that extra income would help if the twins needed anything and would create a nest egg for us. After our discussion, I told him that I would think about the offer he proposed. The money sounded promising for a part-time job. I went home and discussed it with Marcus. I told him that if I took the job offer, I would definitely need his help to care for the twins while I worked. He let me know that he was okay with me getting a part-time job. We were having relationship issues, and I was hoping that absence would make the heart grow fonder. I decided it would be doable, so I accepted the opportunity. The final decision was mine. I took a few days and then accepted the position. My part-time paychecks were not too shabby.

When I wasn't working, I was decorating and buying Christmas gifts. During the summer, the twins and I had discussed purchasing a new vehicle. They selected a Ford Mustang, but not the color. I had been pre-qualified at the bank, so I decided to surprise the twins with the great news. We were all excited. The three of us drove to the Ford dealership. When we arrived, we walked toward the group of Mustangs. I asked the twins what color they liked. My prince ran to the black Mustang, and my princess ran to the red one. They were both good choices, but I told them that since they had selected the vehicle, Mom would select the color. I chose the white Mustang. After that, a salesman approached us; it was an easy sale. We walked inside, filled out the paperwork, and drove our white Ford Mustang home that evening. While driving home, we jammed to some of our favorite songs: "Check Yes or No" by George Strait, "Bohemian Rhapsody" by Queen, and "We Will Rock You/We Are the Champions" by Queen.

As I mentioned earlier, my relationship with Marcus was a bit rocky during this time. He was great with the twins and was always there to help care for and watch them; he was like a big kid when he was around them. However, he started staying out late and would not respond to my calls. He had also been missing work and was smoking more weed. I had suspicions that he was seeing someone else, but I couldn't prove it. It was a gut feeling I had. I had moments when I broke down and cried, yet I just wanted to look the other way and ignore the feeling. I told myself that I had no energy for another broken relationship.

I knew that, as a family, we were going in different directions, but I also knew this was the time to fight for what I wanted. This was not a time to run away. I truly believe that, in time, the truth will come to light; I was just hoping that what I thought was true was not actually the case this time.

I was excited to celebrate the Christmas holidays with the family. My mom had reminded me that we were going to volunteer to clean and decorate the church before Christmas Mass. I loved being with my mom. She had been a volunteer at the church for over 20 years and would always remind me that we had to give back and be grateful for all the blessings God had bestowed on us. I wanted to instill those values and great memories in my twins; I wanted to lead by example. For Christmas, my family had a variety of food, such as tamales, rice, beans, menudo, buñuelos, deviled eggs, desserts, and more. We would gather and listen to music, and later in the evening, we would open gifts. Being around family was fun, but it sometimes brought out drama between siblings. Occasionally, childhood memories caused them to bring up grudges or unsettled disagreements. When these conflicts arose, they would just work them out and the festivities would continue. Within all the chaos, you could see the love among the family.

The next few weeks were a blur. New Year's festivities came and went. I was busy working two jobs, getting the twins ready for school each day, driving from the city to my hometown to drop off and pick up the kids, doing homework, going to the gym, and going on weekend adventures. I reminded myself to breathe and hoped I didn't miss anything along the way. I hardly had time to cook dinner, so we'd pick up fast food or dine in, relax, and enjoy a delicious meal. I couldn't count on the twins' father; he had been distant since he had a new significant other in his life. I wasn't complaining, though; I was grateful that he had moved on. Wearing several hats was tough for me, but I just pushed through for my beautiful angels.

One day during this time, I was doing laundry and noticed lipstick stains on one of Marcus's shirts. I could still smell the perfume on it. I knew it wasn't mine because he had come home late the night before, stumbling into the house drunk and reeking of weed.

When I smelled the shirt and saw the lipstick, I thought, "Can't I just get a break?" I had nothing to say to him or to anyone. I just fell to the ground and wept. While he was still asleep, I kept my composure. I called my mom in the morning and asked her if she would watch the twins for a few hours; she agreed. When I arrived back home after dropping the kids off, I woke him up. He was so hungover. I held the shirt in front of him, and he began to deny it. Then, he began to apologize profusely, kneeling down and crying.

Through his tears, he said, "You have been so busy. I needed more attention. My ex-girlfriend reached out a few months ago. Nothing happened. I love you. We can make it work."

I screamed, "Get out! Get all your shit and get out of my house. I trusted you. I thought our relationship was solid. You were not sexually deprived at all. You should have told me that you needed more attention. Why didn't you come to me before leaning on another woman—the same ex-girlfriend you were with before? I'm so disgusted. Well, you can have each other. It's over. Pack all of your stuff today. Don't leave anything here."

When he wouldn't leave, I began to pack all of his belongings myself. After a few hours, he left. I was devastated and heartbroken. For the next few months, I was a walking zombie. When the twins were with me, I tried to live in the moment. Marcus would call several times a day, but I had nothing to say to him. I needed time to process this unexpected event that had shifted our lives. We missed Marcus, and he missed us too. Every once in a while, he'd come by to pick up the twins for the day. He would also watch them if I worked late in the evenings. I reached out to the twins' father and let him know that I needed his help watching the kids while I worked late and occasionally on weekends. He agreed but gave me grief, saying, "What? Your family or boyfriend can't help you?" I didn't have the energy to argue with him, so I just ignored his comments.

One day, while picking up the twins from my mom's, I noticed a letter from the IRS. They had reviewed and responded to my submission. I was shaking, and my nerves were getting the best of me. I took a deep breath while opening the envelope.

The letter read: "Thank you for your correspondence clarifying the item(s) in question on your Federal Income Tax return. We have accepted your explanation and will complete the processing of your return as soon as possible. If you have any questions, you may write to us or call our office at the telephone number shown. A member of our staff will be able to assist you. If the number is outside your local calling area, there will be a long-distance charge to you. Thank you for your cooperation. Sincerely, Service Center Examination Branch."

I breathed a huge sigh of relief.

Marcus wanted us to work on the relationship; he wanted me to give him another chance. I loved him dearly, but at that time, I couldn't even stomach him. I was heartbroken. It would take time to even consider giving us another chance. Then, one day at work, I met a man who gave me the chills… in a good way. We were immediately attracted to each other. He asked me out for drinks, but I let him know that I wasn't ready for a relationship and that it was too soon. He sent me numerous flower arrangements with boxes of chocolate candy. We started having late telephone conversations. I was truly attracted to him.

I asked my friend Mont for advice about my feelings toward this new man. He let me know that the opportunity to enjoy this new friendship might not come again and that you only live once. He told me to just have fun and enjoy the moment. So, my new friend and I spent the next few weeks having lunch, dinner, or drinks.

I told my mom about this tall, handsome man, and she stopped my parade. She wasn't too pleased that he was going through a divorce and had five teenagers. But there was something about him; I enjoyed his infectious laugh, and his touch was welcoming. I was falling for him. It was electric.

After two months of dating, he presented me with an engagement ring. I was pretty shocked. I gave the ring back, but he placed it in the center of my palm and told me to think of it more like a promise ring. When I told her, my mom was so upset with me; she told me that I had to break it off with him. When Marcus noticed that I was wearing the promise ring, he was furious. But I was living in the moment. I asked myself, "Why is everyone so upset?"

After much thought, I came to the conclusion that my mom was right. I realized that I still had a connection with Marcus. A few months later, I called it off with the new man. After I decided to do that, Marcus and I rekindled our relationship. The hardest part for both of us was learning to trust each other again. I realized it wasn't going to be easy. We just knew that we had to learn to communicate and express how we were feeling, rather than letting our feelings of mistrust fester.

The twins enjoyed school. They especially liked being with their friends, and I was excited to know that they loved learning. They participated in plays, attended Mass, and created so much artwork for me to hang around the house. I found that volunteering at their school was rewarding for me. My twins enjoyed seeing me around the school, and everything was going well for our family. My school semester was coming to an end. I decided that after the semester, I would take some time to focus on my twins and on my relationship with Marcus. Since I was taking core courses, the credits would go toward my major. I truly enjoyed school, but I needed to take a break to focus on other areas of my life. Marcus also started focusing on the family. We hosted more gatherings in our home and were able to enjoy each other's company along with our family and friends.

One Saturday morning, there was a loud bang at the door. The twins were in the bedroom asleep and Marcus had left for work; he worked for a soda distributor. The banging on the door continued as I walked to the front door and peeked through the window. It was Matthew, the twins' father. I thought, "What does he want, especially so early in the morning?" He never just showed up at my house without calling. I was concerned.

I opened the door and walked out onto the porch. He handed me his cell phone.

I asked him, "Why are you giving me your cell phone?"

He replied, "It's my girlfriend. She wants to talk to you. I have nothing to say to her. She wanted me to come to your house to tell you that she has been my girlfriend for the last year."

I told him that I already knew that. I told him that my sisters had informed me when they first noticed him out on the town with her. I reminded him that the town our family lives in is small and news travels fast. He then told his girlfriend that I knew they were dating, but she insisted on speaking to me. He gave me the phone. I grabbed it from his hand and said, "Hello."

She began speaking and said, "My name is Naomi. I wanted to introduce myself. I am Matthew's girlfriend. We have been together for a year now. Since my children and I spend time with the twins, I've been asking to meet or connect with you. I really enjoy spending time with the twins."

When she was done talking, I responded, "Nice to meet you, too. I'm glad you're with the twins' father. I really hope it works out. I have three rules: 1. Treat the twins equally when shopping for toys or anything they ask for. If the twins ask for something while you are out with them and you are unable to purchase it for both of them, don't buy for one and not the other. 2. Unless they get out of hand and need immediate discipline, let the twins' father know what is happening with them. If you have to discipline them, let the twins' father know what happened and what actions you took. And 3. You can expect me at your front door if you don't follow rules one and two. Do you have any questions about the three rules?"

Naomi responded, "No. I got it."

I handed the twins' father the phone and told him, "I can't believe you came to my house so she could introduce herself. I don't care who you date. She didn't need my approval."

I took the time to restate my rules to him. When I was finished, he turned around and walked away. I walked inside and shook my head. I thought, "What the heck was that all about?"

The twins' father had been acting a bit different over the last few months. He was becoming moody, short-tempered, and verbally aggressive. He also gave me the death stare. He had lost weight and looked leaner. I couldn't pinpoint it, but my gut said he was going through something. As always, I kept my guard up. The twins had no idea he came by, and I didn't want them to know. Only my mom and Marcus were aware of this unexpected visit. We focused on having a fun-filled weekend.

I was an avid reader. I found that reading increased my knowledge, relaxed me, and reduced my stress. After reading books, I often reminisced about my childhood, work, friends, and family conversations. These thoughts all had one theme: communication. Everyone had their own style. Communication is key with any family. Knowing this and the issues we were going through, I created "Straight Talk." It was a table conversation that included family, friends, or anyone who would like to be a part of the discussion. It allowed everyone to be heard without any repercussions. Everyone at the table could provide constructive criticism to anyone with no rebuttal. No matter who was sitting at the table, each person had a voice. We listened.

Let me give some examples: if there was a guest who had an odor, another person at the table would express how it made them feel to be around the person who had the bad odor. If my son and/or my daughter broke a lamp or stole a dollar, as long as they were honest and confessed what they did wrong, there were no punishments. But if anyone covered up for the person who had committed the mischief, both individuals would get into trouble. Also, the person who covered up for the other person received double discipline.

Straight Talk worked for us. We began to be more honest and open. When Marcus and I were alone, we had some tough conversations. We talked about things that needed to be brought to light. This was a game-changer for our family. It didn't matter where we were; as long as there was a table, they would tell me things that I wouldn't have told my parents.

One beautiful, sunny day, the phone rang. It was Amber. Her tone was frantic. I couldn't understand a word she was saying. She was yelling. I started stressing out. I immediately became nervous and concerned for her safety.

She screamed, "She has a bat in her hand and is swinging it at him! She is running around the vehicle! She just missed him and hit the vehicle! He keeps running around the vehicle!"

I had no idea what Amber was talking about. All I knew was that her tone was anxious, distraught, and fearful, and that all sorts of other emotions were running through her.

I asked her, "Where are you? Are you safe? Who is running with a bat? Who are they hitting?"

Amber screamed in response, "Naomi is running after Matthew with a bat. She is swinging. She is hitting the vehicle.

I took a deep breath and said, "Repeat what you just said. Did I hear you right?"

She exclaimed, "Yes, you heard me. I am at work. Matthew is being chased by his girlfriend."

I asked, "Are they okay?"

She responded, "Yes, they are both okay. They just left the parking lot."

I was pretty shocked. Amber continued, "Girl, your man is causing drama in front of the salon."

After we hung up, I had to sit down for a minute. I had to take it all in. So many emotions and thoughts started running through my head. I thought, "Does he beat her like he did me? Is she safe? Should I reach out to her? Was this some sort of karma? What about the twins and their safety?"

My anxiety went through the roof. Flashbacks of my past came back to me. I then thought, "Do the twins witness that kind of behavior? She has four kids of her own. He has four kids of his own. What if the stress of all eight was causing this outburst?"

Lately, Matthew had been becoming more verbally aggressive. I thought, "Was it the drugs?" I recently found out that he had been using cocaine—hence the weight loss. I had to be sure that the kids were safe at all times. They didn't need to witness their fighting. I was worried that the fighting was happening in front of the kids. I took a few deep breaths and then called my mom for advice. We spoke for a few moments. She told me to call Matthew, so I called him later that evening. He did not answer my attempts to call. I left him several messages.

As I mentioned earlier, our family recently implemented "Straight Talk." When we sat down for dinner, I asked the twins if they had noticed Dad and Naomi not getting along. They both told me that Naomi and Dad didn't fight or even argue. What a relief it was to hear that from the twins.

The twins had spent most of the summer with their father and his parents. They had a large family with several cousins their age. His parents lived outside the city limits. They had a nice-sized home that sat on several acres of land. The kids had a place to enjoy the outdoors. They played basketball, rode ATVs, tractors, bikes, and go-karts, and sometimes drove Grandma's van. They also bought many pets for their grandkids. The kids always had a blast there. Every time they gathered, it felt like a family reunion. His family was very close. They had their differences, but their unity was incredible. I loved that about them. The family gathered every Sunday after church and spent the day barbecuing, laughing, and enjoying each other's company.

When I looked back at the first time I met the twins' father, I could see a future with him. Being around family is what I loved. I embraced that wholeheartedly. Then, out of nowhere, things went from having a great relationship to feeling suffocated every day. The memories are forever imprinted on my mind. God had saved me time and time again, and I was very grateful.

Summer was coming to an end, and I was so excited for our future. The twins were turning six that year. Why did the school year have to go so fast? I remembered enrolling them in pre-kindergarten, and now it was time to enroll them in kindergarten. I have always been an emotional person when it comes to special moments, especially when it involves the twins, and this was one of those moments.

I reached out to the twins' father to discuss the next few months as they concerned the children. We discussed school, their birthday party, holidays, and enrolling my prince in baseball. He continuously reminded me about the discount I used because of his mother, telling me, "No one would ever do that for you."

He tried to make me feel as if I owed him. Conversations with him were tough; he was always such a jerk. I really hated asking him for anything. It was difficult, but I knew that as a parent I had to communicate with him, regardless of his behavior. I didn't want to ever look back and say I didn't try to do the right thing by him. Our conversations often led to tears, though I didn't let him know they were rolling down my face.

I thought, "Why does someone have to be so difficult? These are our children. We were blessed to have not only one child, but twins." I always prayed, and my mom always consoled me. She was strong and reminded me to look at all the good things I had in front of me.

However, I had had enough of the twins' father. Lately, it seemed like I never did anything right in his eyes. His attitude was intolerable. I was tired of him harassing me during that first year when I picked up the twins from school, and of his continuous reminders about the discount. The twins liked their school, but I dreaded the possibility of seeing him there. I was always scared that he would revert to his old behavior and that the abuse would start up again.

So, I decided to research some private schools in the city. I was hoping to transfer them to a school that was closer. I called several private schools, though I was cutting it close concerning the start of the semester; school was less than a month away. I received a callback from a private school that had two slots available. I immediately scheduled an appointment and was able to tour the school during my visit. It was perfect, but the price of tuition would be much higher because I wasn't going to receive a family discount. I was open and honest about my current situation. I let them know that I was receiving a discount at the current school and asked if they had any tuition assistance.

The administrator answered, "Yes, we have two scholarships for your twins. This will go toward the monthly tuition. Compared to what you are currently paying, your monthly payment for the two of them will increase by less than fifty dollars."

I started to cry. I couldn't believe it.

The administrator continued, "We can register the twins today. Orientation is in two weeks. Tuition is due before the first day of class."

I walked out of the office with a pep in my step; God had given me another miracle. The next mission was to find a daycare in the city. I went home and shared the great news with Marcus. He was so happy because he knew what I had been going through. Within a few days, I found a daycare that allowed me to utilize the government assistance program. That tuition also increased, but the amount was minimal. Uniforms were very expensive, but I had a savings account I could tap into to pay for them. After I made the call to inform the old school that we would not be returning, I contacted the twins' dad to break the news to him. He was furious and began to yell at me. I didn't care what he had to say. I thanked him for his mom's discount and let him know that we would no longer be utilizing it. As he always did in these situations, he threatened me.

The twins were not excited to move to a new school; they had family and friends they were going to leave behind. I told them, "I completely understand your frustration, but you'll also be meeting new friends."

I let them know that the new school and daycare were much closer to home. The drive was easier for my morning and afternoon commutes, reducing my drive time from two hours to one hour. My parents were also sad; they knew the change would give them less time to visit with us. I promised my parents that we would visit on weekends. I also reminded them that throughout the next year, I would be traveling to the larger city, and the twins had the option to come along or visit with them.

The first week of school went well. We were welcomed by the staff and teachers, and the twins enjoyed their new classmates. They were in two different classrooms, which I truly appreciated; I believed this allowed them to develop as individuals, and the school agreed with that assessment. At daycare, they were in the same classroom. The twins transitioned well. I had no idea what the potential impact of two major changes would have on them, so I was relieved that it all worked out.

The twins were ready for kindergarten. They made new friends within the first few days of school, and I was excited to hear about their new best friends. They started the year learning phonics, which involves auditory, visual, and motor skills. They were also line-tracing their first names and practicing tracing numbers, letters, and shapes. In art class, they colored and learned the history of Our Lady of Guadalupe. I loved the fact that the classroom sizes were small. Every day they brought home completed assignments, and we would discuss what they had learned. During dinner, we practiced "Straight Talk." The twins were very open to communicating about their day at school and daycare, and they also brought up any concerns they had.

I registered my son to play baseball, but my daughter wasn't into sports; she wanted me to buy her new books instead. I didn't know if my son was going to enjoy baseball, but he did well. I remember taking him to pick up his uniform; he had a grin from ear to ear. We went to Academy Sports & Outdoors to pick out his gear, and he looked adorable. He tried on several gloves until he found the best fit. There were so many options, but luckily, we had assistance from one of the employees. He also tried on several batting gloves. Once he selected a glove, we moved on to purchasing a bat. I thought there were many gloves to choose from, but when we got to the bat section, I was overwhelmed. My son was measured for a bat by utilizing his weight and height. Who knew that was how they did it? I didn't. He then tried on several helmets to find one that fit his head. I thought, "Safety first. My baby is growing up." We then went to the shoe area to select a pair of cleats. To top it all off, he selected his very own equipment bag. We were all set for his practices and future games.

He made friends quickly, and everyone was very inviting. He was disappointed because I was unable to take him to practice, but Matthew stepped in to do that. Matthew practiced with him both on and off the field. I made sure I made it to his games; sometimes I was late or had to leave early, but I was present. Work, work, work—I had to make sure they had everything they needed.

As I mentioned, my little princess wasn't into sports. She wanted me to take her to purchase books to read. Our favorite store was Barnes & Noble. When we walked in, her eyes opened wide and she grinned from ear to ear. She came prepared and pulled a list of books from her jeans. I smiled. She walked to the information desk and asked if someone could assist her in finding the books on her list. We walked out with a bag full of books. She took after her mom; I loved to read. I encouraged them both to read, but my son wasn't as interested as my daughter was. Still, they supported each other in their goals and interests.

Marcus took my son to practice when I was working, which was most of the time. I made it to his games, though with two jobs, it was truly difficult to make it to each practice. On weekends when the twins were with their father, Marcus and I spent the evenings going out and enjoying each other's company. We also spent time with friends. Our weekends included various activities to choose from: pool, bowling, fishing, movies, the beach, dancing, and parties with friends. To get my workout at the gym done, I would wake up extra early or go right after work. We always had a fun-filled weekend. We both loved to dance; it was nice to have time to drink and be merry, taking our minds off work and the day-to-day grind. I believe this helped us to continue working on our relationship.

The twins were turning six years old. Matthew and I hadn't been on the same page for a long while. I reached out to discuss the plans for the twins' next birthday celebration. He let me know that he wasn't going to be joining us and that his family would be celebrating the twins' party at Peter Piper Pizza. For a moment, I felt sad. I never expected this from him, but in truth, I honestly didn't know what to expect. I wanted the twins to experience both parents celebrating their birth. I accepted the reality that we weren't in a relationship, but I also knew these memories would be imprinted on the twins' lives forever. However, I respected his decision. I never disagreed and just moved on.

With the money I had saved during the year, I had enough to cover the cost of their birthday and Christmas. I decided to have the party at our home. Our neighborhood was near a bay which bordered the city. We lived on a corner lot; to the left of the house, there was a very large piece of land. Behind the house, to the right, and in front were our neighbors' houses. It was a quiet neighborhood. The land we lived on was larger than our "mini-mansion," though the home itself was less than 950 square feet. I asked my family if they could assist in entertaining the guests. They told me, "Let us know what you need. We are here for you."

That year, I rented a moon bounce, ponies, and horses. We also put a small pool in the backyard. I ordered a piñata, candy bags, drinks, a popcorn machine, cake, balloons, and party favors. I also had the party catered by a Mexican restaurant.

We had over 100 people attend. The twins had a wonderful time; it was their first outdoor party and a hit with everyone. We were completely exhausted but overjoyed with the experience. It took a few days to put the house back in order, but I would do it all over again.

One evening, we headed to our local grocery store. I decided it was time to begin teaching the twins to cook utilizing the microwave. My mom taught all my siblings and me how to cook and clean by the age of 12. At the grocery store, we purchased items that could be cooked in the microwave (e.g., Hot Pockets, soups, burritos, beef corn taquitos, ravioli, Chef Boyardee, fish sticks, TV dinners, corn dogs, nuggets, and macaroni & cheese). They were so thrilled. They were gaining their own independence when it came to cooking. I got a kick out of watching them select their food; they would discuss their selections amongst themselves. My son would ask, "What do you want to eat, sis?" and my daughter would ask, "What are you going to eat, brother?"

At meal times, they would take turns warming up their food. While the microwave was running, the twins would grab their utensils, napkins, drinks, and condiments from the fridge. They didn't want my assistance. They would say, "We got this, Mom. You sit down and relax." They would also offer to warm up my food. One of the twins would grab my meal and warm it up, while the other would gather the condiments. These were the moments I cherished. They didn't notice that my eyes teared up. In the next few months, my goal was to teach them to cook their own breakfast, then move on to lunches and dinner. I believed that cooking was a survival skill.

The twins' father had been missing in action during the weekdays when he didn't have the twins. It was nice not hearing from him, but I knew that we had to have interaction every other weekend. The twins missed their dad and called him frequently. That November, the twins each received "Student of the Week" recognition at their private school. The school gave us a sign to display in the yard, and the children were so excited to share the news with their father. Once they told him, however, his response was short. I could hear him ask the twins, "Where is your mom? Is she out with her friends? Did she work today?"

I felt sad and frustrated that the twins had to go through a mini-interrogation. That week, we celebrated their achievement of both receiving "Student of the Week." Marcus and I were both very proud of them.

It was the fall of 1998, and the retail industry was booming. We were expected to work six days a week for the next few months, and our only holiday would be Christmas. We were all looking forward to our holiday party, as they were always a big hit with the company. Our retail store had hired a new sales associate; a handsome, fit, tall young guy walked in through our front double doors. He had a beautiful smile and walked with a lot of confidence. He wore a suit, suspenders, a white dress shirt, a conservative tie, and black dress shoes. He wore his slacks above his belly button, so when he walked, it looked like he was wearing "floods." It was a bit awkward to look at without smiling.

During our regular team meeting, he introduced himself. His name was Manny, and he was 17 years old. He was very personable, intelligent, and ready for the job, eager to learn about the retail industry. We had tailors who worked during store operating hours, and they were very honest with Manny about the length of his slacks. My cousin, who was one of the tailors, lengthened them for him. After that, his attire was sharp.

Manny wore a ring on his wedding finger, so we all assumed he was married. However, he let us know that he was wearing a purity ring, representing a religious vow to practice abstinence until marriage. We were all very impressed and applauded him. Manny and I became very close; he was like a younger brother to me. As soon as he turned 21, we started going to clubs together. Marcus didn't mind me hanging out with Manny and took a liking to him as well. Manny was cool and fun, and he enjoyed going to bars and clubs because he was a hip-hop DJ. We loved taking shots—specifically "3 Wisemen" and "Vegas Bombs." Being a friend of the DJ, I always had requests for my "anthem" songs: "No More Drama" and "Family Affair" by Mary J. Blige, and "Empire State of Mind."

Manny's style eventually changed to a "GQ" look. He always had the latest trends, and wearing suits on a daily basis inspired him to dress to perfection. He especially enjoyed our holiday parties. Manny was one of my best friends.

I remember trying to create a mixtape at home. It was hard recording a tape from the radio; when you heard your favorite songs, you had to remind everyone to be quiet. Otherwise, the recording caught all the background noise. It took a long time to make even an imperfect mixtape to play in the car.

The next few months were fast and furious. Before I knew it, Thanksgiving, the holiday party, Christmas, and New Year's festivities had come and gone. Working six days a week finally ended. I was spent and looking forward to spending time with the twins. I filed my taxes and saved a portion of my return. I did some spring cleaning with the twins. My parents missed them, and now that I was working a normal schedule, I visited my family frequently. During the previous few months, I'd had time for only quick visits. It was nice to enjoy my mom's home-cooked meals.

During the summer of 1999, the stress of my relationship with Marcus and the twins' father became overwhelming. I decided that I needed to get out of town for a few days, so I planned a trip for the twins and me to visit my cousin. My cousin and his girlfriend had moved north four years earlier; they lived about 140 miles away. His girlfriend was the person who referred me to the job I was working. I had been hired four years earlier to fill her position.

We visited them as often as we could. The drive to a different city felt different this time, as if a new beginning were about to unfold. I prayed while the twins slept. Once we arrived, they greeted us with open arms. We spent time at the zoo, touring downtown, shopping, and eating. Afterward, we were all tired from a long day of running around the city, but we had a blast.

That night, I woke up around 3:00 a.m. I couldn't sleep, so I walked outside. They lived in an apartment complex near one of the main highways. It was a beautiful, starry night with clear skies, and the weather was perfect. I looked toward the highway. To the east and west, cars were driving at high speeds, their headlights a blur. At that moment, I felt like this was our new home. This would be the city we would move to. I thought, "Life is too short. Time is passing, and change looks brighter for our future."

In the city where we resided, there were not many job opportunities. This move would give the twins and me endless possibilities. Being around Matthew, I still walked on eggshells. That wasn't living; I was living in fear. I decided I wanted no more fear or drama. I decided that I could either go with the speed of life or stay behind the curve, watching others take chances. I thanked God for allowing me to see what we were missing. I walked inside, excited for our future.

When we arrived back home that weekend, we were refreshed. The twins had no idea that their lives were about to change. Marcus and I had a heart-to-heart talk. I let him know that, over the weekend, I realized I wasn't happy in the city where we lived. I told him I was living in fear of the twins' father and that it wasn't a real life. I asked him to move north with us to a larger city. After his shock wore off, he said yes. I told him that he had one year to say goodbye to his family. I let him know that he did not have to worry about the logistics related to the move; I told him I would take care of it. He agreed.

The next morning, I went to my mom and dad's house. I told them the news of my intention to move. I said we would be moving in one year and that they had one year to say goodbye to the twins and me. My dad was sad.

He told me, "I don't think you should move. Your family is here. You're not going to make it."

My mom then looked at me and said, "Mija, don't sell your house. You might have to come back. I hope you make it. I'll be here either way."

I hugged them both and told them that it would all work out. I called my sisters and gave them the news. They all said the same thing—that I shouldn't go and that I wasn't going to make it. I reminded them that one of our sisters lived in a rural area near the city where I would be moving.

Still, they maintained, "You're the baby of the family. You shouldn't go."

I called my sister, who lived in the city we were moving to. She was excited for me. She told me, "We're here to help you when you move." But she also said, "It's hard up here. I don't know if you're going to make it. It will be nice to have family living closer than where you are now."

It wasn't the excitement I was expecting, but my decision was final. A year from now, we would be moving. Because I feared Matthew's response, I made the decision to give him the news one month before we moved.

For the next year, the plan was to travel once a month to the new city. My part-time job would pay for all the expenses. Marcus didn't want to travel with me; he wanted to spend time with his family and friends. I had to find the best area for our family to live, search for an apartment, research and visit school districts and community colleges, and meet with doctors and dentists.

With regard to my job, I would request a transfer to the new city. They had three retail store locations there. Since I had been with the company for over four years, they had an awesome incentive: if you were with the company for five years, they would give you six weeks of paid vacation. The employee had to accrue three weeks' vacation, and then they matched the three weeks. You could request your vacation throughout the year or all at once. This was perfect timing for us. I was going to request the six weeks off during the summer. That would give us time to explore our new city.

We didn't have Google at that time. Our form of research was utilizing the ethernet ports to establish a connection, and then the computer was ready to start surfing the internet. Ethernet was a dial-up cable. It was a port that plugged into the phone line. This would power the unit. The phone line and ethernet connection were shared. If you were on the landline, you were unable to connect to the internet. While utilizing the connection, you could hear the sounds of beeping, screeching, and dinging. It was an extremely loud connection. If anyone picked up the phone during the connection, you would have to start again.

I decided to use the network of doctors on my insurance to call and visit their offices. At that time, it was much easier than surfing the internet. All I could think about was our new beginning. I often reminded myself, "One year, Reyna. One more year and a new beginning." That was my new mantra.

Throughout the year, I intentionally reached out to the twins' father. I had been avoiding him, but it was time to re-engage for the twins' sake. He was happy to hear from me. He asked if he could see us and spend time as a family. I told him we could. I was taken aback by how quickly he responded. But I had a condition for the visits: the twins wanted to see their brothers. If he wanted to hang with us, they needed to join us. He agreed.

It was nice to see the twins interact with their two brothers. Matthew and I just sat back and watched. We met once a month. I was happy to see when the twins' father would pick up the boys the same weekend, knowing his other kids would be heading over to see my kids. I gave him accolades for that.

I'd drop the kids off after daycare on Fridays. My prince loved wearing his cowboy hat and cowboy boots. My little princess loved wearing fancy dresses. Friday evenings, they would all go out to dinner. He would ask if I could stay and join them for dinner. Sometimes I would stay for dinner, or sometimes I would just visit for a couple of hours. His boys were adorable. They took a liking to me.

The year flew by. Before I realized it, we had less than two months to go before our move. Everything was falling into place. We had begun to pack and give away items we didn't need or want. The twins were also on board for the move; I promised them that we would be back to visit family throughout the year. They were looking forward to spending summers with his parents and mine. I also agreed to drive them back to spend time with their father during holidays and birthday celebrations.

Marcus reminded me that we still hadn't found a renter for the house, but I knew we still had time. I believed that it would all work out. My friends and I met for lunch at Golden Corral before the move, and I asked them to spread the news that a rental house was available. My plan was to place an ad in the paper. During our conversation, an employee was cleaning the tables near us. He stopped at our table and greeted us; he was the manager.

He said, "I couldn't help overhearing that you have a rental property available next month. My girlfriend and I would be interested. We are planning to marry and would like to move in together before our wedding day. When can we see the house?"

I replied, "How about Friday?"

He agreed. We exchanged contact information, and I provided him with our address. That evening, I told Marcus the great news. The manager's timing was perfect, and he and his fiancée were on time to see the house. We gave them the "nickel tour," then walked back inside to the living room to discuss their thoughts about the place.

Before I could ask if they were interested in renting, he took a wad of cash from his front pocket and announced that they would like to pay the deposit and first month's rent. We all laughed.

I responded, "I won't be taking your cash today. Let me set you up with my attorney. He'll be drawing up the rental agreement for the two of you to sign. You can leave him a check or money order for the deposit and first month's rent." That evening, we drank a few beers to celebrate.

I dreaded reaching out to the twins' father to give him the news that we were leaving. Over the past year, we had been in a slightly better place, and I was about to bring that to a halt. He had a temper, and I wasn't ready for it. I thought, Here we go.

One evening, I got the nerve to call him. I asked if he had time to chat for a few minutes. He was available and open to listening.

I then told him, "We are planning to move next month. I have been doing research for about a year. We are moving up north; this will give the twins and us a fresh start. I'll be transferring with my job. The twins will not be attending a private school, as I am unable to afford the new private school rates. I have selected a top public school for them to attend. I reached out to an attorney and confirmed there is no restriction requiring me to stay in this city. I learned that I am only required to give you notice and provide you with the new address for their school and our residence."

I continued, "We leave in a month. I am willing to meet you halfway for your visits. On some of those weekends, I will drive all the way to visit my family and friends."

For a few seconds, there was silence.

Matthew finally answered and said, "You're not taking my kids. I don't give a shit if you want a fresh start. You're not taking my kids."

He then hung up the phone. So many emotions ran through my body. I took several deep breaths, then sat there for a minute and thought, "We are doing this, Reyna. It's a new beginning. You've got this."

I omitted the date we were actually moving during the conversation; I didn't want him to show up and cause a huge scene. The twins also didn't know our departure date. My sister, her husband, and his family were ready for us. My sister's husband would be driving the U-Haul, while Marcus and I would be driving our own vehicles. When the twins' school year ended, they spent a few days with my parents.

For the next month, the goal was to avoid the twins' father like the plague. The twins' drop-off and pick-up location was at my parents' home. Matthew would enter the house every time to greet my parents, hoping I was there.

A couple of weeks before our move, as Marcus and I were having an intimate conversation, he asked, "What do you think about staying and not moving up north? Is it too late to cancel? I'll pay all the fees and costs you have incurred. Do you really want to move away from your family and friends? What about the twins? Are you thinking about the impact it is going to have on them? We can stay here and move to a new home."

I was blown away. I thought, "Was he being serious? Was this an 'Aha! I got you!' joke?"

I sincerely asked, "Do you want to move? Are you being serious?"

He hugged me and said, "I was hoping that you would have dropped this dream of yours to uproot us to another city."

My jaw dropped and my heart sank.

I told him, "I love you, but we leave in two weeks. You can join us or move back with your parents. I'm not going to beg you. This is your decision. It's your life. We can see if our relationship will stand the long distance. If you had any hesitation or concerns, you could have mentioned them during the planning. You said nothing. I'm sorry. I've been mentally preparing myself for a year. I truly feel this is where we are meant to grow. From the day I went to visit until today, I feel the same."

We held each other without saying a word.

Marcus then said, "I'll give my notice and request a transfer. I don't want to lose my family."

I shook my head, shrugged my shoulders, and said, "I can't believe you hadn't given your notice. You really don't want to go. You can stay. Don't do something you'll regret and place the blame on me. We'll try the long-distance relationship."

I took a few minutes to regroup my thoughts. He followed me and said, "I honestly want to go. It wasn't fair of me to tell you when we were about to move. I'll give my notice first thing in the morning. If they are unable to transfer me, I'll find another job."

That summer, we moved 140 miles north. It was our second chance. I couldn't help but wonder if my relationship with Marcus was slipping away. We moved in, and boxes were everywhere. I wasn't worried about unpacking because I had plenty of time. Marcus's job had an opening and he was able to transfer, but he worked long hours. The twins and I were off for the next six weeks.

Early one morning, I called my two sisters. I asked if their kids could stay with us for the next few weeks. My only request was that they pack clothes, a pair of tennis shoes, and a backpack for each child. I told them I would pick up the kids in the next couple of days. My sister from my hometown said she would drop off my nephew by the end of the day. Her husband was heading to the laundromat to wash all of his clothes while she went to get him a backpack and a pair of new tennis shoes. My sister who lived in the same city also told me she would be dropping off her girls by the end of the day. They owned their own embroidery shop; she left work to get the two girls packed and ready to go to Tia's (Aunt's) house. By the end of the day, we had a house full of five kids, including mine.

I planned out our schedule and activities for the upcoming weeks, and the kids chimed in. Marcus worked on Saturdays, but he was off on Sundays. We spent Sundays by the poolside while Marcus barbecued for the family. We did so many activities: the Tower of the Americas, the River Walk, the Alamo, the zoo, walking trails, and playing at several different parks throughout the city. We had picnics, visited museums, went to movie theaters, ice cream shops, restaurants, swimming pools, malls, cathedrals, theme parks, and so much more. There were some days when we just filled up the car's gas tank and drove around the city. It was exciting; you could see the joy in their facial expressions.

Our favorite restaurant was Ruthie's, an outstanding family-owned Mexican restaurant. They had fluffy flour tortillas, great menudo, carne guisada, and delicious ranchero sauce. Whatever you chose to eat, it was great, and the price was reasonable for a family of seven. Our time together was soon coming to an end, but these memories would forever be imprinted. The past few weeks were exhilarating—what a way to begin the next chapters of our lives!

The twins would be heading back with my nephew soon. School wasn't scheduled to begin for a few more weeks, and their dad would be spending time with them. We were so blessed to have spent time together without a care in the world. Now, it was time to join the workforce and go back to work.

Marcus was enjoying the new atmosphere at work. As for me, my first day went well. I had met most of the employees throughout the year, and the layout of the store was similar to the one I had just left. The clothing trends were on point.

We had a few weeks before the twins would be home, so I asked Marcus to take a few days off. He had no idea that I had planned a getaway to Indianapolis to visit Mont and his wife, who had moved back home to Indiana. A couple of days before our departure, I surprised him with the news. We headed to the mall for some last-minute shopping. Around the time of our arrival in Indianapolis, a jazz festival began on a Thursday and ended the following Monday. This was a way to spotlight Indianapolis' rich jazz heritage through an annual event. We spent our first night at a hotel near Mont's home. His wife decorated our room with candles and fresh flowers and left a basket of goodies for us to enjoy.

On the first night, Mont's brother invited all of us to watch a boxing match. His brother was very chill, just like Mont. We spent time with his family and friends and enjoyed some good ribs and side dishes. Over the next couple of days, we enjoyed some excellent music. Mont and his wife took us to some local restaurants to enjoy authentic fried fish; it was delicious. We flew back on Monday morning. Marcus and I had a fantastic weekend.

The next weekend, I headed to my hometown to pick up the twins. Summer was over, and they would be enrolled in the second grade. They had an after-school care program that charged a small fee for the kids to join while parents were still at work. It closed at 6:00 p.m. Since Marcus finished work earlier than I did, he planned on picking them up around 5:30 p.m. My schedule usually ended between 6:00 p.m. and 9:00 p.m., which allowed me to get the kids ready for school in the mornings.

Depending on the weather, we would either walk or drive them to school. Luckily, the school was located across the street from the apartment complex. I also registered for two classes at a local community college.

Fall was in full swing. The kids had met some of their classmates during the summer, as they lived in the same apartment complex. Our jobs were going well, and Marcus had made new friends whom he hung out with quite frequently. We went home for the holidays later that year. The twins' eighth birthday was celebrated at a roller-skating rink, and my family drove into town to enjoy the festivities. It was so much fun; I couldn't remember the last time I had been on roller skates. We laughed the entire time. Matthew and his family didn't join us, as he had a separate party for the twins. I drove down for the day so they could enjoy the festivities with his family.

School was going well for the three of us. My relationship with Marcus was also going well; he wanted to go out more and explore San Antonio. Sometimes he wanted to explore with just the two of us, and other times with his friends. We both enjoyed going to the movies, shopping at the mall, and trying new restaurants.

In hindsight, I thought our relationship was going well. I suppose that is what I get for thinking. One day, I received a call from his mother. She asked, "How is everything going?" I told her about all the good things we were experiencing. She then began to paint the picture Marcus had described to her. His mother was a registered nurse. Since the first week we moved into our apartment, Marcus had called her every Friday to ask for money. He claimed that we had been struggling to eat and survive in the new city. He told her we had been living there for over six months. I thought, "What the heck?"

His mom told me that the amount of money he requested had increased in the last few months; it had started with $50 requests and was now up to $200 a week. She then told me that we should move back if we were financially unable to pay our bills.

I apologized to her profusely. I let her know that we paid our bills and had money in our savings account. I asked her to keep our conversation between us, as I wanted to do some investigating of my own.

Marcus was out with his friends one day. I never went through his stuff; I only ever put his clothes in the dresser drawers or hung them in the closet. But today was different. I decided that I was going to search every place in the house, beginning with his dresser and our closet. I found a box containing cocaine and weed. I also found bank statements with only Marcus's name on the account; what's more, the statements indicated a large negative balance. We had a joint bank account where our payroll earnings were deposited, but the credit card bills were addressed to me. Several credit cards had been opened in my name, with a combined credit limit of over ten thousand dollars. I thought we only had one credit card open.

What a fool I had been. But wait, it gets better: he also had a cell phone bill with a new number. I looked at the bill and called the most frequent number I found on the statement. It was a strip club in the Houston area. This was where his ex-girlfriend worked—the same one I caught him with when we initially met.

I thought, "How could I be so stupid?" I was a full-time mom, working and going to school. I just wanted a better life for all of us, but I didn't see the signs. In that split second, everything shattered. I wept for hours. He got home late, and I was too mentally and physically exhausted to even confront him. The next day while at work, I made some calls regarding the open balances on the credit card statements. They confirmed that I had a balance and that the minimum payments were being met. Marcus was asking his mom for money to cover the cards and the cell phone bill. I called my bank to request a personal loan to consolidate my vehicle and all the credit card debt in my name. He had to go, but there was no way that I could afford all the minimum payments on my own. After three days, I was approved for a large personal loan to consolidate everything.

I asked my sister to take care of the kids for the weekend, and she was more than willing to do so. I asked Marcus if we could spend Saturday evening alone. I told him I would cook dinner and that we could spend quality time together. He had no idea that I was going to confront him. I wondered, "Would he be honest enough to tell me the truth?" I had no idea how the night would go, but I had been through too much to let anyone destroy what I was trying to accomplish for the future.

Before we had dinner, I asked him to sit next to me on the couch. I grabbed us both a beer. I had slid a folder with all the proof underneath the couch.

Very calmly, I began to tell him, "Tonight, our conversation will change both of our lives. Your mom reached out and let me know that you had been asking her for money since the first day we arrived. Apparently, our family has been struggling to eat and survive in the big city. After my research, I called her back to give her the true picture of what I found in a box. Do you know what that might be?"

He kept quiet. His eyes grew wider. Fear and anxiousness entered the room.

I continued, "Well, you wouldn't guess what I found? I found a box of goodies. I found drugs, unpaid debt, a bill for a new cell phone, and a bank statement. I want you to hand me that cell phone NOW!"

He grabbed it from his back pocket.

I continued and said, "I hope it was all worth it. We're done. We have been together since 1994, but today we celebrate the end of our relationship. Let's make a toast to the year 2000, when my ex-boyfriend fucked it all up. You lied to me. I explicitly told you not to come with us if you were going to blame me for the change. Your actions showed me that you did."

Marcus finally responded and said, "They weren't my drugs. I'm not leaving this house." I begged him to leave, but he continued, "This is my family. I helped raise the twins. I'm not their father, and I don't love her—I love you. Nothing ever happened. You can't make me leave. I'm never leaving you. You're mine forever."

I shook my head from side to side.

I took a swig of my beer and said, "Listen here. You only have two options. Option 1: Leave in five days and pay the full debt off by acquiring a loan to pay off the credit cards. Or, Option 2: Leave in five days, and I'll take on the full debt. You can take all the furniture in the apartment except what is in the twins' room. I'll give you enough for your deposit and pay for your first month's rent. In addition, I will pay the fees to open your own utilities. These are your only options. Pick one!"

He began to cry and said, "I'm sorry I let you down."

After a few hours of going back and forth, he picked option two. He did not want the money for the first month's rent, nor did he want any money for the utility fees. He said I could keep all the furniture; however, he did want the money for the down payment on his new apartment. He said that I could pay off all the incurred debt. What a man...

I was a survivor. I knew we would be fine. He packed most of his clothes that evening. After packing, he said, "I'll be back on Monday for the money to put down on my new apartment."

We never even touched the food. I was devastated. I couldn't even look at him. That night, I drank and cried until I couldn't drink or cry anymore.

CHAPTER 6

FRIENDSHIP

In the midst of all this sadness and drama, true friendships began to bloom. One day at work, I met Jeff, the manager of the retail store I was assigned to. After only a few minutes of conversation, I knew Jeff was a cool guy. He got along with everyone. Jeff was ranked as the number one salesman in the store. He was 5'10" and wore three-button dark suits, buttoning the top two and leaving the third one undone. Dark suits were his color preference, but he would choose light-colored dress shirts to brighten his suits. His collection varied in color and pattern; he had exceptional and modern taste in dress shirts and business casual apparel. His shirts were either point or spread collar types with button or French cuff models, and they ranged from dark to light. Blue twill, purple, pink, navy blue, wine, white, grey, lavender, off-white, red, and gold were just some of the colors in his collection. And let's not forget the most important accessory: Jeff had the perfect neckties to coordinate with his dress shirts. To complete the ensemble, he rocked Oxford dress shoes with a black buckle on the side.

The team trusted and respected Jeff, which made our work environment more engaging and productive. I enjoyed going to work. After we had worked together for a few months, our store won a sales contest. The prize was dinner at a fine-dining restaurant; we all agreed on a steakhouse. Five employees RSVP'd for this elegant experience, including Jeff and me. We dressed for the occasion and met at Ruth's Chris Steak House. Everyone was welcoming and offered excellent customer service. The steaks were tender, flavorful, juicy, and cooked to perfection. They also had delicious side dishes to go with the steak. We were all pretty full but still made room for dessert. It was a wonderful evening.

Our friendship bloomed organically. One day while at work, Jeff approached me and asked if I could take his daughter to gymnastics classes. I asked if everything was okay, and Jeff explained that he felt out of place; he was the only male sitting among the women waiting for their children. Practice was twice a week. I picked up his daughter, Luna, and we headed to the studio. As we entered, the staff greeted us both. Luna walked into the studio, and they guided me to a waiting area with a window so parents could watch the class without being in the same room as the students. Luna was so flexible; I was in awe. She had been attending gymnastics for several years.

The twins were eight years old when they met Jeff's children, Luna and Luke. Luna and Luke came to visit their dad every summer and on holidays; they were five and eleven years old, respectively. There was an instant connection between the four of them when they met.

That summer, we purchased season passes to Fiesta Texas. They loved the theme park, which offered live entertainment, roller coasters, water rides, a wave pool, kids' rides, adult rides, and a variety of dining areas. Jeff wasn't a morning person—he was more of a night owl—so I would take the kids to the park. Each one of them had their own backpack filled with snacks, a Fiesta Texas cup for free refills, and cash. If I had to head to work, Jeff would pick them up. Afterward, they would head to Dave & Buster's for dinner, which featured a full-service restaurant, a bar, and a video arcade.

When I arrived to pick up the twins from dinner, Jeff would be hanging out at the bar. My favorite adult beverage was a Cape Cod (commonly known as a vodka cranberry). Without fail, my drink and appetizers would be waiting for me; this helped me unwind from the long day. Jeff had a VIP card from Dave & Buster's. To earn a VIP card, you had to play a certain number of games and earn many points. The card offered various discounts. Seeing the twins run toward me made my heart smile; I felt so much better when I saw them.

I was still an emotional wreck. I was trying to put the pieces together, one step at a time... one day at a time. I kept telling myself, "This too shall pass." My twins were my everything; they brought me so much joy. I wanted them to be safe, to enjoy the journey, to be kids, and to laugh and create memories with family and friends. I reminded myself that they, too, had lost someone they cared about. We all missed Marcus. He had been part of our lives for several years, and it would take some time for our family to heal. But we had each other. When Marcus was free on weekends, he'd pick up the twins for the day or an overnight visit.

As the summer was coming to an end, all four kids wanted to spend more time at the theme park. One week, the six of us went to Fiesta Texas every day. The late afternoons were the best time to go because the lines for the attractions were shorter. People who had arrived early in the morning were walking out of the park, exhausted, so the crowds thinned out.

Since we only had a few hours before the theme park closed, Jeff and I would have the kids select one side of the park to enjoy. They were not allowed to roam to any other side. Without any lines, they were able to get on the rides several times. Jeff and I would enjoy a drink while the kiddos enjoyed the attractions; we would wave our hands as they passed us by.

On weekends, the girls would have sleepovers at Jeff's. They would rent Blockbuster videos and eat junk food all night. For their part, the boys preferred overnight "lock-in" computer gaming arcades. When they went to one of these places, Jeff or I would go in to register them. We would drop them off by 10:00 p.m. and pick them up at 6:00 a.m. The kids played computer games all night. Fiesta Texas and Dave & Buster's were our two favorite entertainment spots. Meeting Jeff and his kids was a true blessing.

While I was with Marcus, I also met Olivia. She was a college classmate in my speech class. During one session, the instructor asked us to go across the room and introduce ourselves to someone new. I introduced myself to Olivia, and we hit it off well. She was ten years younger than I was, but that didn't matter to either of us.

Olivia and I hung out on weekends; she was my party buddy. We'd go to the club and dance all night. Olivia liked to drink alcohol, while I preferred to smoke weed. Olivia would drive us to the club, and I would drink water and soft drinks. By the end of the night, I no longer had a buzz, so I drove us both home. Marcus was jealous of our friendship. Dancing helped take the edge off my stress.

The twins and I went back home for the holidays. The trip was short because I had to work. It was our peak season (the usual "six days a week for six weeks" schedule). The twins had the option to come back home with me or stay with their dad for a few extra days. The kids missed their family. Both sets of grandparents and Matthew shared the responsibility of caring for them.

When the twins were gone, all I did was party. I partied like I didn't have a care in the world. I couldn't shake the broken heart and another failed relationship, so this was my time to dance and have fun. I would think, "How could this happen to me again? Why did it happen? What signs did I miss? How did he rack up my credit cards? When did he get another cell phone? Where was I through all of this? Was I just too naïve to see the person he was?" I had trusted him. Now, I had all these questions and no answers. But I reminded myself that God had a plan and that I just had to walk the journey—no matter how hard it was. I reminded myself that these emotions would pass. I'd been through the wringer with Matthew; what I was going through now was tough, but not compared to what I had endured in the past. I knew I had to focus on the present moments with the twins. I had to stop looking back at what could have and should have been, but wasn't.

The holiday break was over, and the three of us were back to our normal routine. The twins and I were doing well in school. We would go to a Barnes & Noble twelve hours a week; they would enjoy a hot cocoa while I enjoyed a café mocha. I would leisurely read or do my homework. My daughter was an avid reader, but on the other hand, my son did not like reading at all. He didn't like going to Barnes & Noble and thought it was boring. So, he and I made a deal: we both agreed that when we went to the bookstore, he was not to read one word or letter of the alphabet. He was only to look at pictures and photos. If he did read, there would be consequences: he would be grounded for one month and spanked three times. We shook on it and sealed the deal. He was so happy that he didn't have to read.

In less than three weeks, he was asking to read a series. I reminded him of the consequences, and he would shake his head and walk away. A few days later, before leaving the house, he asked to speak to me. His hand was behind his back, holding a belt. He handed me the belt; I looked into his eyes and turned him over to face the sofa. I waited a few seconds, then turned him back to face me, and we hugged it out. I couldn't spank him for wanting to read. My prince went on to read fifty-nine books in the Hank the Cowdog series that year. He did better in school, too, averaging 97% in all of his classes. He loved reading.

There were several occasions when the twins just didn't get along. If they continued to argue, I would stop everything or pull over into a parking lot. I would then make the twins get out of the vehicle. I'd let them know that it's okay to not get along, but they would have to come together to discuss the issue and make amends. The twins were stubborn sometimes; I think they must have gotten that trait from me, their dad, my mom, or someone else in our family.

Their disagreements went like this: first, they would tell me that they were never speaking to each other again. In response, I'd look at them and let them know that I had nowhere to be and that I could stay in the parking lot until they talked and hugged it out. During one of their disagreements, we stayed outside the vehicle for a few hours, their arms crossed and their faces bearing serious expressions. Second, they would usually complain about how hot it was and say they wanted to go home. However, I would not interrupt the process of reconciling their differences.

I had learned over time that you have to discuss the issues and then hug it out. The disagreements would eventually resolve when they would both say "sorry" at the same time and hug. But that alone was not good enough for me. I insisted that they discuss the concerns before hugging. I would then wait on them. A few minutes would pass, then they'd chat and sincerely hug it out. This happened on several occasions. Eventually, when an argument started, I would let them know that I was going to pull the vehicle over, and the twins would immediately begin to discuss their concerns, apologize, and hug it out.

Telling the twins' father that my relationship had ended was pretty tough. He was already angry with me because I moved away; he felt that I had ripped the kids away from him. I promised him that I would meet him halfway whenever he wanted to see them. Since moving, I had kept my promise. We always went home for all holidays and birthdays because I never wanted to keep them from their father. But that wasn't the only reason it was tough. After I told him about the breakup, he began to shout through the phone for a bit. I could hear him cursing at me, so I just put the phone down until he was done. His yelling brought back a lot of unsettled emotions from our past.

When the twins weren't with me or their father, my sister, who lived in a rural part of the city, would occasionally take them on weekends. She had two girls who were a few years older than the twins. She was a strong woman who had faced many challenges growing up; despite those challenges, she had remarried and was doing well in life. My sister and her family loved the outdoors. They enjoyed camping, fishing, barbecuing, swimming, theme parks, water parks, and so much more. They were a family that was always on the go. When I was free, I too would partake in their adventures.

As a mom, I was always trying to protect the twins from being emotionally hurt. The recent breakup with Marcus was hard for them. "Straight Talk" helped them get answers to questions they had. Marcus was with me when "Straight Talk" was implemented; he was well aware of the light as well as the deep conversations we'd had in the past. The twins asked us some difficult questions—sometimes of both Marcus and me, and sometimes separately. They would ask things like, "Why did you both break up? Will you be getting back together in the future? Why does he have to move out? Whose fault was it? Did we have anything to do with the breakup? Why didn't you try to work it out? Why don't you love each other anymore?" and, "Why can't we continue to be a family?"

They were able to express their feelings to both of us. Marcus admitted that he messed up and assured the kids that it wasn't their fault. Marcus also told them that he loved us all. We cried and hugged during the conversations. We both reassured them that the relationship ending had nothing to do with them. I felt there was inner healing for all of us. We were honest about our feelings; it was emotional and painful, but we got through it. Over time, you could see the change in the twins' posture. They were more relaxed. We had several conversations throughout the next few months.

Second grade flew by. The kids enjoyed school. We had morning and bedtime routines. The evening routines went well: after they showered, brushed their teeth, and selected their clothes to wear in the morning, they placed their backpacks near the front door. I placed all signed paperwork in their folders and made sure that they were ready for bed. My little princess was an early riser. Once she was up, she'd get dressed; very seldom did she have difficulty waking up. On the other hand, my little prince was not a morning person at all. I would have to drag him out of bed. I didn't actually drag him off the bed, but that is what I wanted to do. It was incredibly frustrating, and yelling didn't get him up any faster. Once he was out of bed, he was okay. It just took a bit to wake him, and I did my best.

I tried several techniques to wake him. I would start with "Good morning," sweet kisses, and hugs. If that didn't work, I would turn on the light and say, "Wake, wake!" I would try rewarding him for waking up and so much more. It got better, and eventually, he would wake up without any issues, but then it would get worse again. I would have to pull the covers off, and eventually, he would get up. We did this routine for several years. I also wasn't a morning person, so I had to push myself to wake up.

The elementary school contacted me on several occasions because we had too many tardies. We had so many, in fact, that the three of us were required to attend four hours of Saturday detention. The weekend we attended detention, the school was facilitating SAT testing. All the classrooms and the auditorium were occupied, so they had no space for us. The administrators had us sit in an office. During our detention, the twins worked on school projects. After that day, we all agreed to try harder to never be late. All three of us learned huge lessons. The funny part was that we lived only a few minutes away from the school.

The move to the big city was emotional for all of us. With our routines in place, the twins developed new skill sets and built healthy habits. Visiting their dad and family each month made the transition easier, and the twins adapted well to their new school.

The daily schedule provided at the beginning of the year was structured well and presented within a small booklet. It included a welcome note from the teacher, tips on ways parents could support their children at home and school, and a daily checklist for parents. There was also a "Get to Know the Students" one-pager entitled "These are My Favorites," which covered items such as their favorite color, pet, ice cream flavor, sport, game, day of the week, place to visit, thing to wear, restaurant, food, school subject, possession, and song.

School started before 8:00 a.m. Once they arrived in their classroom, the teacher took attendance and the class listened to the morning announcements. The students read, had a bathroom break, and learned math, spelling, and handwriting. The twins had good penmanship and were also learning cursive script. After lunch, they had story time and another restroom break, followed by classes in English, writing, social studies, and science. Before school let out for the day, the students had one last bathroom break, packed their backpacks, and moved into a homeroom or attended a music class. Lastly, they attended a physical education (P.E.) class. Throughout the week, students also visited the computer lab, attended rhythms, and went to the library. Second graders worked on projects that involved research and critical thinking.

Some of their assignments included learning Spanish words, the United States map, geography, division, multiplication, word problems, math vocabulary, "greater than" and "less than" concepts, ordering numbers, anatomy, problem-solving, and sign language. They also created pretend passports, voter registration cards, and driver's licenses. The school encouraged the students to create stories and staple them together as books.

During "Red Ribbon Week," they made a booklet and pledge cards related to the "Just Say No" program. They unscrambled letters to find hidden messages and read stories about drugs and medicines. They also learned to read medicine labels and studied tobacco and its effects on the body. After long days of school, homework, and dinner, their dad would call to chat with them. He would then ask to speak to me; once he heard my voice, he became a complete jerk. He would get upset for no reason, and if I had any questions, he would become agitated. I believed the drugs he was using were causing him to be more verbally aggressive. In response, I would simply ignore him and hang up the phone. I was always grateful that we had moved away from the drama.

Before I knew it, summer was around the corner. The twins were heading back to my hometown to spend time with their father and both our families. It had been almost a year since we moved, and I thought about how quickly time passes. I was still emotional and tried my best not to let the twins see my sadness. I knew I would miss them terribly; I cried every time they left to visit family. They are my babies, and I didn't like being away from them. We talked every day, and I told them that I would be in town to visit.

I was looking forward to some personal time and planned to hang out with Olivia during the summer. My personal time would involve going out and having some fun. During those trying times, I had focused so much on making sure the twins were happy that I shoved my emotions deep inside where no one would notice, choosing to just smile instead. However, I knew I couldn't do that forever. My plan for the summer was to allow myself to feel every emotion. I planned on taking the summer off from school and decided to go through the process of healing. I would pray, cry, yell, workout, party, and work—repeating that routine until I finally felt better.

I had been through so much in my past. I kept telling myself that this failed relationship did not define me and that I was meant to be successful—that I would fulfill all of my goals. I resolved to always put God first and to let go of what I couldn't control. I decided to trust in His journey for our lives.

Work had been going well. Our district manager was moving employees to different locations, and I was selected to move to a store closer to home. I knew the majority of the employees at this location; we'd met during our holiday party. I'd also picked up merchandise from that location in the past. I was told I would be moving at the end of the summer. I realized that change was constant in my life, but I trusted God, so I embraced the changes. I was grateful for my job. My employer was flexible with my school schedule, and my bosses were aware that I had twins. They gave me time off for any appointments I had with the kiddos.

The twins' school year ended, and we headed out of town to visit family. We were so excited. I missed my parents, especially my mommy; I was her baby girl. When we arrived, we spent the weekend with my parents. Mom's hugs and kisses were the beginning of my healing. While the twins were enjoying their time with their cousins, I would lay my head on my mom's lap and she'd play with my hair. When she did this for me, tears rolled down my cheeks. She knew I was hurting. I didn't have to say one word; she just knew. Leaving my mom and moving to a new city was the hardest thing for me. Even though we spoke daily, it was still tough.

She told me, "Baby, I love you so much. I'll always be here for the three of you. You can pick me up anytime to stay with you and the twins. Know I am only a phone call away. You're always in my prayers."

We had a great weekend. The twins' dad picked them up that Sunday evening. I let him know that I would be calling every day. In response, he gave me a death stare. He didn't say one word, but he smiled when he locked eyes with the twins. The kids hugged and kissed me before they left. Watching the twins leave was emotional, and my mom held me. I left soon after. My drive back to the city was less than two hours.

Being home alone for the next few weeks was difficult. I put my plan in motion after a few weeks, and I started seeing the light at the end of the tunnel. The summer flew by. Before I knew it, it was time to pick up the twins. I missed them so much. Their dad rarely let me talk to them; when I called, he was rude. He told me the kids were busy playing and that he'd have them call me later. Then he'd hang up, and I wouldn't hear from them. The twins went to my parents' home during the week. My mom would call me when they arrived. When we spoke, the twins would ask why I hadn't called them while they were at their dad's. I explained that I did call, but they were out playing with their cousins.

The twins were excited to come home. When I picked them up from my parents, their father was there. He was just there to annoy me. He could have dropped them off and left, but no—he waited for me. When we locked eyes, he gave me a look like he was about to attack. He never let the twins catch him doing that, but they knew something was off between us.

He would whisper in my ear, "Take care of my kids or I'll come after you. You'll f****** pay for anything that happens to my kids. Watch your back."

Then he'd give me their bags and walk away. I would get sick to my stomach, but I knew I had to keep it together. Even though my parents were near, I was scared. Memories of the physical trauma he caused me flashed before my eyes. I remembered the impact his actions had on others who witnessed him harming me, and that what they had seen could not be unseen. But I didn't let any of my emotions show; I pretended like his words didn't faze me. I knew this reaction pissed him off.

The twins ran into my arms and almost knocked me down. I cried with joy. They were taller and looked beautiful. We then said our goodbyes.

After I picked them up, we had plans to see my sister and her children. I also planned to spend time with Jeff and his kids. On the drive home, they told me all about their summer; they had a blast. The twins asked how my summer went. I told them, "It was good. I worked and had some fun with friends." They would often worry about me.

School was starting in a few weeks. Jeff and I planned a vacation to South Padre Island. We spent a week buying everything we needed for our trip. South Padre Island had so many attractions: water sports, boat tours, dolphin watching, horseback riding on the beach, an amusement park, seafood restaurants, and many more family activities. Jeff and I agreed on expenses for the trip. He didn't want me to pay for much. He told me, "I am doing great financially. Let me bless your family. You can get us on the next trip."

He was very generous. I was humbled and thankful. All I paid for was our breakfast and expenses when I had the girls with me. He paid for lunches, dinners, activities, and the condominium that overlooked the beach. It was beautiful and spacious, and the food was excellent.

The first night, my daughter had a hissy fit at dinner. My little princess didn't like anything on the menu. She wanted a grilled cheese sandwich, but it wasn't listed. Jeff told her that she could ask for whatever she wanted, and they prepared it for her. Jeff explained that restaurants accommodated most special requests. He told her that if they have the ingredients, it can be done, albeit with an upcharge. Everyone else enjoyed what was on the menu. She didn't have another fit through the remainder of the trip. We had such a great time on the beach.

One evening, we went to a theme park that had bungee jumping, go-karts, mini-golf, a Ferris wheel, rock climbing, and a giant swing. Luke, Luna, the princess, and I decided to bungee jump. I was last in line. I was geared up and ready to go, but I kept overthinking the jump. I stood on the edge for a couple of minutes, though it felt like a lifetime. I asked the attendant to push me, but he said their policy was not to touch the party jumping and that they were unable to assist. I chickened out at the end; I just couldn't do it. Everyone was yelling for me to jump, but I couldn't. Oh well... I tried.

Jeff, Luna, and the princess got on the giant swing. It was really high. When the swing dropped, you could hear the girls screaming so loudly. When we met up with them after the ride, they were so excited. The girls said they were scared, but they had fun. The next day, the boys planned to go on a guided fishing outing. The girls decided to go horseback riding on the beach and shopping. The girls had never been horseback riding, but I had been before. My last experience had not gone well.

When we arrived, I explained to the staff members who were selecting our horses that during my last ride, the horse walked, trotted, and then galloped. They had to run to my rescue to help me stop the horse. They reassured me that they were going to give me a mature, older horse. A staff member was assigned to watch me throughout the ride, but the horse had its own ideas. It walked slowly for a bit, but what happened next was scary. The horse went from walking to galloping. It jetted past all the other horses; it felt like he was running a freaking horse race. I was so f****** scared.

The staff riding with us began following alongside and behind me, giving me instructions on how to stop the horse, but the horse didn't listen to my commands. The other riders were pointing at me and freaking out as well. One of the staff members grabbed my horse's reins; once they pulled on them, the horse dropped to the ground. I was scared shitless. For the remainder of the ride, someone held the horse's reins. The staff apologized. The girls did well and had no issues.

The next day, my muscles were sore. That same day, the boys went on a private charter fishing extravaganza. They caught some fish and gave them to the guide. My son and Luke didn't know how to fish; when one of them cast their line, they ended up hooking the guide's eye. What a debacle! We all made it back safely to the condominium and had stories to share about the day. We just laughed. The week flew by, and we were exhausted because we had done so much in such a short time.

My angels were soon entering the third grade. We had a couple of weeks to finish our school shopping. Before orientation, we had to buy general school supplies: things like backpacks, three-ring binders, No. 2 pencils, colored pencils, pencil sharpeners, erasers, pens, composition notebooks, loose-leaf paper, glue, highlighters, red pens, folders, zippered pouches, scissors, boxes of Kleenex, and rulers. We enjoyed shopping for school supplies and clothes.

My little princess didn't like me to do her hair. She loved wearing it half-up, half-down with a bow in the center. The twins were turning nine years old in the next few months and had decided that Peter Piper Pizza would be their birthday celebration venue. The twins submitted a birthday wish list a month in advance; they also submitted a Christmas wish list six weeks prior to Christmas Eve. I was glad I had a savings account and money invested in the stock market

The twins going back to school meant that my college semester was about to begin. We were looking forward to the teacher, parent, and student orientation, where expectations would be laid out for the three of us. The teachers expected the students to learn social studies and science. In math, students were expected to learn addition, subtraction, multiplication, and division tables, as well as equations and word problems. They were also expected to read and write large numbers. In reading and writing, they were expected to explore a wide variety of books, define and pronounce complex words, write in cursive, and understand nouns, verbs, and adjectives. Furthermore, they would use thinking maps to organize ideas and learn prefixes, suffixes, and homophones.

My princess asked if she could take piano lessons in the fall, and I agreed. I had no idea how I was going to afford a piano, but someone at work told me to go to a pawn shop to purchase a gently used electric keyboard and stand. I thought that was a good idea. We were able to find an electric keyboard in great condition.

Some of my daughter's friends were taking lessons, so we reached out to the instructor and set up an appointment to meet with her. I soon learned that the lessons were expensive. The instructor informed her that piano lessons were not always fun; she was a tough teacher, but my daughter agreed to practice and not give up. So, we signed a contract. My princess was so excited and ready for the challenge. My son wanted to play basketball or football but had a hard time deciding.

Every day, I reminded the twins that they were beautiful and that they could accomplish anything as long as they put the work into achieving their dreams.

I couldn't believe that it had been almost a year since Marcus and I cut ties. During our "Straight Talk" conversations, the twins brought up some of their fondest memories of Marcus. They both recalled fishing. Marcus took them both on their first fishing experience, and they always had a great time. Since they fished near the house, it was easier to come back home when they forgot something, which happened often.

The twins knew that fishing required being patient while waiting for the fish to come. They would cast the line and wait. When one of them felt the tug of a fish, they would get excited and be ready to assist each other. If the fish got loose while they were reeling it in, they would encourage each other, saying there would be a next time to catch one. They always had fun. Listening to them speak brought joy to my heart; you could hear the excitement in their voices. I was grateful that Marcus taught them skill sets that I didn't know.

The twins also discussed their summer fun with the family. They were glad to be home, yet they still missed them dearly. They also talked about conversations with their father. He told them that he wasn't happy that I took them to another city. He told them that if they ever wanted to, they could come live with him and his mom. I explained to them that I never "took" them. I told them that their father was aware of the plan and that moving to a larger city opens doors to more opportunities that would benefit the three of us. I reassured them that once I graduated college, I wouldn't need to work two jobs. I asked them to have patience with me and trust in my decision to move us.

School was going well for the three of us. We continued to go to Barnes & Noble to do our homework and read new books. Reading is something we enjoyed, and it was a hot topic in our "Straight Talk" conversations. My daughter's favorite book was Harry Potter and the Sorcerer's Stone, a novel by J.K. Rowling. We went to watch the movie Harry Potter and the Sorcerer's Stone with Jeff, Luna, and Luke. There were long lines, and many of the kids wore costumes. Princess and Luke were more excited than the rest of us. We sat one row below the last row of the theater. Sitting left to right facing the screen were Princess, Luke, Luna, Prince, me, and Jeff. When we sat down, my princess wondered why we sat her next to Luke. Once the movie started, she realized that Luke had read the book and was also a fan of Harry Potter. For the rest of us, we just wanted to support their love of the movie, but after watching it, we all became fans.

At work, we were ramping up for the holiday season. Our hours of operation were about to change. During this peak season, we worked six days a week and between eight to 10 hours a day.

I hadn't been on a date since my breakup with Marcus. I wasn't really looking to date anyone, and then I met Ken. He was a client of mine. He was extremely polite, confident, and optimistic. He was tall with a medium build and a cute butt. He was an executive at his organization. Ken asked me out on a date, but I politely declined. I wasn't really ready to date; I knew one day I would be, but it wasn't the right time. Ken was persistent in asking me out for several weeks. He sent flowers and notes wishing me a good day. He was aware of my long hours and brought me food. He'd come by to shop and called during the week to check in on me.

Finally, I caved and went on a date to a Japanese steakhouse. When he picked me up at the apartment, he was early. He looked adorable in his grey mock turtleneck and jeans. As always, I was running late. He waited patiently for me and told me not to rush. After I finished getting ready, we walked toward his white Corvette. It was a beauty; I love sports cars and trucks. He opened and closed the door for me. When we arrived at the restaurant, I was about to open my door, but he gently grabbed my hand and said, "Let me get every door for you." I was impressed; I was used to getting my own door.

He was funny and listened attentively. We had a wonderful evening. He walked me to the door and gently kissed my lips. I walked inside, and he walked back to his vehicle. I was happy to see the twins. My babysitter was my neighbor, who also worked at the retail store. The twins were excited to see me, too. They asked all about him. I responded by telling them that he was just a friend, but inside, I was actually looking forward to our next date.

That year, I made reservations for the twins and me to stay at the Embassy Suites by Hilton during the Thanksgiving holiday weekend. With all the family gathering, my parents' home was crowded. My mom welcomed everyone to stay over, but we opted out. My family would join us at the hotel in the evenings. There was an indoor pool and jacuzzi. My family enjoyed the free happy hour; the kids swam while the adults enjoyed the jacuzzi.

When the family gathered, my siblings would recall family events or stories from our past. We'd laugh for hours listening to the stories. Since I was the youngest, they'd make fun of me all the time, and I'd just laugh with them. My mom and sisters were great cooks. They never really wanted me to help; again, because I was the youngest, they assumed I couldn't cook. But they were wrong. I was allowed to open canned goods—nothing more than that. My twins would get annoyed with that, but I'd explain to them that it was okay with me. I would tell them that we could just relax until the food was done. Because I was not needed in the kitchen, we'd sit and watch football with my dad.

The twins spent half the day with us and the other half with their dad. He'd come by and pick them up. Their dad would come inside the house to say "hi" to all of my family, but I'd go to a bedroom and hide from him. No matter where I went, though, he would find me and say, "I'm taking the twins, be back later."

In response, I would look down and nod my head. If we were alone in a room at these moments, fear would overtake my body; the memories of him yelling or hitting me would flash before my eyes. His voice was enough to make my skin crawl. Mom would find me afterward. She would hold me for a bit until I composed myself. My mom knew exactly what to do. Sometimes she would tickle me until I had to go pee.

The twins spent the Christmas break with their dad and rotated days with my family. That year, I drove back to my hometown to visit the family for a couple of nights. Then, I drove back home to get ready for work. The twins spent New Year's Eve and winter break with their dad. He had a very large family, and they would all gather at his parents' house. They would pop fireworks with their cousins on New Year's Eve. They would have family dinner and stay up most of the night. They loved it. They did so many outdoor activities while they were there.

As for me, I partied with my friends. When I spoke to the twins at midnight, I could hear the joy in their voices. After our call, I cried. It was tough not being with them. Being a single mom sucked.

My work hours were exhausting, but I just pushed through. I did continue to date Ken. For Christmas, we agreed to give each other just one gift. I explained to him that I was on a budget, and he agreed. For our date, I went over to his home. It was a very nice one-story, three-bedroom, two-bath house with a two-car garage. He had lighted candles and a wine pairing with cheese and fruit. He also ordered food for us to enjoy for dinner. I was impressed with his presentation.

When it was time to exchange our gifts, I had one box with two shirts in it to give to him. When he brought out the box for me, I was surprised by its size. He was really excited for me to open it. It was one large box with 12 gift boxes inside. I turned to him and shook my head; I told him that I could not accept these gifts. I reminded him that we had agreed on only one gift.

I told him, "Yes, I did go over by one, but this is too much."

But he insisted and replied, "I had fun shopping for you. Please, I insist. Inside each box, there is a gift receipt. You can return them if they are not to your liking."

After opening all the gifts, I was overwhelmed with joy. The gifts were perfect. We had a wonderful evening.

After the holiday break, the twins were excited to come home. They had a blast with their family and received so many gifts. With their birthday and Christmas being so close together, we had a large number of toys and clothes in our apartment. The twins were good about donating toys and clothes to our church or giving them away if we knew someone in need. We were blessed and extremely grateful.

After settling in, we sat on the couch, cuddled, and watched movies. Before I knew it, they fell asleep. I loved these moments. My babies were growing up right before my eyes. I always got emotional when thinking about them weighing under seven pounds at birth; now, they amazed me with their curiosity and conversations. I remember thinking that it was truly an honor to be blessed to rear such beautiful kiddos. I was lucky to have a boy and a girl.

Retail peak season was in full swing, and I worked almost every day. The twins and I went back to school. I thought to myself, "Here we go again." We continued to go to Barnes & Noble; going there kept us on track to complete our homework assignments and do recreational reading. I read over 20 books on how to rear twins during their teenage years. It was important to me to have different perspectives from other parents who had raised twins.

Being single and saving money was difficult sometimes. Since they were also in extracurricular activities, I did my best to save money for special occasions or for just treating ourselves and creating memories. Occasionally, we'd get all dolled up and have a nice evening at a fine-dining restaurant. Giving the twins opportunities to experience new things was wonderful. I would make reservations, and once we arrived at the restaurant, we would be greeted and seated at our table. The server would pull each of our chairs out for us. The twins were impressed when the server placed napkins on their laps and menus in their hands.

I'd then tell them to order anything from the menu, instructing them not to concern themselves with the cost. My prince and I loved a good steak and shrimp, but my princess was only interested in the macaroni. Sometimes I would lean over to her and whisper, "You can order anything. Mom has enough money to pay for it."

The server would then arrive at our table, but my princess would often not be ready. My son and I would place our orders first. Eventually, my princess would close her menu and say, "I would like the macaroni." After she placed her order, I would tell the server that she could have ordered anything, but all she wanted was macaroni.

On this occasion, the server leaned in a bit and smiled. He told my daughter, "Macaroni is my favorite. It's made fresh here by our chef. You're going to love it."

When the food arrived, the macaroni was a hit. After that day, I never questioned her food choices again. The dinner and the experience—along with many others we had—were exceptional.

My sister and her family also created new adventures for my twins. They continued to visit my sister every other weekend. When the twins were gone, I'd hang out with Ken, Olivia, or friends from work. The weekends were never dull; there was either a bunch of us hanging out, or Olivia and I were at a club drinking.

During one of my vacations, I was invited to celebrate my colleague's bachelorette party on a Carnival cruise ship to Cozumel, Mexico. During our excursion, the girls wanted to enjoy the beach. I did not want to do that, so my friend and I ventured out to experience the ancient Mayan paradise kingdom of Tulum. During the other days, we laid out by the pool and relaxed. The ship had fine-dining restaurants, casual eateries, and 24-hour all-you-can-eat pizza. They also had a few clubs where I could dance the night away.

Ken and I had been hanging out for a few months. He invited me over to his house one evening; we had plans to head out to dinner from his place. When I arrived, he was a bit nervous. He asked me to walk to the kitchen. As we stood in the doorway, he asked if I liked the appliances and accessories.

I replied, "Yes, they are nice. Since you live here, you have to like them."

He replied, "I've never cooked in this kitchen; I prefer to dine out. I purchased this house because I did research and the school across the street is the best elementary school there is in San Antonio. If you don't like the appliances or accessories, I can replace them to your liking. If you have any debt, I'll write a check to pay it off. Also, I prefer that you drive a BMW. You can pick out a BMW for you and the twins. We can sell your Mustang and you can keep the profit."

He then placed the following items on the kitchen island and said, "Here is my checkbook, bank statements for both checking and savings, a statement of my return on investments, and my yearly salary."

He had additional documents that he then placed on the kitchen island and continued, "This is everything. Do you have any questions? This is all yours. I'm financially in a great place in my life. I want to begin a future with you and your family."

I took a step back and immediately became overwhelmed. He was still talking, but for a split second, I couldn't hear what he said. I truly liked Ken, but I wasn't ready for this huge commitment. I wanted to take this slow. We were on different sheets of music; he was ready to move in and become a family. Ken was a good guy, but the twins and I were still working through our emotions from my last relationship. Ken hadn't met the kids yet, but he was ready to step in. I thought, How admirable of him.

I was standing there looking like a deer in headlights. Ken asked me, "What are your thoughts? It's a lot to take in, but I'm ready."

I agreed that it was a lot to take in. I appreciated him expressing how he felt and wanting to provide for my family. His foundation was solid.

I finally responded, "May I think about this?"

He lowered his head and nodded. He then grabbed his documents and walked into the other room. I stood there and thought, Oh my God! What just happened?

I felt so sad because I couldn't say yes to his offer. This was a huge decision, and he had put himself out there. I noticed his expression went from one of excitement to that of someone who had just had his balloon popped. He walked back into the kitchen and asked if I was ready to head out to dinner.

I said, "Thank you for choosing me to become part of your future. I just need time to think."

He hugged me and told me, "I understand. I'm not going anywhere."

After returning from my sister's, the twins asked how my weekend went. They knew about Ken but hadn't met him. I told them work was uneventful, that I went out with friends, and that I met up with Ken. I told them that it was a good weekend. I then asked them, "What do you both think about me dating again?"

They replied, "We're happy that you are putting yourself out there. But we're not ready to meet anyone or have someone else in our lives. We want it to be just us for a while. Marcus was part of our lives for seven years. That's over 75% of our lives. We want a break."

Their answer crushed my heart. My babies were being vulnerable and expressing that they weren't ready to put themselves out there. The twins needed time to heal. They wanted me to have fun and meet someone else, but anything beyond that was just too soon for them. That night, I fell asleep crying. I asked God, "Why bring a great guy into my life if my twins and I aren't quite ready? Why?" I then thought, "Would Ken wait if I explained to him how we felt?" All I could do was talk to him and be honest. He would have the option to continue to date me and take it slow or decide to move on.

I called Ken the next day. We had a deep conversation. I thanked him for putting himself out there and for being willing to provide for us. And then I told him that we needed to take it slow. I also told him that he didn't have to pay off my debt or buy me a vehicle. I suggested that we get to know each other and then see where it goes. I told him that after a few months, we could revisit his proposal.

I gave him the options. Before I could finish, he interrupted me and said, "Excuse me. I'm not going anywhere. Let's take it slow."

A few months passed. Along the way, Ken earned an executive promotion that would transfer him to St. Louis, Missouri. It was where the largest call center in the company was located. This was an opportunity he'd been waiting for and couldn't pass up. The company was giving him a bonus and paying for his moving expenses. They also offered to assist in selling his current home and purchasing a new one. Ken let me know that this new position would require him to work long hours.

It was tough to say goodbye. In the end, I told him, "I'll visit when you settle in."

Another school year flew by. The twins and I ended the year on a good note; we all passed our classes. But we needed a change of scenery. The apartment had too many memories from a past we were healing from. We'd been living there for almost two years. While the twins went to their father's house for the summer, my goal was to search for a new apartment. I had my eye on a three-bedroom, two-bath, 1,400-square-foot apartment. I stopped there frequently just in case something became available. While I was in search of an apartment, my renters decided to move out. They had given me their notice. It was a bit stressful knowing that I needed to quickly find a new renter.

During the last couple of years, I had made a small profit with my investments. I had put away any extra money I earned in a separate account. The money was to be used for repairs to the property or any unexpected expenses that came up. The tenants were great. They were always on time with rent, and I hardly had any repairs in the past two years.

When I traveled back to my hometown to visit the twins, the twins' father wasn't happy. He complained that the summer was his time. He'd give me a hard time, but I didn't care. I'd pick the kids up anyway. When I did, we would spend time with my parents and family. My mom reminded me to ignore him. It was hard to do because he was such a jerk; his voice was enough to turn my stomach. My mom, the twins, and my nephews and nieces would hop into my vehicle and go into the city to enjoy a movie, dinner, the beach, or shopping. Between my visits, I'd stop by the house to clean, and my dad would do minor repairs to the home.

During one of my visits to my house, when I happened to be there alone, a young lady knocked on the door. She was looking for a place for her mom to live. She began to explain that her mom was part of a state-run program; the state was paying for her mom's rent. If the house were available to rent, the state would pay me directly. We toured the house and she loved it; it was perfect for her mother. I asked if her mom would also be touring the house.

The woman replied, "No, I know she'll love it because I do. I'm also the executor of her estate."

She went on to say that they wanted to move in immediately. To this, I replied that I would have her contact my attorney. I continued by telling her that once the documents were signed and the security deposit was in hand, she and her mom were welcome to move in. Within a week, the documents were signed and checks were mailed—one for the deposit and one for the first month's rent. The transaction was like a beautiful row of falling dominoes. I had been worried and stressed, but God had a plan. The house was vacant for only one month, and the new offer doubled my profit. Since there was only one income in our family, this would definitely help us. The twins' father's child support was so inconsistent that I couldn't rely on it.

After a few weeks of searching for an apartment, I was successful in finding a suitable place. The apartment was located at the intersection of a very nice community. The complex had great outdoor amenities: a swimming pool, basketball court, community clubhouse, large park, and beautiful large oak trees. The apartment itself was 1,036 square feet and had two bedrooms, two bathrooms, a fireplace, and a private covered patio balcony. You could access the balcony from the living room and each of the bedrooms. We moved from a first-floor to a second-floor apartment. It would be ready in August, just in time for the start of the new school year. I couldn't wait to give the twins a tour of the new place. While they were with their father, I started packing all of our belongings and hired some movers. We needed a fresh start. Change was constant, and we did our best to adapt.

When our schedules aligned, Ken and I talked for hours. I was hoping to keep the spark alive, but we knew we were both going in different directions. He was focused on his career, while I was focused on my kiddos and completing my college degree. I thought, "Sometimes you meet people and it just isn't the right time." It was frustrating to come to that conclusion. We were both looking forward to my future visit; he had purchased a home and was excited for me to see what he selected.

The twins were back in town, and there was so much to do before the school year. I was glad they had opted out of playing sports. They were going into the fourth grade. We moved into our new place before the school year started, and they loved it. They were ready for a change in scenery.

First, we had to unpack and go through their current wardrobes. I decided to donate the clothes they had outgrown. I purchased new clothes, shoes, and school supplies for them. It seemed that as the kids got older, the list of school supplies got longer. Thankfully, I had a savings account. Sometimes I nearly drained all of the funds in the account, but I avoided this by working a second job. I did this to ensure we had money in savings, that our bills were paid on time, and that we had funds to travel. Investing money in the stock market really helped. With that profit, I was able to purchase all of the items on their birthday and Christmas wish lists. I also had money to purchase gifts for the family. I put any extra money I made into savings. I was happy that the twins had a routine of submitting their wish lists a month in advance.

One evening, we sat down for dinner; we were having chicken and some sides. My choice of beverage that evening was a cold beer. I sat at the head of the table, with my son on my left and my daughter to my right.

My son began a conversation and said, "Mom, we have something to tell you."

I reminded him, "Remember, in Straight Talk you can tell me anything. I won't get upset."

He then looked at his sister and asked, "Should we tell her?"

My princess nodded.

He then said, "Then you tell her. No! I'm not going to tell her. This is your idea!"

They went back and forth like that for a couple of minutes. I continued to enjoy my meal and acted like their conversation didn't faze me.

My son then asked, "Aren't you curious?"

"Yes," I responded. I continued, "If you don't feel comfortable, you can both tell me when you're ready."

My son then responded, "Okay. We'll tell you. We know where babies come from and how they are made. Adults lied to us."

I began to get a bit nervous, but I kept my poker face and didn't say a word. They both stared at each other.

He then said, "When we were at Dad's, we went to our family Sunday barbecue at our grandparents' (Dad's parents). Our twin cousins told us that they could show us the truth about how babies were made."

The cousins my son was referring to were identical twin boys. They were six months younger than my twins.

My son then told me a story and said he was told, "You just have to ask your parents for a dollar. Meet us in Grandma and Grandpa's bedroom. Don't tell anyone. If they ask, tell them you're going to watch a kids' movie. There were over ten cousins that showed up in the bedroom. One of the identical twins had a video in his hand. He walked back and forth in front of the T.V. and said, 'We found Grandpa's videos. It shows how babies were made. We're going to show you this video. If you tell anyone what we're about to show you, you're going to answer to us.' He then put the videocassette in the VHS, and it began to play."

My princess interrupted and yelled, "Mom, they were killing her! There were two men on top of her. They were killing her! She was yelling. We all closed our eyes, but we could still hear them."

I realized the children had found Grandpa's porn videos. When my daughter started yelling, I had just put a piece of chicken in my mouth. I nearly choked on my food; I lost my appetite.

After they were done, they both looked right at me. I asked them, "Are you both okay?"

They replied, "Yes, we are good."

I then asked, "Do you have any questions?"

"No questions. We hope she is going to be okay," they responded.

I had no words. They finished their dinner, and I excused myself. I let them know that I was going to check the mail near the front office. They asked to come along, but I told them I wanted to go alone.

"Okay. We'll get ready for bed," they said.

I took the keys, a beer, and my cell phone. I walked outside the apartment and chugged my beer. I then ran down the stairs and called the twins' father.

He answered the phone in typical fashion: "What!"

I asked him, "Do you know your kids watched a porn video at your parents' house a few weeks ago?"

He replied, "What?!"

I continued, "They told me everything."

To this news, he laughed and answered, "Ohhh… I remember giving them money. That day the boys were together. The girls were by themselves. They were very quiet. I didn't know. It's too late. It already happened."

I angrily asked, "What the f***! Why didn't you ask if everything was okay? Everyone noticed their behavior was different."

He answered, "I didn't think to ask."

I just hung up the phone. I couldn't even speak to him any longer. I walked back inside and held the twins. It was a "Straight Talk" night that I will never forget.

School was going well for the three of us. The twins were in the 4th grade and turning 10 years old. I thought, *Where does the time go? Before you know it, they will be walking the stage, graduating from high school. Every memory matters.*

I felt as if I'd been going to college forever. My schedule didn't allow me to go full-time. I remember thinking that one day I would have to change that, but for now, all I could manage was part-time. Even though we had moved further from school, we pushed ourselves to get there on time. No one wanted to experience another Saturday detention. The twins made friends; they had transitioned from private to public school well.

They decided they wanted to celebrate their 10th birthday at a bowling alley with friends and family. A few weeks after their birthday celebration, an administrator at their school called and asked me to come to the office. When I got there, I received some shocking news. The administration had made a mistake no one caught. I learned that our old apartment complex and the new complex were not in the same geographic area and that our current residence did not fall within the school district limits. They apologized for not catching the mistake. I told them that the first apartment complex was located right across the street and that we had been living there for two years. I was then told that the district line runs between the school and the apartment complex and that we would have to move immediately.

I asked the administrator to allow us to delay the move until after the Christmas holiday break. Waiting until then would give me time to register the kids in a new school. Waiting would also give the twins time to say their proper goodbyes to their friends. The principal agreed. During the visit, I was also told that the new school already had the transfer paperwork and that the date would be revised to reflect the delayed transfer. They also handed me some documents which contained information about the new school and a copy of the transfer slip.

Delivering the news to the kids was not easy. We had the conversation during dinner. The twins were so sad and upset; they didn't want to move to a new school. I explained that the error was never caught by the staff. As I told them what had happened, I wondered, *Why should their error affect them?* But then I reasoned, *It doesn't seem fair, but they have to follow rules mandated by the school district. We had no choice.*

I felt like crap after our conversation. It took a few days for them to be okay with the move. Shortly afterward, we drove by the school; it was so nice. The school had been recently built, and our new place was closer to it. We were happy that our current school administrators agreed to let us stay for a few more weeks. In the meantime, we continued our daily routine.

During that time, the twins planned to stay with my sister for a weekend. I had planned to attend our yearly holiday party. My girlfriends at work decided to carpool and meet at my apartment; they were excited to see the place. When they arrived, I gave them a "nickel tour" of the apartment. They thought it was adorable. We then had a few drinks. Before we headed out, we took photos in front of the white brick fireplace. We were all wearing formal gowns and heels; I enjoyed getting glammed up for special occasions.

When we arrived at the party, the guys were smoking cigars. We joined in. I wasn't into smoking cigarettes, but I did enjoy an occasional cigar. We had an awesome DJ, and we danced all night. The food was excellent. Everyone coming together from the surrounding stores was awesome; we were able to connect and get to know each other. The best part was the balloon drop at the end of the evening. Everyone would get on the dance floor. Countdown! We danced until the lights went on. Our holiday celebrations were a blast!

We loved our new neighborhood. There was a shopping center near the apartment complex. The kids had opted out of sports for the semester, but one day on a drive, we noticed a martial arts school. We stopped to take a peek inside. They welcomed us in, and I spoke with the Master. He offered the twins a free lesson. Before I left, he recommended that I join a different type of martial arts.

During dinner that night, we discussed the martial arts school. I explained that it was a school focused on developing confidence, discipline, character, focus, and respect. It was more than just kicking, punching, and getting the next color belt—it was especially focused on fun! The twins were ten years old when they joined.

I signed up for Taekwondo, which emphasizes kicking. The twins were not aware that I was taking lessons. I told my Master that my twins were enrolled in martial arts as well.

In reply, he told me, "I'll prepare you." And then he asked, "When the time comes, they will challenge you?"

I shook my head and said, "My twins wouldn't do that."

Upon hearing my answer, he smiled and walked away.

After each lesson, the twins would come home and show me their new moves. One day, I walked into the living room to find the twins wearing their uniforms. I started freaking out, thinking I'd missed a notice for an additional lesson or a competition.

They said, "No, Mom. You're fine. We want to challenge you."

I replied, "Wait, there are two of you and only one of me."

They laughed and said, "We're just kids."

They took turns coming at me. I kept knocking them down. They both charged me with kicks, but I was able to strike back and knock them onto their butts.

After being knocked down a few times, they asked, "Mom, how did you do that?"

I told them, "I don't know," and just gave them a wink.

Refusing to quit, they said, "Wait! You need to fight us with one hand behind your back, and you have to kneel. You can use your legs, but you can't stand up."

I told them that it wasn't fair at all. They were standing in front of the fireplace and asked me to stand on the opposite side of the living room, kneel, and place my hand behind my back. The twins turned to look at each other, then turned to face me and bowed. With a short shout, they got into their martial arts fighting stances. I was surprised by how serious they looked.

They ran toward me, shouting and throwing kicks. I used a leg kick to knock them both down. They both fell and looked at each other. They rushed me several times but had no success. Finally, they gave up.

My son enjoyed the lessons, but my daughter opted out after the three-month contract expired. My son continued with his lessons until the spring.

The holidays flew by. It was always exciting to see family and enjoy time together, but sometimes it was stressful—especially the interactions with the twins' father.

The twins were set to finish the second semester of fourth grade at a new school. We had no idea what to expect in the new environment, even though we lived only five minutes away. As we drove to school that first morning, we were nervous. The elementary school had been built five years earlier, and the building and grounds were beautiful. Everyone welcomed us. I took the day off just in case the twins or a school administrator called me; I wanted to be nearby. The twins had a great first day. They had been dreading it, but overall, it worked out well.

My work gave me a pair of San Antonio Spurs basketball tickets, and I took turns taking the twins. We always had fun, and the seats were great, too. My dear friend Jeff had resigned from the company the previous year, but we still hung out; he was my best friend. Manny and Olivia were also my best friends. I'd visit Manny when I drove back home or when he came to visit me. In January, a sales position opened up at the original store location—the one I had been promised when I first moved to the city. I enjoyed my time at my current store, but I was looking forward to transferring to the new location.

My relationship with Ken didn't work out, but I hadn't given up hope on love. In the fall of the previous year, I met Peter at work. He was a customer who had come in to purchase a tie. I assisted him, and after we selected the tie, we walked to the register. I proceeded to gather his information to generate a new customer profile.

I asked him, "What is your name?"

"Peter," he replied.

I took a deep breath and sighed.

He gave me a look and said, "Wait! What was that about?"

I apologized and told him that it had nothing to do with him.

To this he responded, "Wait, you have to tell me. I want to hear it. You took a deep breath and let out a huge sigh."

I was so embarrassed.

I replied, "I am so sorry. Okay—I know a guy named Peter, and every time I hear his name, my stomach turns."

He exclaimed, "Wow! That sucks. Just use my middle name, Andrew."

I said, "I like that better. I'll do something even better than that—I'm going to skip the customer information and just continue with the purchase."

After I completed the transaction, Andrew walked out the door. I felt so bad; I truly didn't mean to offend him. That afternoon, Andrew called me at work.

He started out by saying, "Hey, it's me—the guy who had the first name that you didn't like. Now I'm on a 'middle name basis.'"

I laughed and apologized again for my earlier behavior.

Rather than being offended, Peter replied, "I thought it was funny. You should have seen your face; it was priceless. I want to take you out for coffee."

"Thank you, but no thank you," I replied.

"Why not?" he asked.

I responded, "You're a nice guy, but I am not ready to date."

Peter quickly replied, "Not asking for you to be my girl—just out to coffee."

"I am going to opt out. Thank you," I said.

Not to be deterred, Peter said, "Okay. I'll call you every day until you say 'yes.'"

True to his word, Peter called every day. I finally agreed to meet for coffee. What happened next was so unexpected; little did I know that my life was about to go through another roller coaster. I felt mesmerized, and the chemistry between us was electric. I couldn't even breathe. I thought to myself, "What am I feeling? Is it just me, or is it mutual?" We said our goodbyes. Andrew walked away, and as he did, he said, "I'll see you soon."

Over the next few days, we spent hours on the phone. I told him all about Ken. I also told Peter that no one had met my twins since Marcus was a part of our lives.

During one of our conversations, he said, "I'm scared too. I felt something between us at the coffee shop. It was unexplainable."

I let out a deep sigh.

He continued and said, "My son's name is Peter. I hope he won't make you sick when you meet him. Peter is my only son, and he is my everything."

I replied, "I'm not ready for that. We're not ready for that."

Andrew asked where I lived and about my work schedule. I didn't think anything of it. On another occasion, Andrew called and asked, "Are you home?"

I replied, "Yes, we're just chilling."

A short time later, during our day off, I heard the doorbell ring. I answered it and discovered that Andrew and Peter were at the door. The twins asked who they were. I introduced them to Andrew and Peter; I told them that Andrew was my friend.

Andrew then said, "We wanted to know if you all wanted to hang out. Are you going to let us in?"

I moved away from the door, and they walked in.

As they entered, I whispered to Andrew, "What are you doing?"

He replied, "I am taking a chance." I just wanted to grab and kiss him, but I couldn't. The chemistry was truly electric. In a split second, we both felt the energy between us grow. The five of us had a fantastic day. The twins were also drawn to him; he was easygoing, cool, funny, patient, confident, handy, thoughtful, and optimistic. I asked myself, "How could I be falling in love with a man I hardly know?"

So, I called Jeff. When he answered, I told him, "I think I'm going crazy. Every time I'm with him, I feel like I'm walking on clouds—like I'm free-falling and can't stop. It's a feeling I can't control."

Jeff laughed and said, "You're in love! Let go and enjoy the moment. Love doesn't always show up, and these moments don't come often."

I told him, "I can't do this again."

He replied, "Yes, you can. Now, live and welcome love. You said it yourself: you're a hopeless romantic."

Andrew and I spent almost every day and weekend together. Driving over to his place, my heart would pound with the anticipation of being in his arms. He had a foot fetish and was always massaging my feet; I loved every minute. It was hilarious when we finished each other's sentences.

The five of us spent New Year's Eve together. Before leaving his house that night, I looked back at him, asking myself, "Is this a fairy tale relationship? Is he really the one? Have I crossed every boundary that I said I wouldn't for a man I hardly knew? Snap out of it, Reyna! He loves you. Enjoy the moment like Jeff mentioned. Love doesn't come around every day."

But then, Andrew went missing in action (MIA) for a week. I called his cell phone, his work, hospitals, and morgues. I was going crazy! I was panicking, thinking that something tragic had happened. I cried for days and felt such deep sadness.

I didn't go to work; I couldn't function or even eat. The twins were staying with my sister.

In the midst of this, there was a knock at the door one day. I looked through the peephole, but all I could see was a bouquet of white roses. I didn't think anything of it, assuming someone had the wrong apartment. I opened the door. It was Andrew! I just hugged him and exclaimed, "You're alive!"

He replied, "Of course I'm alive."

We kissed and hugged. Afterward, he said, "I just needed some time to think about our relationship." He began to apologize profusely.

In response, I blurted out, "Are you fucking kidding me? How selfish are you? I was worried sick! I thought you were dead. All you could think about was yourself? You couldn't have just told me you needed a break? I would have given you all the space you needed. I'll never force myself or a relationship on anyone. What were you thinking?"

He began to explain, saying, "The feelings between us were so beyond me that I needed to step back. Reset. I'm in love with you. I wanted to make sure that it was something that was best for me and my son. I'm here. I've made my decision. I want you."

I took a deep breath and responded, "This week, you showed me that you are a selfish man. You didn't think about me or my twins; it was all about you. You could have told me that you wanted space. This past week, I was a mess. I can't be with someone who doesn't think of us. What happens when you feel uncomfortable with a future decision? Are you going MIA again? You'll do it again and again and again. I will never go through this again. I need you to leave."

He sat there and wouldn't go. He told me, "I'm not leaving. We're meant to be together."

I got up and walked to my bedroom to go to sleep. As I walked away, I said, "Let yourself out."

After a long while, he walked into my bedroom and said, "I'm sorry. I'll be leaving."

I heard the front door close. I grabbed the pillow, sunk my head into it, and started yelling. I was devastated. We deserved more than this, and I wasn't going to settle.

Andrew called every day, but I didn't have anything to say to him. I was just trying to pick up the pieces. I thought, "What is wrong with me? What did I do to deserve this? Communicate! All he had to do was communicate!"

Olivia was by my side through the ordeal. She had never met him, but she had seen a photo of him and his son. Andrew kept calling and calling. I agreed to see him, but I was determined to keep my "brick wall" up. Over the following weeks, we got together for coffee and occasional dinners. It was so hard for me to see him because I loved him with my every breath. We had not reunited; I couldn't trust that he wouldn't break our hearts again. My twins are precious to me. Andrew wanted us to fight for the relationship and told me we could take it as slow as I wanted, but I told him I was not ready. I explained that, though I loved him, he had hurt me deeply. I also told him that I had not felt so vulnerable in a very long time, and it was going to take time to trust him again. In the end, he told me, "I'll wait."

On a Saturday morning shortly after this, I remember going into work for a pre-shift meeting. While I was on the way, Olivia called.

She yelled, "Andrew is married! I'm sitting next to his wife. I walked away to call you. I'm here at a baseball game, and I think he's the coach for his son's team. Send me a picture of him and his son. What is Andrew's full name? I'll call you back when I confirm it's him."

I told her his name was Peter Andrew. A few moments later, Olivia called again.

"Bingo, it's him," she announced. She continued, "He's walking toward us with his son."

I responded, "Best friend, do me a favor? He's never met you before. Go and introduce yourself. Tell him that you're my best friend."

Olivia agreed and said she would call me back. A few moments later, she did.

"Bestie," she said, "I walked up to him and asked, 'Your name is Peter Andrew?' He said it was, so I continued, 'My name is Olivia and I'm Reyna's best friend. I just spoke to her and told her you were here with your wife. That was your wife sitting next to you, yes?'"

Olivia went on and said, "His jaw dropped."

At that, we both started laughing. My stomach went into knots, and my emotions went haywire. After our conversation, I just shook my head and thought, Thank God, He saved me again. With his secret now revealed, I called him all day, but he didn't answer. He finally called back later that evening. He tried to explain that he was separated from his wife and that he had been planning to tell me.

I started yelling, "If I had known you were married, I would have never dated you! We are done! It's over. How stupid of me to think that maybe I should give you another chance! 'Everyone gets cold feet,' I kept telling myself. 'Have a heart, Reyna.' Never call me again!"

And then I hung up on him.

Over the next few days, I refused to take his calls. I was determined to be serious this time. What a fool I had been! He tried almost every tactic to get me back. I loved him so much, but seriously? Enough was enough.

Not long after that, a male friend of mine came into town. I had not seen him since high school. He asked me if I wanted to hang out; I did not have any plans, so I agreed. Things went well, and we started catching up. He asked me if I was dating, so I told him about my most recent relationship and the drama surrounding it.

My friend had some thoughts about Andrew. He said, "He is a player. He plays women all the time. He thinks he'll be back and you'll allow it. I bet he's done this before. He's also a good liar and has his own playbook."

But then he added, "You're a good girl, and I wouldn't play you. Please know that I care for you and won't allow anyone to take advantage of a naive woman."

Shaking my head, I responded, "What are you talking about? He's not coming back! He doesn't have a playbook; he just lied to me."

At hearing my answer to his thoughts, he smiled at me and said, "You're beautiful, and he doesn't deserve you. I'm going to make sure that he stays away. I promise. You'll thank me one day. For now, you're going to be extremely upset."

And then, in a split second, he grabbed my waist and hair. He pulled my hair so that my neck and chest were exposed to him, and he then gave me two hickeys—one on my neck and one at the top of my breast. He let go quickly.

When he had finished, he announced, "You're welcome!"

Stunned, I thought, *What just happened?* I then went to a mirror and saw what he had done. In disbelief, I exclaimed, "*What the fuck did you do?*"

Thinking nothing of what had just happened, he went back to ironing his clothes. After a moment, he said, "I just saved you from an asshole. He'll be back. Once he sees your hickeys, he'll turn it around and you'll be the whore. He'll quickly forget that this was all his fault. Mark my words."

I left there pretty upset. Andrew called and showed up at my house almost every day. I avoided him like the plague.

Not long after all that, I remember dropping off the twins with my sister for the day. Andrew had been at my apartment watching me because I wouldn't take his calls. Once I arrived home, he begged to come inside to chat. The hickey on my neck was gone, but the one on my chest was still there. I told him that we had nothing to discuss. Not taking "no" for an answer, he tried to convince me to let him explain himself. He went on and told me that our love was unique and we should get back together. He told me that he would divorce his wife.

To this, I responded, "You need to stay with her and work it out. We're done!"

He wouldn't leave and begged to come inside. I thought, Whatever, and I let him in. We ended up talking for hours. We kissed and made passionate love. Words can't describe how electrifying it felt when we made love. We fell asleep and woke up in each other's arms. I forgot the hickey on my chest, and he didn't notice it. We made love that morning. During the moment, he noticed the hickey and jumped out of bed.

He accusingly asked, "Is that a hickey on your breast?"

I quickly sat up and tried to explain what had happened, but Andrew was not hearing any of it.

He exclaimed, "No! You're a whore. To think that you truly loved me. I was willing to get a divorce for us."

I desperately tried to explain, "It's not what you think. My friend said you would react like this and blame me."

He got dressed and walked out. I thought, We are done. Four months with him passed so profoundly fast that in just a blink of an eye, it all came to an end.

Looking back, it was in those days of wild and nonstop emotions that my healing began. I'd been here before. When I was fourteen years old, I fell in love. Look what that got me! I became a single mom of beautiful, precious, and innocent twins. On top of that, he blamed me for taking the kids away. Yet, he didn't take accountability for what he put me through. I forgave him, but I will never forget what he did.

I thought, Way to go, Reyna! You suck at relationships. *Why be a hopeless romantic? Maybe romance isn't in the cards for you. Focus on the twins, school, working out, and the journey of being the best single mom there is. Live life and take it day by day. You can't change what happened; you just have to look forward to a better tomorrow. The struggle is real! I hate this…*

The twins and I continued our routine. During our daily "Straight Talk" conversations, they expressed that they really liked Andrew. I told them I had hoped it would work out with him, but explained that the situation was complicated and I was sorry it didn't work. I told them that I liked him, too, and that one day they would understand; but for now, we should enjoy the meal and our journey.

When the twins were 10 years old, they started learning to cook on the stove. They began by learning how to cook breakfast. Over the next two years, they learned almost everything I knew how to cook. They had fun taking turns as the "lead chef." My babies were growing up. We also continued to read at Barnes & Noble or the public library. As for me, I kept reading books on how to raise twins during their teenage years. For the rest of the school year, we enjoyed the amenities of the complex. While I used the gym, the twins would play basketball, enjoy the playground area, or swim. The gym overlooked these activities. My prince loved to play basketball, and my princess loved to read.

In January, the twins also attended Catholic classes (catechism) to receive their sacraments. Internally, I felt a nudge to call the church and ask if they were seeking volunteers. Before I knew it, I was assigned to co-teach with two veteran volunteer catechists at the church. They had over 15 years of experience and were very kind and patient. They told me that it was going to take time to learn, but they would be there to mentor me. I was extremely nervous and had no idea what I was doing. I owned a Bible but hadn't spent much time reading it; I hardly knew any scripture.

The class addressed various religious-based topics in a classroom setting of approximately twenty 6th-grade students. We created group-based activities to increase material retention, such as religious games and plays. We motivated students to learn more about Catholicism, with an emphasis on current events. After a month in the classroom, one of the teachers had to resign for medical reasons. We had many intelligent students who were more familiar with the Bible than I was. There was one student who was so bright that his questions had to be written down; the teachers would then either contact a priest for assistance or conduct research to provide an answer. The book provided for the class was very detailed, and preparing for the weekly lessons required a lot of reading. I learned so many scriptures during that time.

Two months passed, and the lead teacher informed me that she would no longer be volunteering. She told me her doctors said it was time for shoulder surgery and she could not postpone it. My jaw dropped, and I could feel my stomach tying into knots.

I told her, "I'm so sad that you will be leaving. There is no way! How am I supposed to teach these students without you?"

She smiled and answered, "God has been preparing you for this. You're ready. The Holy Spirit will guide you and give you the words to respond."

That was our last class together. Going forward, I would have to teach and plan our end-of-school party. The kids had been earning "Holy Bucks" by playing religious games, and there was going to be an auction. I prayed for guidance. I prepared the lesson plans and studied the Bible. I had to trust myself and use the knowledge I had gained to teach the students.

The first Sunday, the young boy asked me a question. I said a prayer before responding. My heart started racing. The words just started falling out of my mouth. I could hear myself speaking. When I was done, he nodded. Yes! The response was sufficient. What a relief! From that moment, I had so much confidence.

It was time to plan the party. I reached out to Claire's and Academy Sports. I asked them if they could donate gifts for the students or discount some items. They were unable to donate but were willing to give me a discount. I was so excited! Each item I purchased was less than five dollars. At Academy Sports, they discounted basketballs, soccer balls, and boys' sporting goods. At Claire's, they discounted jewelry for the girls. To top it all off, at work, a client agreed to do a free magic show. The party was a hit. My journey as a catechist teacher ended in May 2008. There was always a waiting list for my class.

School was going well for the twins. The school focused on guiding the students academically, supporting and empowering them to be successful. Assisting the twins with their homework and reviewing their completed assignments allowed me to recognize that the school truly challenged them to be creative, visualize, plan, and practice critical thinking. One of their social studies projects focused on Texas history. They were instructed to select and research a person who had influenced Texas history. They were also instructed to generate a biographical facts report with the data. They were required to support their facts with citations. The students were given one week to complete the assignment.

Fine arts, science, English, math, reading, and writing were their core curriculum. The school also had music and physical education courses.

For Mother's and Father's Day that year, we drove back home to spend time with my parents, their dad, and the rest of the family. Spending time with family was a sort of healing for me. I loved hearing the noise—the running around, yelling, and enjoying a home-cooked meal—that is, unless my dad was barbecuing. When he was grilling, we had to keep a lookout. If we did not, we knew we would be eating overcooked barbecue.

I recall opening my Mother's Day gift that the twins created at school. They made a 12x18 designed envelope. On the outside, it read, "Happy Mother's Day, Mom." They drew a house with the three of us inside. They each made a card and a paper teacup. The cup had the same typed note on the outside, which read: "A cup of tea to say thank you for all the things you've done, and wishes that the day will bring you happiness and fun. Happy Mother's Day! Love…"

On the outside of my prince's card, it read, "TOP 10 Reasons why I love you." He wrote out ten reasons. The first one read: "Thank you, Mom, for giving us what we want for our birthday." The second one read: "I love you because you are the best cook…" and so on. The ten reasons why he loved me were so adorable. It melted my heart. On the outside of my princess' card, it read, "Happy Mother's Day!!!!!" It had a flower pot cut out of construction paper that was glued to the front cover. Her words had been typed out and glued on the inside. They read:

"You fill my heart with joy every day. I think of you no matter where you are. All day, every day, you're on my mind. Thinking of you. You do everything to make me happy all the time." The rest of her words also melted my heart. I cried after reading their cards. They were the best gift ever!

As the twins got older, they loved playing jokes on me. I loved it when they whispered their plans in front of me or when they were close enough for me to hear them. I'd have to act surprised because I could hear everything. I remember one of those times. It was in the late spring of 2003. We had just arrived at the apartment complex, and I was going to get my mail from the cluster mailbox units, which were located on the opposite side of the complex from our apartment. As we were driving toward the units, we had the windows down. I heard the twins whispering, so I lowered the radio.

I heard one of them say, "When Mom gets the mail, let's jump out the window and act like we have been kidnapped."

I couldn't believe the plan. I thought, What were these kids thinking? But, okay. I'll go along with it. I opened the car door, closed it, and walked toward the mailbox. I grabbed the mail and turned back toward the vehicle. They were gone. I didn't even hear them jump out of the car; it was so quick. I drove off toward the back of the complex and parked far enough away, but not too close, to our apartment building. I decided to call Jeff and told him about the twins' plan. He asked what I was going to do. I told him that I was going to place a note on the front door.

While I was talking to him, I found a piece of paper and wrote the following: "I could not find you, so I left for the police station."

Then I told Jeff that I would just sit and wait. I told him that I would call him back once I placed the note on the door. He said I was crazy for doing this, but I responded, "Nope! They wanted to prank me. The prank will be on them."

As I walked toward the building, I could hear the twins. I ran up the stairs and left the note on the door. I stood next to the building. The twins read the note and ran toward the front office. I ran back to my car and called Jeff. I told him, "In a few minutes, they'll be calling me from the front office. I'm not going to answer the first time; I'm going to let it go to voicemail."

Jeff laughed and said, "After this is done, I hope they learn their lesson."

We chatted for a bit. As we talked, I noticed another call coming in. It was the twins again. I told Jeff to hold the line. I answered the phone and, with a distressed voice, I asked, "Where are you? Are you both okay? I'm driving toward the police station."

They had me on speakerphone, and I could hear the fear in their voices. They started crying. One of them said, "Mom! Mom, we're safe! Come back. It was a joke. We didn't mean to scare you. Please come back. We're safe, Mom!"

I told them that I would turn the vehicle around and come back to the apartment complex. I instructed them to stay inside the front office and told them that I would be there soon. They responded, "We'll be here, Mom. We're sorry. We love you."

I switched back to the call with Jeff. He couldn't believe they would pull such a prank. He asked, "How long are you going to wait before you drive to the front office?" I explained that I had to wait at least ten minutes because I told them I was heading to the police station. It was an emotional moment, but I had to laugh. These kids. I couldn't believe they would play this type of prank on me. What were they thinking? This is serious. What if the prank went wrong? What then? I'm glad it didn't and that they were safe. I wanted to teach them a lesson: never play pranks that scare the living shit out of anyone. This is not cool.

After a few minutes, I drove to the front office. The twins were watching the front door; I could see them as I drove up to the parking spaces. The apartment manager greeted me. The twins ran toward me and started crying. We just hugged. I thanked the manager for watching them, and then we drove home. That evening, the twins didn't leave my sight. They explained the prank wasn't supposed to go like that; they were originally going to meet me at the front door of the apartment. We then discussed the seriousness of pranking, especially a prank that involves something like faking a kidnapping. They promised that they would never do that again. This prank was terrifying. I never told the twins the truth until years later. During one of our "Straight Talk" conversations after they had graduated high school, I finally revealed what really happened.

My relationship with the twins grew closer. A few months later, with the help of the kiddos, I realized they needed their space; my babies were getting older. I also realized that we really needed a three-bedroom apartment, which would allow them to have their own rooms. During the week, I continued to stop by the apartment complex that I'd been eyeing for over a year. I got to know the ladies in the front office of our future complex, and after a while, I didn't have to stop by as often because they remembered me.

One day, out of the blue, I decided to stop in. It had been a while, and I was still on their waiting list for a unit. The lady in the front office mentioned that they might have one available. The family that was next in line had confirmed they were interested but had not returned any calls for over a week. They asked me if I was still interested. Was I interested? Of course!

I was then told that management gave potential new tenants a couple of weeks to come in and pay their deposit. According to their procedures, the move-in date was one month after the deposit was given and the contract was signed. That gave the current tenant time to vacate the property and allowed the staff to perform an inspection, make repairs, and prepare the property for the next tenants. They told me they might call me in the next few days and to be ready with a security deposit.

I left with a huge smile and went straight to the bank to get a money order. This complex was less expensive than our current apartment. If we got it, the new apartment would be larger—increasing from 1,036 to 1,440 square feet—and would offer three bedrooms instead of two.

A few days later, I received the call I was hoping for. I immediately left work and drove to the property management office to sign the contract and drop off my deposits. It worked out perfectly; my current lease ended around the same time we needed to move into our new place. I decided to move our things while the twins were visiting their dad. I thought, "Soon, we will be living in a spacious apartment." I also decided to buy a new living room set to replace the one we had been using for eight years. I gave away the old furniture since a local store was having a sale with 0% financing, and I didn't want to miss that opportunity.

With the move, the kids would be attending a new school. I had budgeted for their school supplies and clothes, but I was short $100. Around this time, the twins' father was driving with them from my hometown to the city, and we had agreed to meet halfway.

When they pulled up, I noticed his girlfriend was with them. It made me happy that they were together because, with her there, he didn't bug me as much. During this brief meeting, I pulled him aside and asked if he could give me money for the twins' school jeans. I told him that the average pair costs $15 and that I was planning on buying them a half-dozen pairs.

In response, he called to his girlfriend and said, "Bring me the cash."

He proceeded to show me a large bundle of money. In fact, he put it right in front of my face and announced, "I make a lot of money, but it's not for you. I have my own needs."

Turning back to his girlfriend, he continued, "Put it back in the truck and get me my checkbook."

He then made a check out to me… for $45.

I exclaimed, "Are you kidding me? You have needs? Drugs are not a need. This check won't even pay for four pairs of pants. We have twins together. You have a bundle of cash, and you wrote me a check for $45? These are your kids, too!"

To this, he nonchalantly shrugged his shoulders and dryly said, "Not my problem. Maybe you shouldn't shop at expensive stores. This is all I'm giving you."

I became very upset and screamed, "What the fuck is wrong with you! The jeans are on sale. That is a low price for kids' jeans. You don't pay me child support consistently, and when you do pay, it's less than $200 a month for two kids! I don't ask you for shit! When I do ask for anything, it's for the twins. It has never been about the money for me! All I ever wanted was for you to have a relationship with your kids. You can take this check and shove it! I want you to remember today. You're going to pay for this!"

I then ripped the check to pieces and threw the bits of it in his face. You could see the anger in his eyes, but I didn't care. I just walked away. True to my word, the next day I contacted the Attorney General to request back child support and a review of his income.

Both my best friend Olivia and my dear friend Britney from my hometown got engaged that year. Also, both of them asked me to be their Matron of Honor. So, I had to plan two bachelorette parties. Olivia chose Las Vegas as the place to celebrate her bachelorette party. Britney and her party drove into the city to celebrate hers. Both parties were a hit. Olivia and Britney were both ten years younger than me. Both of the weddings were in November, and they were two weeks apart. They both looked stunning in their wedding gowns. It was an honor to be part of their celebrations. Since the girls' wedding parties were younger than me, I decided to hire a trainer to work out five days a week for a period of six weeks. When the sessions were complete, I was in the best shape of my life.

Shortly after, I went to visit my parents. When I walked in, my dad stared at me with a worried expression. He asked me if I was alright, to which I responded, "I'm feeling great." He walked away and went into my mom's bedroom. I could hear him asking her to come to the living room. As they were walking back, I heard him say, "I think something is wrong with Reyna."

A moment later, my mom appeared. She looked at me and gave me a huge hug. My dad asked if I needed money for groceries. He told my mom to go bring me cash from the other room. She walked away to get the cash.

But I interrupted and said, "Dad, we have groceries. We're alright."

He started calling for my mom. My dad started asking me questions. He asked, "Are you doing the snow white? Roll up your sleeves so we can check your arms."

I started freaking out. I turned to my mom and asked, "Mom, what is Dad doing? I have no idea what snow white is."

My mom started to explain when my dad interrupted her and, in an accusing voice, asked, "Are you doing cocaine? Are you doing drugs? Why are you so thin? You look sick. You look as if you're going to die."

I was in complete shock but still managed to blurt out, "Dad, Mom, I'm not doing any type of drugs. I decided to work out because I am the Matron of Honor for two weddings. That's it. Nothing else."

My dad told my mom to double the amount of cash she was going to give me. After instructing my mom, he turned to me and ordered, "Go buy some food and gain some weight. You look sick. Mija, we care about you."

My mom agreed with my dad. I left there totally blown away; here I thought I looked fantastic, but to them, I looked like a malnourished daughter. I left my parents' home feeling so confused. I thought, "What just happened?" I had no idea why they would assume the worst.

At this time, I had known Liam for a few months. He was a client who had come into the store every weekend for the last six months to purchase a new garment. I had no clue he was even interested in me. I only realized it when, one day, another salesman announced, "Hey, here comes Reyna's guy!" as he saw Liam's car in the parking lot. I looked outside and, sure enough, there was Liam pulling up in his Bronco.

I just laughed the comment off. I thought there was no way this attractive guy had any interest in me. When I mentioned this, my comment was met with, "Yes, he is! He doesn't buy from any of us."

Once they mentioned that he was interested in me, I got nervous. Then I started thinking about it. As I did, I thought, "Oh my God!" Memories quickly came to mind. I remembered that the girls and I would have him try on garments that were too small; he knew it and would play along. I then remembered that every time he visited the store, he would spend an hour just to select one shirt.

In appearance, Liam had a sharp jawline, green eyes, and brown hair. He was tall, fit, muscular, toned, and lean. He had a barrel chest and a thin waist. He looked as if he were ready for some sort of competition; he looked like a bodybuilder. One day, Liam drove up in a new black Suburban XLT. I didn't recognize him at first. The girls and I were checking him out as he walked into the store. Then he took his sunglasses off and smiled. At that very moment, I felt an instant attraction. I thought, "What just happened?" I was so nervous that I could feel myself beginning to blush.

We walked away from everyone. Then he said, "I'm not here to buy anything. I want to be honest with you. I am recently divorced, single, and was not a perfect husband. After the divorce, I had to do a lot of reflection. I went back to church and focused on healing; I'm in a better place now. I cheated on my wife with a stripper. She has a martial arts background and punched me when I told her. She knocked me to the ground—I deserved it. She was good to me, and I messed up. We've been talking for over six months. I don't need all the clothes I bought, but I'm drawn to you. Let me take you to lunch today."

I smiled at him and replied, "Thank you for your honesty. You've been through so much, but I'm unable to go to lunch."

Then, from across the room, one of the salesmen yelled, "It's not busy! Go to lunch with the guy!"

Soon all of them started yelling, "Go to lunch!" My boss waved for me to go, too. Lunch it was. I was so giddy. Halfway through our meal, I asked him, "What is your date of birth?" When he responded with the date, I exclaimed, "Let's go!" and placed my napkin on my plate. To make it clear to him, I continued, "We're done! Let's go."

Surprised, Liam asked, "What did I do? Please."

Staring back at him, I just gave him a look. Finally, I said, "I'm sorry, but your date of birth is the same month and day as my ex—and he cheated on me with a stripper."

He reached out, gently took my hand, and said, "We might have that in common, but I am a different man. These are the qualities that I have to offer."

He then rattled them off, and I completely ignored him. I heard him say, "I'm not your ex. My name is Liam, and I want to get to know you better. You felt the connection when I walked in today; I felt it the day I first laid eyes on you."

I told him that I would have to think about it, but that I could not make a decision in that moment. He held my hand and said, "Let's finish our meal. We're already here."

I thought, 'How could I say no to this man staring at me with beautiful green eyes?' Well, I could enjoy the view, but this would be our first and final date.

He called me at work every day. After two weeks, I gave in to him. The following Saturday evening, I heard a knock on my apartment door. I looked through the peephole. He looked freaking hot! I started jumping up and down in excitement. I turned away from the door and took a deep breath. I then turned back toward the door to open it. He was very complimentary.

A few moments later, we were on our way to a club. Once inside, we decided to sit down and chat for a bit. While I was talking, he grabbed the back of my neck, gently pulled me closer to his lips, and kissed me. Liam's kiss sent chills down my spine. We had a wonderful evening. When he walked me to the door, we kissed for a long while. He walked away. I went inside and closed the door. Quickly, I looked through the peephole to watch him walk away. He stopped to look back toward the door. I turned to lean my back against the front door and just sighed. We went on a few more dates. One of the dates was at a nearby bar. When we arrived, the place was pretty empty. Before we knew it, the place was hopping.

During this date, I noticed that Liam was locking eyes with other women. The girls kept waving at him. I asked him what he was doing.

He replied, "It's okay to check out a girl when she's passing by. It happens. We all do it. When you begin to flirt with her and you have someone with you—that is completely wrong."

He kept denying he was doing anything. When I came back from the restroom, the girls had approached him. I just grabbed my purse and walked out. I had my dear friend Jeff pick me up. He wasn't going to disrespect me. Liam tried to call a few times, but I ignored his calls. He kept calling the store when I was working and my cell phone when I was not. He even came into the store. He wasn't taking "no" for an answer. He would wait at the store until I spoke to him.

All the other salesmen kept telling me that I should give him another chance. They told me that guys are stupid and that they mess up. They would tell me things like, "Reyna, it's obvious that he cares. He won't stop calling or coming by. He looks like a sick puppy."

I called my friend Mont for advice. Mont is an honest and forthright person and has been my mentor for many years. After our conversation, I called Liam. We met up and discussed my concerns. He made it clear that we had only just met, but he wanted to become exclusive with me.

Mont and his wife invited us to visit. He told me to invite Liam. We traveled on our first vacation to St. Petersburg, Florida. Mont owned a one-story home right near the beach. Before entering the backyard, we had to walk through Mont's man cave. Their back patio was an oasis. It was landscaped, and there were plants everywhere. They had a wooden gazebo, chairs, sofas, and an avocado tree. We sat there, and Mont gave us words of wisdom. He told us that it was important to relax and appreciate life, and that it was important to learn through our experiences; that experiences need to be lessons learned. Mont and his wife were so cool. They were so calm and relaxed.

The weather in Florida was nice. Treasure Island Beach was beautiful. Mont's wife and I went clothes shopping almost every day. That gave Mont and Liam time to get to know each other. In the evenings, we went to listen to jazz music and enjoy cigars. Mont lived maybe half a block away from a church. The Sunday before we left, I walked to and visited the church. I needed some quiet time with God.

I prayed and cried. I thought about how my last two relationships hadn't ended well. I thought about how I was attracted to Liam, but also about the doubts I still had regarding our relationship. I reasoned that being attracted to someone is good, but it isn't a reason to stay if you don't trust him. I left there feeling at peace; I decided to "let go and let God."

Liam and I had our time alone while we were there, and our conversations went well. We both decided not to rush the relationship. We decided to take it slow. In 2004, a year after we met, Liam moved in.

"Taking it slow." I now laugh at that phrase. We tried to slow it down, but I was in love. I thought to myself, "I am setting my personal boundaries: be yourself and do not lose yourself in the relationship." I had dreams to graduate from college, own a home, travel, and put the twins first in every decision I made. I had to be true to myself and my desires. We deserved to be happy. What Liam did in his past relationship was horrible, but he had asked for God's forgiveness. I was not going to hold that against him, or anyone else trying to repent. We all have our flaws.

When the twins met Liam, they thought he was the Hulk. They slowly built a relationship. I remember him asking me if he could take the twins out on his own because he wanted to spend the day with them. He suggested that I have a "girls' day" with my friends. He was good to the twins, and they approved of him.

Liam was hardly home. He worked and went to the gym six days a week, and he also attended church five times a week. Together, Liam and I attended church six times a week. Since we attended on Sundays, I gave the twins the option to join us, but they opted out. Our schedules were tight. We had work, college, after-school activities, traveling, church, the gym, and weekend outings as a family. "As a family"—that had a nice ring to it.

Liam owned a Harley-Davidson motorcycle. I had never been on a motorcycle before. We would drive around town and sometimes take day trips to nearby small towns. Liam helped a lot with the twins; he would pick them up from school and take them to their after-school activities. After work, I would join them, and he would head to the gym once I arrived. We were a family, and I was loving every minute.

In the meantime, I started receiving consistent child support. We had gone back to court to resolve the non-payment and past-due support. The twins' father was so upset with the new amount. I hadn't wanted to report him, but he had flaunted wads of cash while denying us help.

Not long after that, we went to visit my parents. Matthew hadn't met Liam yet, though he knew I was living with someone. He arrived at my parents' house to pick up the twins, stepped out of his truck, and had an angry look on his face. He didn't notice Liam at first. When he finally locked eyes with him, he immediately stepped back and got back into his vehicle to wait for the twins to come outside.

Things were different after that. My dad hadn't met Liam either. When I introduced them, my dad asked Liam to go meet my mom and then come back outside. Nice! Dad wanted some alone time with Liam for a man-to-man conversation. Mom and I chatted about Liam, and she told me it was time to set roots in San Antonio. She said it was time to buy a home—that apartments were nice, but a home was what we needed. I told her I would think about it and promised to research buying a house.

On the way home from our trip, Liam was quiet. Finally, he said, "Your dad approached me. He told me that you were his baby. He told me that I was a big guy, but if I hurt you..." then he pulled out a gun, pressed it against my waist, and said, "Capiche?" I nodded. Then he offered me a beer.

I apologized for my dad's tactics and replied, "You should have told me while we were there."

Liam looked at me and responded, "No way! He had a gun. I stayed put until you said we're leaving."

I apologized again for my dad's behavior.

The twins were in middle school; my angels were in the 6th grade. I was working full-time and going to college. It was rough. It felt like I was on a very slow pace to graduate because I had so many more classes to take. I would get frustrated, but I pushed through it. Liam was supportive of my goals. We spent Thanksgiving apart; he flew home to visit his parents, and the kids and I drove back home.

Once we were back home, I rented a room at the Embassy Suites by Hilton. The kids and I loved to stay there, and my family did, too. It was nice to see everyone gathering together—my aunts, uncles, cousins, and friends. I'd visit Manny and Britney; since I had moved away, we would party whenever I was back. It was just like old times.

When we got back into town, we celebrated the twins' birthday at Dave & Buster's. Liam and I picked up their closest friends. They spent the afternoon playing games and enjoying dinner. We all had fun. Last year, the twins' father drove to the city to assist with their 11th birthday. The twins wanted a slumber party, so the boys slept in tents in the backyard of the apartment while my daughter and her friends slept inside. I would do anything for my kiddos.

The twins had been acting out and getting in trouble at home, especially my son. He had been pushing the envelope. Disciplining the twins wasn't easy for me because they would join forces against me. They would defend each other and tell me that I was wrong. Sometimes, they were able to make me second-guess myself, so I'd call my mom for advice. I would also call Jeff, my best friend, to go over the scenario and get his input.

The twins and I had several "straight talk" conversations, but they didn't seem to help. When the twins got in trouble, their punishment involved doing things they did not like to do. For example, my son loved to play outside but didn't like to read unless he was in the mood. So, I would make his punishment reading a book and giving me an oral report. My daughter loved to read but didn't like going outside, so her punishment was going outside to play. They would get so upset because the other person was getting to do what they actually enjoyed.

My son would push the envelope so much that, sometimes, I would make the decision to spank him. We would discuss why I made that decision. We talked about the fact that his acting out was not going to be tolerated and that it was unnecessary. I acknowledged that we all get angry at times and that we all need to take a moment from time to time. I told him that he may need to go outside to regroup his thoughts and emotions. He told me that he understood. After some time in his room, he'd come out to apologize.

I always tried to give them words of encouragement. I encouraged them to think about their decisions and to make wise ones. If they intentionally made the wrong choice, there would be consequences. I told them, "Do the things you love to do." My babies knew I loved them. I told them they were beautiful and that I loved them every day, so they would never forget it.

The twins were both in band; she played the clarinet and he played the trumpet. I couldn't afford to buy their instruments, so we rented them from a local music store. I was lucky growing up because my parents were able to buy mine; my mom made payments until it was paid off. I would talk to the kids about my time in band. The twins were required to attend summer band, and they had to maintain good grades to remain in the program.

The twins were so cute when they practiced their instruments in their bedrooms. I would lean against their bedroom doors to listen, or they would play in front of me. I was so proud of them. They were required to wear white dress shirts and black slacks for their concerts, and the boys had to wear black ties. We also participated in fundraising activities for the band.

One evening during dinner, we had a conversation about making San Antonio our home. I told the family about the conversation Mom and I had. I explained that if we planned to make this city our home, we needed to plant roots. The twins and Liam were on board with the idea. I knew I would have to contact a bank and pre-qualify to purchase a house. After much discussion with Liam, we decided the home would be under my name. Since his divorce, his credit score was extremely low, and he was still trying to recover financially.

The twins wanted to be part of the north side of the city. After researching, I decided I wanted us to live in the northeast area. However, the twins mentioned that they didn't want to continue in that school district because of the high school; they preferred the high school on the north side. My daughter had her eyes on a magnet school there as well. We agreed that we would look in both areas. My twins said they would be praying every night for God to find us a home on the north side. I just smiled and told them I would pray as well. Liam liked both sides. We agreed to look for a brick house that had three to four bedrooms, two bathrooms, a two-car garage, and a fireplace. With that, I began to search.

A friend referred me to a realtor named Mike. The four of us went to his office to discuss what we were looking for and to determine the next steps. He explained that it could sometimes take weeks or months of looking at several homes before finding the right one. He assured us that there wouldn't be a problem finding us the perfect home; he was so nice and genuine.

I had not yet contacted a bank for financing, so he asked if we were pre-qualified. We explained that I would be the only person applying for the loan. He asked us to follow him and introduced me to some mortgage brokers and the manager. The manager and his assistant sat us down. Mike said he would return to his office to research homes in the northeast and north side areas and that once I was pre-qualified, he would narrow the search. A little later, I learned that I was pre-qualified. I was instructed to produce copies of many documents for the loan. We left the office very excited and celebrated by going out to dinner as a family.

The twins and I had just finished school. I remember that before they went to visit their dad, they had two weeks of band practice. I asked their dad if I could keep them an extra week; he wasn't happy, but he agreed. I also remember that my vacation would begin in two weeks. I couldn't believe that I had earned my second six weeks of paid vacation. Ten years had flown by, and I was still going to school part-time. I loved that my employer worked with my childcare and school situation.

As far as the house-hunting went, we viewed several properties. I remember not feeling ready for the move; I liked the apartment cost and the convenience of having someone else responsible for maintenance issues. A new house would require maintenance, lawn care, and so much more. But I convinced myself that since we had started on this journey, I had to follow through on the commitment I made.

Later that spring, my dad mailed me three different packages. He didn't include a letter with them, only the gifts. The first package contained a red mini boxing glove. When I received the package, I called my dad.

I asked him what the boxing glove was for, and he answered, "Mija, when life knocks you down, you get back up and fight. Do not stop fighting! No matter what, never give up. Love you, Mija."

A few days later, the second package arrived in the mail. This package contained a pair of extra-large black binoculars. Again, I called my daddy to ask him what this gift meant.

He answered, "Mija, keep your eyes wide open and your mouth shut. You'll learn a lot if you just listen."

Not long after that, the final package arrived. This one contained a poem. It was an 8x10 inspirational Footprints poem. Though this one was easier to understand, I still called to ask my daddy why he sent it.

He answered, "Mija, you're never alone. God has you. Cast your worries on God."

My dad was a man of few words, but these three gifts were impactful. I was his baby girl, and he adored the twins. I felt so honored to have a father who loved us dearly.

Not long after this, I noticed that the front door was slightly open as I arrived home from work. I called Liam to ask if he was home. He let me know that he had picked up the twins and they were out running errands. He told me not to go inside and said they would be there shortly. I noticed my neighbor outside relaxing on the patio and asked if he had noticed anyone coming out of the apartment. He told me that he saw a guy carrying stuffed pillowcases; he didn't think much of it because he thought it was my boyfriend.

I called the front office to ask if any maintenance workers were in my apartment. They checked and told me to stay out of the apartment. They also told me that they had contacted the police. Liam arrived home before the police arrived. The twins and I went to the neighbor's, and Liam decided to enter the apartment. A moment later, he came back out and announced, "Someone broke into our home. They are gone."

We walked back into our apartment without touching anything. It was ransacked. There were piles in the center of each room. My guess was that they had plans to come back and haul the rest of our stuff out of the apartment. As I looked around, it appeared that they had entered through our bedroom window. The police arrived shortly after this and took our report. We felt violated, helpless, angry, sad, and afraid. We were so overwhelmed by what had happened that the twins and I started crying. Liam remained calm through all of this; he suggested we go out to dinner and step away from the scene. I thought that was a great idea, and we felt at ease with that plan.

I knew I had renter's insurance. My policy covered all of our personal belongings, furniture, electronics, clothing, and so much more. Even though we didn't feel safe, I knew that we were physically safe and that those items could be replaced.

The twins wanted to go to their father's as soon as band camp was over; they didn't want to be around the apartment. They trusted me to find the perfect house for us. In the meantime, we all made a list of our missing items. It was so sad that one of the items they stole was the gift my dad had recently given me: the extra-large binoculars.

After summer band camp ended, I prepared to take the twins to see their father. I asked Liam if he would like to join us to visit my parents and drop off the twins, but he did not take me up on my offer.

I brought some boxes home from work that week and started packing the apartment in preparation for a move. I didn't know where we were moving to, but I knew that when the time came, we would be ready. We looked at nearly three dozen properties, but we still hadn't found one by the time the twins came back from their dad's.

On the drive home, and for the next few weeks, they told me stories about their summer vacation with their father and our families. We kept searching for a house while the twins went back to school. Searching for a home was stressful for me; in spite of that, I recently decided to enroll for the fall semester as a full-time college student. I decided that attending school on a part-time basis wasn't cutting it, and Liam supported my decision. On a different note, Liam was a bit needy, and we discussed my concerns. He reassured me that it would be okay because we lived together, but I made him aware that the little free time I had would be going out the window. I explained that I needed to buckle down and graduate.

It was about this time that a university recruiter began calling. He repeatedly asked if I had time to listen to the benefits of attending their private Catholic school. At the end of each call, I politely asked him to call me back the following month. I did that because I didn't think I was ready for a university; I had convinced myself that I was fine at the community college I attended. However, I didn't realize that I had already completed enough credit hours toward my four-year degree. I then began to think I was definitely ready, but I also knew I needed a push.

At the retail store, there was a guy named Paul who was the manager of the Tuxedo Department. I told him about the recruiter who was contacting me. He picked up the phone and called his wife. When he hung up, he looked at me and said, "You have a meeting scheduled with her this week. I'm not asking if you are free to meet with her; you'll be meeting with her. We'll work your schedule around the meeting. She works five minutes from here."

I was completely taken aback. A few days later, I went to her office. She was a financial advisor for a great company who specialized in helping people achieve their life and career goals. She was extremely welcoming. She told me that we would begin in a few minutes and that we were waiting for another colleague to join us. A few moments later, her colleague arrived and sat right in front of me.

Paul's wife began the conversation by telling us her husband had called and told her that I was "dodging" the university.

She continued, "We are here to tell you that we've been to the university and graduated. We are here to empower other women and provide moral support for those seeking a college degree. Do you know the percentage of Hispanics who graduate from college? It's low. The program the school offers is called ADCaP (Adult Degree Completion Program). The school developed it specifically for individuals who are working full-time and have a family. Each course is eight weeks in length, and the program allows you to go back to school full-time."

She went on to share, "I didn't have to go back to school. I did it for my dad; that was the last promise I made to him before he passed away. I earn over $200,000 a year here. I didn't need a degree to do what I do, but I kept my promise to my dad, started ADCaP, and before I knew it, I graduated with my bachelor's degree. I just completed my master's degree."

The other lady then began to tell me about her journey. She said, "I read the ADCaP guidelines and policies. I, too, was unsure of the program. I had a meeting with the Dean of Students and told him that I would be attending this program, but if it did not follow the program outline, I would sue. As an advisor, I earn over $125k in annual salary, and I don't need the degree. But… my mom passed away, and this was the last promise I made to her. I didn't pursue my master's degree then, but you just have to put in the work; it's doable."

I thanked them both for their time.

A few days after our meeting, the recruiter called for the third time. I was happy to hear from him and scheduled a meeting for the following Friday at the university. As I was sitting in the lobby waiting for the advisor, there was a lady sitting next to me. I told her all about the meeting I had with the two other women and added, "You know, God always has a plan." She winked at me when a gentleman called my name.

She then stood up and said, "Ma'am, you're here." As I turned to look at her, she continued, "I'm his manager. I'll be auditing the meeting you both have, if that's okay with you."

I nodded. Once we were all in his office, she asked the gentleman how many credit hours I had. He replied that I had 67 credit hours.

She then turned and asked me, "Would you like to begin classes on Monday?"

I replied, "Yes!"

He began to explain to his manager that there was no official transcript on file and that I hadn't applied for financial aid.

In response, she told him, "Please register her for two classes. She'll request her official transcript. I'll be her mentor until she graduates. We're heading to my office to select her degree and outline the next few years. I will also assist her with applying for financial aid and researching any scholarships we may have."

I thanked her profusely. She replied, "God has a plan for you. Don't forget that."

That Monday, I met a classmate who became a very dear friend and academic mentor who forever changed my life. On May 10, 2008, I graduated with my Bachelor of Arts in Business Administration with a concentration in Management.

In September 2005, the mortgage company that was assisting me with my loan asked if I wanted to work part-time for them as a loan officer. I accepted their offer, as this would allow me to pay for any unforeseen future expenses. In this position, I was responsible for pre-qualifications, credit analysis, client-to-loan matching, loan processing, and closing sales. I had to be well-versed in building relationships within a demographically diverse market by effectively selling solutions to multicultural and multilingual groups.

I had been working various second jobs since I moved to San Antonio. I met Linda, a realtor who worked with Mike. She asked me if I was interested in buying a pool table. I told her that I would love to, but we had not yet purchased a house to put it in. I explained that my apartment was too small for a pool table. She told me that she wasn't in any rush. Later, Linda sold me her husband's pool table—though he had no idea. She went on to tell me that she and her children had purchased a new home without him knowing. She explained that the furniture in their current house was to be sold at a garage sale in a few days.

When I arrived at the garage sale to pay her for the table, her husband was walking down the stairs. He started looking around, confused by all the people in their home. Linda had placed a "For Sale" sign in the front yard, and while this was happening, the children were posting price tags on everything. His expression was priceless. She held the pool table for me until I finally found a property.

Liam and I had visited over 40 properties. I remember not wanting to see another house, ever. Around this time, Liam got a call from Mike, who said that he'd found the perfect home for us.

Liam picked up the twins and bought them dinner. When I arrived home from work, they told me the news. I tried to opt out, but no one was going to allow me to stay home; I was told that we were going. The twins were eating dinner and planning on doing their homework right after. For their part, the kids told me to go look at the house, mentioning that it was on the north side.

I changed from my business casual clothes into something more comfortable. Liam mentioned that after seeing the house, we could pick up dinner or dine out.

Not long after, we all walked into the house. Within 15 minutes of looking around, I knew in my gut this was the one. I decided to place an offer. It was a two-story brick home. If you remember, I had wanted a brick house since I was a little girl; my dream of owning one was finally coming true. It had three bedrooms, an office, a formal living room, a family room, two full bathrooms, a two-stall garage, a fireplace, and a huge backyard. There were dozens of mature trees on the lot, and the home was located in a cul-de-sac. We made an offer, and not long after that, it was accepted.

Two months before I found my forever home, my long-time renter moved out because she needed full-time healthcare. I put that house on the market, and it sold within a couple of months. The same week I closed on that sale, I closed on my new brick house. With the help of the twins' father paying child support for one full year, I qualified to buy my dream home. His payments included an increase in support as well as a portion of the past-due support.

In October 2005, we moved into our new home. A few months after we moved in, however, the twins' father quit his job. That meant he would no longer have to pay child support.

CHAPTER 7

BROKEN HEART

While the journey of finding a new home was long and trying, finally finding it meant a fresh start of sorts for us as a family. I think that made us feel happy and safe. I was so grateful that my dream of owning a brick house finally came true. The twins were especially excited that we moved to the north side of town. I remember thinking then that this was where our family would grow, thrive, and form new friendships.

The neighbors were so welcoming to us. There were six families that lived at the end of the street, which was a cul-de-sac. A woman and her son lived in the house to our left. Next door to her was a couple who had just become "empty nesters." Next to them was a couple who had two children. The last family on the left side of the street was a couple with a young daughter. To our right lived a couple who had a daughter and three-year-old twins (a boy and a girl). I remember them bringing us all kinds of desserts. It felt as if we belonged; it seemed like they were all waiting for us to arrive. I remember thinking that this had been God's plan all along.

The move was exciting. The twins were so happy and felt all grown up because their bedrooms were upstairs. They finally had their own privacy. Even though they shared a bathroom, it was large enough for the two of them. We decorated their rooms with things they liked. They were also looking forward to playing pool as a family. The master bedroom was downstairs. While I had enjoyed apartment life, moving into our house changed my perspective; I realized there was no better feeling than this.

During movie nights at home, we would gather downstairs. We watched movies and ate popcorn and pickles. Our favorite movie was Remember the Titans. It was based on a true story—an inspirational tale about an integrated high school football team overcoming racial tension in 1971. From this movie, we learned about trust, coming together as a community, respect, overcoming difficulties that are out of your control, navigating the unexpected, and so much more. We also loved going to the cinema as a family.

We had a bookshelf that we placed in the small, open office upstairs. My princess asked me to purchase books for her. She told me she was the only one who didn't own the new series of books going around the school. As often as I could, I purchased all the books she wanted. I remember her asking me to buy her a spiral notebook to keep track of her collection. I was so proud of her reading habits. I wasn't aware, however, that she was allowing her friends to "check out" her books. I was curious as to why her friends were borrowing books they supposedly already owned. She then mentioned that they didn't actually have the new series and that she was the only one who did.

When she told me this, I responded, "Really? You lied! You told me that everyone had them."

She responded, "I thought they did."

I shook my head and thought, *What could I do?* I had already purchased a bookshelf full of books. I kept purchasing books for her until she turned 16. After that, I had her check them out from the public library. I remember that when she was 18 years old, she sold them all—and kept the profit.

I was so proud of myself for instilling good reading habits in the twins. Since going back to school, I hadn't been able to read as much as I wanted to. When I did, I focused on books that discussed rearing twin teenagers.

Along the way, there came a moment when I wanted to know the purpose of a woman. I thought, "How do I find my life purpose? How am I expected to act, speak, dress, groom, and conduct myself?" I became very curious about these things, so I started looking for answers. I asked several women about their life experiences and their understanding of what they thought the purpose of a woman was. I also decided to turn to books for answers. I went to the local library to check out some books on the subject. Some of the authors I read were Judge Judy, Patti LaBelle, Betsy Morscher, and Barbara Schindler Jones.

I had a conversation with my managers and explained how I was feeling. I remember asking them if I could read during our downtime at the store. They had no objections to me reading on one condition: if a client walked in the door, I had to put down the book and assist them. I agreed to that condition. We were usually pretty slow at work, which gave me the opportunity to read thirty books in one month. My cup was full. I learned so many life skills, greater empathy, lessons, and viewpoints, gaining an understanding of the purpose of a woman through so many different authors.

I learned that as women, we should inspire hope, love, support, patience, gentleness, goodness, self-control, and peace. I also learned that we should celebrate life and live for today. I learned that women should be doers, givers, and forgivers. I learned how important it is to trust, to respect, and to be healthy. Beyond all this, I learned to expect to be prosperous, joyful, thankful, blessed, confident, positive, hardworking, fearless, and courageous. Even more, I learned that to be all of those things, I needed to show up and know that I am worthy; I needed to strive to be beautiful, happy, and pure in heart; to rebuke anxiety and fear; and to be resilient, motivated, grateful, reliable, and educated. I saw all of this as a snapshot of my life purpose as a woman. Lastly, I learned that I needed to put God first and that we are God's masterpiece.

In November of that year, after the twins' laser-tag thirteenth birthday celebration, we invited my family to visit. We wanted to have a combination housewarming and November birthday celebration for the twins, my niece, and my sister, whose birthdays were two days apart.

Whenever we had a family gathering, there was a lot of drinking, laughter, games, and some drama. It never failed that someone would bring up a past concern that was never resolved. The event could have happened several years ago, but the person who brought it up would make it sound like it was a recent event. I never looked forward to the drama.

Before they arrived, Liam and the twins went to the store to buy some last-minute items. I remember being so tired before anyone even arrived! I remember lying on my bed and praying, asking God to bless this home and to grant us peace, joy, love, family unity, laughter, compassion, and beautiful memories. I remember thinking, "God is great."

We had a fantastic time. There was no drama at all. My family was up until early the next morning; we laughed all night long. The next morning, it felt like I had gone to the gym and finished an intense ab workout. I thought about the night before and my dad pulling me aside. He hugged me and said, "I'm so very proud of you. You have a beautiful home. I love you so much, Wabi. You make me proud." That melted my heart.

The next afternoon, my family drove to my sister's house. We had decided to go to her place for Thanksgiving. Liam decided not to go. I remember thinking that was odd, but I respected his decision. As we prepared the Thanksgiving meal, the kids played outside. My sister's husband prepared the turkey, and everything was delicious. We drank, played games, laughed, and then laughed some more. The following day, we said our goodbyes, and my family returned to their homes. I remember everyone hugging each other before they left and that it took a while; I had a large family. I specifically remember Mom and Dad holding me tight. They looked at me and told me again, "We love you. We're so very proud of you. You take care of our twins. If not, they'll call us, and we'll have to make a special trip just for you."

The twins heard what my parents said to me, and my parents winked at me in return. It was hard to live in a city without them; my mom was my best friend. However, I knew they were only a phone call away. Tears rolled down my face as I watched them drive away.

The next Sunday evening, Liam was not himself. He asked if we could go out on a date, and I agreed. We got all dolled up and went to a local restaurant. Once our drinks and appetizers arrived, Liam began expressing his feelings. He told me, "I'm happy your family had a wonderful time in our home. Looking at you and the twins all smiling was nice." He then abruptly added, "Your mom doesn't like me."

My eyes opened wide. Liam continued, "When you were in the other room, your mom pulled me outside onto the back patio. She started smoking a cigarette and said, 'I don't like you. My daughter is in love with you, but you don't love her. You love the thought of her. One day, the clouds covering my daughter's eyes will move. Sooner or later, your true self will break through; then, she is going to see the real you and leave. I hope it's sooner rather than later. I know you don't want to be here with us, so why don't you head out and get some sodas? I'll let her know you left for the store. No need to rush home—take all the time you want. You love the streets, so have a drink and come home late tonight.'"

I was in disbelief. He asked me not to tell my mom.

"Is this the reason you left to get drinks and came home right before bed?" I asked.

He nodded.

"Is this the reason you didn't join us for Thanksgiving?" I asked.

He nodded again.

I told him I remembered repeatedly asking my family where he was, and I recalled their replies: "Let him be. He's a man. This is his home; he can come home anytime."

I apologized profusely. I told him my mom was brutally honest about her opinions, but I reassured him that I wasn't leaving. I reminded him that we were in love and that this was our new beginning. I insisted my mom had to respect my decision.

When we arrived home, Liam went to shower while I tucked the kids into bed. Then, I went outside to call my mom; I was furious. When she answered, I told her Liam had explained what happened between them. I told her this was my life and she had to respect my decisions.

She listened and then responded, "Mija, I told him exactly what I witnessed myself. It's only a matter of time. Have fun and enjoy the moment. I'm sorry he couldn't handle the truth. Love you, baby girl."

I had to compose myself before entering the house. My mom was honest to a fault and far too blunt. I loved her, even though I didn't always agree with her. Liam, meanwhile, was so understanding.

Over the next few weeks, the twins had band practice almost every day after school as they prepared for their Christmas concert. Liam and I agreed to split the decorating duties: he would handle the outside, and I would do the inside. We all went to select a tree from a local lot; it was beautiful.

One evening shortly after we got the tree, I went on a mission to purchase decorations. Hobby Lobby was the popular place to go, as they carried a variety of items for every season. I remember the Christmas aisles being overwhelming, and I had no idea where to begin. Since all the decorations were half off, I knew I wouldn't be leaving empty-handed. You could tell who the professional decorators were, and everyone was kind enough to help me select my items.

At the end of an aisle, I heard a lady ask a gentleman for assistance with making a wreath. He grabbed all the items and placed them in her basket. Watching from afar, I took mental notes. He described the design to her with such simplicity; he also mentioned to her that he was a professional decorator. I thought, "Bingo! That is my guy." I walked toward the wreaths and placed the exact same items he had selected into my basket. I knew that I had to approach him, so I walked straight toward him and asked, "Sir, I couldn't help overhearing that you are a professional decorator. We just moved into a new house. I don't have a clue how to decorate or where to begin. Really, I am starting with a clean slate."

He peeked into my basket and winked. Then he said, "Good choices. Do you have a piece of paper to sketch the rooms you would like to decorate?"

I pulled out a piece of paper and a pen and quickly sketched the floor plan of my house. Looking back, it was a terrible sketch, but he got it. After looking at my "artwork," he asked, "Do you mind if I put some items in your basket? I'll explain what to do with them in a few minutes."

"Yes!" I happily replied.

And with that, he started placing decorations in my basket. I saw garland, Christmas lights, another wreath, bows, ornaments of all shapes and sizes, stockings, candles, a sleigh, Santa Claus figures, reindeer, tablecloths, a tree topper, ribbon, red berry stems, and so much more go into my cart. When he was finished, he explained in detail how to create beauty in my home by keeping it simple. He also offered me this tip: always purchase things on sale. He went on to explain other things, such as how to save money by not buying lights that are embedded within the garland. Instead, he suggested wiring them together because it is less expensive in the long run to replace the lights, and the garland will last for a long time. He mentioned that Hobby Lobby is a good place to begin and gave me tips on how to change the design over the next few years.

I was so grateful for his help. I thanked him, and he replied, "You're welcome and good luck. You've got this." Then he waved and walked away.

When I got back to the house, I decorated the staircase with garland. It took a few days to wire the lights and garland together. I also added red bows and red berry stems, placing the extra-large red bow at the foot of the staircase. In the living room, I placed lighted garland on the fireplace mantel and around the top of the walls near the ceiling. I hung extra-large silver ornaments from the lighted garland on the ceiling and added more red berry stems.

It took me a week of decorating to use everything I had purchased. It turned out beautifully. Liam did a fantastic job outside, and the family loved it. We placed our gifts under the tree; the house decorating was complete.

It seems like time flew by, and before we realized it, the Christmas band concert had arrived. The children wore white button-down shirts, black bowties, black vests, black slacks, and black dress shoes. The concert was so nice and reminded me of my own days in band. After their performance, we celebrated at a nice restaurant.

A few days later, the four of us celebrated Christmas on Christmas Eve. It was nice and peaceful as we opened gifts. On Christmas morning, the twins and I drove to my parents' house. Liam opted out, and I understood why.

The twins stayed with their dad for the holiday break. They loved spending time with him and visiting with their cousins. He was an overprotective dad, especially with his little princess. When he came inside to greet the family, he avoided me. Actually, he didn't even say "hi." I assumed that meeting Liam had changed his tune a bit. Though it had been several years, I still wondered what had happened to the 15-year-old guy I first met. I found the change in him mind-bending, but then I accepted the reality of what he had actually become.

All along, I had been working on a better tomorrow for my family. I couldn't help but look back when I saw him. I still felt uncomfortable when our eyes met; I realized that the man I once knew was no longer there.

It was always tough leaving the twins. I had to remind myself that it was only for the holidays and that they would be home soon. I recall teaching the twins Cumbia and Tejano dance at a young age. When we attended parties and the DJ or band played those two genres, the twins would get on the dance floor and dance. I loved seeing my children bond. When they danced, our family and friends would make "oohing" and "aahing" sounds. The kids would glance at me, and in response, I would give them a great big smile, nod, and place my hand on my heart.

As my son grew older, his emotions changed. He started experiencing mood swings that affected all of us. We began having more conversations to discuss what he was experiencing. I hoped our "Straight Talks" would provide topics I could research to provide him with better guidance. I realized my son was going through puberty, and since I didn't have the knowledge to guide him, I read about it. The books provided good tips and techniques, many of which we tried. He felt frustrated because he couldn't understand what was happening inside of him, and it was hard for him to explain his emotions. Sometimes he became so agitated that although I wanted to hold him, he preferred to be alone. So, we gave him the space he needed and created boundaries. I thought that perhaps spending time with his dad would give him an opportunity to chat about puberty.

My relationship with Liam grew closer. As I reflect on our relationship now, I realize that he wanted constant attention. I had to remind him that I also had two children. We did so much together; however, going back to school full-time cut our time together in half. To add to the stress, I also held a part-time job as a loan officer. Looking back, I guess this was the first time Liam experienced me being away from home for long periods.

In the meantime, peak season at my full-time job arrived. We worked six days a week, which was a large time commitment in itself. I did my best to read and complete my assignments as soon as they were assigned. Initially, he was supportive of my decision, but our relationship started changing when I wasn't able to hang out as much. He liked to go out several times a week. On my drive home from school or work, he'd call and tell me to stop and meet up with him. When I arrived, he would have my drink and food ready. We went out every weekend; he wanted us to get all dolled up for drinks, appetizers, and dinner. I loved going out with him, and we also went on double dates with Olivia and her husband. I couldn't get enough of him, but eventually, I had to start saying no.

Liam attended some of the children's after-school activities, but other times, I was the only one in attendance. I missed spending quality time with the kiddos, and they missed having "mom-time" with me. School was also a priority. Liam became more distant and started treating the twins differently. I sensed that something was "off." I kept reassuring him that school would be over soon, but I didn't think things would change so quickly.

When we initially moved in together, Liam whispered in my ear that he wanted to have a baby with me. He was aware of what the doctor and my mom had recommended, and he knew that I had undergone a procedure. Yet, he kept pressing me to make an appointment with my gynecologist. I repeatedly told him that I was unable to have any more children due to the procedure.

I thought, "Wait! What is he thinking? A baby!! My tubes are tied; it is impossible to become pregnant." Still, he begged me to go to the gynecologist, so I agreed and scheduled an appointment. When the date arrived, he took the day off to join me. My doctor was positive that the tubes could be untied through a procedure called a tubal ligation reversal. They would reopen me and untie the tubes so I could have a baby again. He had hope. As I was lying on the bed, I started thinking, "If this procedure works, we could have twins. Oh my God!"

During this visit, she noticed something on my ovaries: cysts. She prescribed medication to treat them and scheduled a follow-up for three days later. She told me the medication should shrink the cysts, but if it didn't work, they would grow larger. If the cysts increased in size, surgery would have to be scheduled. Three days passed, and we went back to the office. It was then that I learned the cysts had grown to the size of a tennis ball.

In February 2006, I underwent a laparoscopic cystectomy to remove them. The doctor also peeked to see if I was a candidate for the tubal ligation reversal surgery. Post-surgery, the doctor reported that the cysts were successfully removed; she actually showed them to me. Then, she reached out and took my hand. She proceeded to tell me I was not a candidate for the reversal procedure and that she was sorry to inform me of that. She explained that I was not a candidate because the doctor who performed the initial procedure had cut and burned the tips of the tubes. Liam bowed his head. He didn't have to say a word; you could see it in his posture. He was crushed.

The doctor recommended that I stay home for a week, noting that if I felt better, I could return to my normal schedule in four to five days. My goal was to get back to normal in four days. During that time, I was unable to drive or do anything, so I sat on the couch and watched TV.

Unexpectedly, I was able to observe the twins' daily routine, as well as Liam's. Everything felt so robotic. No one even spoke to each other. Liam came home, showered, and left for the gym. He would then return, shower, eat, and leave the house again for a couple of hours. The twins would come home, eat, do homework at the kitchen table, and then go to their bedrooms. Watching this was a huge eye-opener for me. I thought, "What happened? What did I miss?"

I asked the twins why they weren't speaking to each other. They responded, "We speak to each other upstairs. Liam doesn't really talk to us unless you're around. He's never around. We say 'hi' when we see him, but that's all. He offers us food when he's cooking."

Wow! I felt so sad. I couldn't believe Liam and the twins didn't really speak or have a relationship. Liam was hardly home, but I had never noticed because he was always home when I walked through the front door. I had a conversation with Liam about what I had witnessed. He told me that this had always been his routine. He explained that, since my schedule was jam-packed, he went out for drinks on his own. Liam also mentioned that the twins were getting older and didn't need an adult hovering over them. He said that if they needed anything, they could ask him.

I tried to wrap my mind around this whole scenario. The twins didn't seem to be bothered by it, but for me, it was weird—it wasn't right. On the fourth day of my recovery, I went back to work. I didn't last very long and had to come home halfway through my shift. My family worried about me. When I got home, the twins asked, "Mom, you're home! Are you okay? We only see you before school and a few hours before bed... unless you're working the early shift or have no classes scheduled in the evenings."

I promised the twins and Liam that I would be home more. I felt so guilty for going to school full-time; I wasn't going to stop, but my work schedule had to change. I stayed home for the remainder of that week. The twins started watching TV with me in the evenings, and Liam didn't go out for his evening drinks; instead, he spent time with us.

When I returned to work, I spoke to the managers about my schedule. They changed it so that I worked only one evening and was allowed to leave early during the week. As for my second job, I reduced my in-person schedule to one day a week; any time I spent working beyond that, I did from home.

A few months passed, and we were all settled into the new house. My son was not a morning person, and it took so much effort to wake him up. Princess, however, woke up with no problem. To help the situation, I decided to make a deal with them. I hyped up what it would be like if they owned their own alarm clocks, trying to sell all the features and benefits to them. I even went to a store prior to taking them with me; I spoke to a salesman and asked how to best promote the benefits of an alarm. My plan was to bring them to the store and let them select any alarm clock they wanted.

The twins were excited to select their own clocks, but my deal came with a condition: I would no longer wake them up in the morning. I told them that they were old enough to wake up on their own, and they agreed. The salesman greeted us when we arrived at the store and pointed us toward the selection. This is when I announced to them that there was no cost limitation. There was such a large variety that they asked the salesman several questions. After narrowing down their choices, they turned to me and placed the ones they wanted on the counter. I reminded them that they would have to wake up on their own and that "Mommy" would no longer be there to wake them up. They agreed. When we arrived home, they set up their alarm clocks. Before we had left the store, the salesman explained all the features to them. My plan worked; my son woke up on his own. I was so happy, as we had overcome a huge hurdle.

The following weeks and months were filled with school, college, school activities, the gym, volunteering, sacrament classes, church, work, and traveling. My son's personality was changing, and changing quickly. His behavior was putting a strain on our family; his anger, rudeness, disrespect, and emotional breakdowns were having a negative effect on us. After these outbursts, he would apologize and cry. He would tell me, "Mom, I don't know what's happening inside of me. It's hard to control my emotions. I do the techniques, but the anger just comes out."

My heart melted in sadness as I listened to this. I wished that I could take the anger from him. I started researching counseling options and anger management classes for teens. With the twins, our conversations were an opportunity to encourage them and teach them strategies to implement in their daily lives. I believed, and still believe, that knowledge is power. For me, it was better to have more information on a topic than to have no knowledge at all.

I read several books on managing his behavior and possible solutions that might help my son. One day, as I was driving to work, I noticed a roadside billboard promoting teen classes. I called the number on the sign and learned that the organization offered anger management classes for teens. I thought, "Bingo!" Not long after, my son began attending counseling group meetings with other teens, as well as one-on-one sessions. They gave us several tips that truly helped.

There were days when my son would come home frustrated, wanting to be alone. The counselor told us that we needed to give him some space, explaining that he needed an hour to decompress after school or when he became emotionally frustrated. I was encouraged to check on him after an hour but was instructed that if he needed more time alone, I should give him that space to decompress. My prince was required to exit the room for dinner and to let us know he was doing better. The counselor also recommended purchasing a punching bag, so I bought a free-standing red heavy bag for him. I also bought him boxing gloves, hand wraps, and other accessories. Additionally, I purchased a weight bench with a squat rack and an arm and leg developer. Lastly, I bought an abdominal toning machine, an ab-cruncher, and a crunch roller. My idea was to make it a fun family workout.

Another technique the counselor recommended was deep-breathing exercises. I had never heard of tearing or crumpling newspaper to reduce anger, but he explained that this technique helped individuals vent their frustration by tearing paper into pieces or crumpling it up. Once the anger or frustration had passed, one could simply throw the newspaper away. We tried everything. The counselor also informed us that individuals who receive anger management counseling and incorporate these techniques achieve positive results. After a few weeks, we did see a decline in his anger.

Liam didn't understand; he felt boys should be disciplined and that I was too soft. We had agreed before our relationship began that I would be the only person disciplining the twins, and he had consented to that. Liam and I were on the same page regarding rules and boundaries for the family, but not every boy is the same. I knew I was not just sitting back and allowing my son to break the rules. I believed it was important for the twins to feel supported by both of us. The situation was not easy for anyone. I reminded Liam that no one ever said parenting was easy and noted that he did not have kids of his own. Sometimes, it was hard for him to understand me.

One day during this period, my daughter came home from school and mentioned a book that was popular; there was even a waiting list to check it out from the library. During one of our study trips to Barnes & Noble, she found it. My son had also heard about the book, so I agreed to buy it. They went off to study and enjoy some leisure reading. To this day, I can't recall the exact title, only a part of it: Preteen for the Soul.

The book had four sections: the first for preteen boys, the second for preteen girls, the third for parents, and the fourth for family discussions. The chapters focused on etiquette—the "dos and don'ts" of social behavior. Some of the manners included were apologizing when a wrong is committed, asking for permission, making eye contact, saying "excuse me," "thank you," and "please," shaking hands when greeting someone, hygiene, using appropriate language, opening doors, being kind, asking questions, and having table manners.

Other topics included how to treat others and what to expect during puberty. The book provided visuals of the body and explained the types of changes to expect as they grow. It was perfect. The parental chapter encouraged parents to read the entire book to learn what their kids were reading. It also provided one-on-one conversational questions for chats with both boys and girls. This book informed me about how kids feel going through puberty and how this stage of life can affect all of their relationships.

It provided the perspective that puberty is different for everyone. It explained that bodies don't change overnight and that a teen will experience many different emotions. Those one-on-one conversations bonded us and helped us build trust. The last chapter was for everyone in the family to read. It explained what to expect if someone in the house was going through puberty and the differences between the experiences of a boy and a girl. After reading the book, we all had a better understanding of what puberty entailed.

It was cute to witness when one of the twins was going through an emotion. The other twin would remind them that it was puberty they were experiencing and that, in time, it would pass. I remember replying, "Yes, I recall." He or she would sincerely apologize, and then we would all brush it off.

School was going well for the twins and myself. Liam had his normal routine: work, the gym, and then off to a nearby happy hour. He would drive his Suburban, Bronco, or Harley Davidson. He invited me every day, and I would join him whenever I had time. Since I started dating Liam, we ate out often, especially at nice restaurants. The twins enjoyed the experience of trying new foods, though sometimes the food was an acquired taste for all of us. Liam wanted us to get dressed up; I eventually grew tired of being dressed up all day only to have to dress up again in the evening. The kids didn't mind, though. Liam didn't like me wearing T-shirts, as he said they were too casual, so we got rid of them. I didn't own a single T-shirt, even though I thought they were nice to sleep in or wear on a daily basis. That changed when I got together with Liam; I slept in silk garments and just went with the flow because I wanted to make him happy. He was still sad that I was not able to conceive a child for him. I felt horrible, but we were working through the pain.

My son's anger was like a boomerang, which was extremely stressful for us. He continued attending counseling and working out daily, but he was no longer interested in playing the trumpet. He told me that he wanted to try out for football, and the coach encouraged him to try out in the summer. My daughter's plan was to remain in band throughout middle school. Juggling all of the activities was tough, and I appreciated Liam opting in to be there when I couldn't be. My mom was always worried about the stress I was under, but it felt normal to me. I had to push myself for my family; failing was not an option. I reminded myself that this was only for a short time and that the chaos of overworking and school would subside one day.

Around this time, my mom and I had a conversation. She knew I loved massages but didn't take the time to go; she also knew that I didn't like spending money on myself. She told me that I needed to do better at taking care of myself. At that time, I was getting massages every six months. My mom convinced me to budget for quarterly massages, and I agreed. When I received my raise, she asked me to add another massage, but I told her there was no need. She asked if they made me feel less stressed, and I replied that they did. She then told me to do it for myself. My mom always knew best.

Since I held two jobs, the massages truly helped. I felt a sense of peace and relaxation; I felt lighter, less stressed, and more energetic. They also reduced my pain after many workouts. One day during a session, my massage therapist informed me that he had signed a huge contract. He felt that his blessing should be shared with others, so he gave all his regular clients a decrease on their hourly rate. My mom told me to use the money to invest in additional massages, so I began going once a month. My mom and dad gave me money to add additional sessions each month until massages became a monthly routine. At that time, I had been with my massage therapist for many years. When he went on vacation, he took six weeks off at a time. Because he was gone for so long, he liked to tell his clients that they could "cheat" on him.

The twins enjoyed having friends over on weekends, and they also liked going to their friends' homes. As a mom, I was extremely protective of them—I mean really protective. Before the twins could visit their friends, I had a few requirements for the parents. Each parent had to provide their driver's license number, a list of everyone who lived in their home, and disclosure of whether they owned any guns. If they did own a gun, I needed to know if it was in a locked safe. Most of the parents provided me with that information. Every once in a while, I would get a "deer in the headlights" look from a parent, which was understandable. The ones who didn't provide the information said it was easier to allow their kids to come to our home instead. The twins did not like me asking all these questions. They hardly ever went to their friends' homes—that was, until they met another set of boy/girl twins.

Their mom invited us over to her home. The two sets of twins played in the other room. During our conversation, I realized that she was just as protective as I was. When I mentioned the information requirements I had for parents, she started yelling. She exclaimed, "Oh my God! I do the same thing! The kids don't like it when I ask the parents anything."

I was excited that we met. We immediately called the twins to the living room, and I let them know that we had something in common that they disliked: we both had the same information requirements for parents. Everyone started laughing and sharing embarrassing stories about asking other parents for information. We never exchanged driver's license numbers or anything else; our connection was instant. The twins became best friends with her twins, and all four of them were in band together. As moms, we never minded if the twins went to each other's homes.

That summer, the twins wanted to stay in the city for a few weeks, but their father wouldn't budge. He wanted them on time and not a day late because he had plans with them. We arrived a couple of days early to spend time with my parents and family. Their dad picked them up on a Sunday evening, but his demeanor was "off." The twins called one evening and mentioned he no longer had a girlfriend. In April 2006, the twins' father had ended his relationship with his girlfriend of nine years. I thought, "No wonder their father looked sad."

I had one week off before my summer courses started. Liam and I had a wonderful time hanging out like we did when we first met. During the summer, we had date nights with other couples; Olivia and her husband joined us for most of them. Liam didn't like it when I spent time with Olivia alone; he wanted to be with me all the time. Still, Olivia and I squeezed in some girl time. When we were alone, Olivia noticed our relationship was a bit off. She observed that Liam had changed, noting that he was a bit cold to her and anyone who came near me, and that he was becoming possessive. I explained to Olivia what we had been going through over the last few months.

To this she responded, "You're not his property. You're too good for this guy. Why can't you see what I see? Liam likes to flirt with girls when you're not around. In time, you'll see him for who he truly is. I'll be here for you when he is gone."

I loved the fact that she was honest and kept it real with me. My friend from school also mentioned that Liam was becoming possessive. I remember thinking, "First my mom, and now my friends." I called my friend Mont to get some advice.

He told me, "Men are simple, but we also slip. We're not perfect. Men need their space, but the more space you give them, the more they venture out. Keep your eyes open. He's a nice guy, but he might have some habits you weren't aware of. Also, keep in mind what your mom and friends are telling you."

Just when I thought we were doing well, I began to worry about my relationship with Liam. Now I had to keep my eyes open and pay attention. My relationship was crumbling and I had no clue. I knew that crying about it wasn't going to help, but I couldn't help but cry for a few days. Liam reassured me that we were okay. At that point, I didn't know what to think.

When the twins came back from their dad's, they ran into my arms. Tears started rolling down my face. I noticed they had grown taller and that their conversations were more adult-like. They shared many adventures and stories about their time with their cousins. They also pointed out that their dad's girlfriend had spent some of the summer with them. I was hoping they might work it out since they had a long history together. Selfishly, I also knew that if she were there, it would keep him busy—and away from me.

The twins were ready to enter the 8th grade, their final year of middle school. My son started football practice, while my princess attended summer band sessions. The expenses for the twins had definitely increased; back-to-school supplies, clothes, equipment, school fees, and recreational activity costs all added up. The twins also returned to Sunday classes to complete their sacraments, and I returned as a catechist volunteer teaching Sunday school.

My second job helped cover these additional expenses. Meanwhile, my full-time college classes were becoming more challenging. The instructors were very nice, and I enjoyed going to school, though I had to take out student loans to pay my tuition.

In spite of all the positive things going on, my son's attitude problems returned. His mood swings were back, and I hoped that football would help him learn to manage his anger. During our "Straight Talk" conversations, the twins mentioned they were tired of me teaching them life lessons; they wanted to learn on their own. They complained that my explanations were like PowerPoint presentations projected onto the wall, and they disliked how I explained scenarios and all their potential effects. They even expressed that they did not like it when I moved the dishes around in the cabinets.

In response to their complaints, I told them, "Mom loves you so much that one day you'll thank me. You're the most beautiful beings, and I love and care about you deeply. Our conversations are an opportunity for a teaching moment. Life isn't easy. You have to hustle, never give up, and maintain the right mindset. You need to be ready because change is constant; you shouldn't be stagnant."

Late pick-ups from school became frequent because it was hard for me to leave work, and Liam had started working overtime. At my job, we recently hired a young high school graduate named Priscilla. She was a beautiful young model and very sweet. One day, I found myself in a pickle and asked if she could pick up the twins from school and take them home. Without hesitation, she agreed. I called the school to let them know Priscilla would be picking them up. There was an instant connection between the three of them, and she began helping me out several times a month. Even when Liam's overtime slowed down, Priscilla continued to pick them up. The kids enjoyed her company, and she eventually started occasionally babysitting them on weekends.

One weekend, Priscilla asked if her friends could come over while she babysat. I thought, "The more the merrier," and agreed. When the four of them walked into the home, they looked as if they had just walked off a runway shoot. They were all gorgeous, confident, and respectful, with great smiles and a graceful presence. The girls were so nice and looked forward to spending time with the twins.

Liam and I headed out for the evening to enjoy dinner and a Spurs game. It was nice to have an employer who gave us passes throughout the year.

I was in disbelief that the twins were turning 14. I told myself many times how quickly time flies! I found myself tearing up at the thought of fourteen years of watching them grow. I thought about how they were so dependent on me at birth and were now growing to be independent. The twins wanted an intimate birthday party with their closest friends and selected California Pizza Kitchen. It was a casual restaurant, and they each invited two friends. There was a total of six teens sitting at a round table. Liam and I sat at the bar because the twins wanted space from the adults. It was a cozy celebration.

We drove home for Thanksgiving, though Liam opted out of going with us. We stayed at the Embassy Suites in town because my mom's house had become too crowded. We had an awesome time; it was always nice to come together as a family. We were blessed to be surrounded by family and friends, and the food was delicious. I loved when Mom said the table grace; her prayer over the food was beautiful. The twins spent half the day with their father. The trip back home was short. I wished that we could have stayed for a few more days, but I had to return to work. So, off we went; the peak season at the store awaited.

A couple of weeks later, on a Sunday, my son called me at work. He told me, "Mom, my friend called. He said that they found some cats in their backyard. Would I like to have them bring one over for the day? His mom would bring cat food, cat litter, and a box. If we don't like the cat, we can call them tomorrow."

My immediate response was, "No!" But he replied, "Mom, I'm sorry. The cat is already here. They dropped her off earlier. We named her Sassy. I'm sorry I didn't call you first. She is so cute and she is over six weeks old."

I told him to call his friend and request that the cat be picked up. To this he argued, "Mom, what's one night? My sister likes her too. Just one night."

When I arrived home, they both greeted me at the door with Sassy. They said, "Here, Mom. Isn't she so cute?"

I took one look at her and said, "Yes, and she'll be going back tomorrow." Not to be denied, they said, "Please, just hold Sassy for one minute."

I grabbed her and gave her right back. I wasn't ready to care for a kitten; I knew that this responsibility would eventually fall on me. I asked the twins to go upstairs and get ready for school, telling them that dinner would be ready in an hour. The twins came down for dinner a bit later with the cat sitting on my son's shoulder. They were so excited about Sassy.

I asked them why they had named her Sassy. They responded that she had come with a name they didn't like, so they renamed her. It was as simple as that. Before the twins went to bed, they asked if we could keep her. They promised that they would be responsible and take care of her. As they walked away, I told them that I'd think about it. Afterward, I started washing dishes and cleaning the kitchen. Sassy started meowing excessively. The twins asked if I could watch her because they weren't able to sleep.

I shouted, "No! She is your responsibility until tomorrow!"

Sassy continued to cry. My son came down again and said, "She won't stop crying."

I caved, and he handed her to me. Since I was washing dishes, I placed her on my shoulder. Sassy cuddled up underneath my neck. That night, she slept on my chest. Sassy became part of our family. She was so hyper and mischievous, and we loved her.

Christmas was fast approaching. Liam made plans to visit his parents. He was becoming a bit distant; we were growing apart but were trying to hold on. The twins were ready for their holiday break. For me, another semester was completed, and I only had a few more to go. Going to school full-time was tough on my relationship with the twins and Liam. At this point, I had been in school on and off for seventeen years. I had to push through because I was tired of being a part-time student. My mom and dad were proud of me and encouraged me not to give up.

We drove back to my parents' house for Christmas. The twins stayed for the break with their father. I had some time alone before Liam came back from his parents' house. It was nice to have a quiet home, but I missed him so much. I was looking forward to our time together. When he arrived, I surprised him by taking some extra days off from work.

We brought in the new year and discussed taking a family trip. After researching several cities, we agreed on Destin, Florida. Our goal was to go on our vacation during Spring Break. We discussed our relationship and recognized something was off; he wanted more time with me, and I missed having our daily outings after work. I reminded him about the conversation we had prior to my making the commitment to go to school full-time. It was definitely taking away from our time together. I promised him that after graduation, I would have plenty of free time, but I don't think I convinced him. On the drive back from my parents' house, the twins mentioned that Liam had become a bit more distant. They noticed that he had purchased a mini-refrigerator for the garage and told them they were not allowed in it. They agreed, thinking that everything they wanted was in the main refrigerator.

When we got back to the house, I looked inside the mini-refrigerator. I saw that he had his own groceries outside; there was a duplication of almost everything. When I confronted him about it, he brushed it off. He explained to me that this would allow the twins to have more for them in the main refrigerator. He suggested that I keep the inside stocked with food and he would keep the outside stocked. He told me not to make a big deal of it and that more was better. He went on to say that, if I looked at them, both had the exact same items. He told me that there had been times when he got home from work craving certain foods, only to find there were none to be found. He reasoned that the garage refrigerator would guarantee food for him to eat.

I let him know that this made me feel like there was a division coming between us. I told him that the one thing I didn't understand was this: why can't anyone go into the refrigerator if it wasn't a big deal? He told me that, again, I was overthinking it. He said that he would buy for the outdoor unit and that I could buy for the inside refrigerator so the kids wouldn't have to come outside in the heat. At that point, I realized that we had come to a roadblock in our conversation. Liam had his mind made up. That was concerning to me, but I felt that I had to respect his request.

We drove back home to celebrate my sister's birthday in mid-February of that year. Liam declined to go with us. My son loved all his aunts, but he was closer to my sister, who called me "baby sister." We laughed all weekend and enjoyed some great barbecue.

That Sunday, before our two-hour drive home, we stopped by church. There was a mass in session. While we were there, they had two kittens in a small cage with a blanket; they were giving them away. The twins ran up to me and stated, "Sassy needs a sister."

Shaking my head, I flatly replied, "No! Sassy does not need a sister."

But they persisted, "Please, Mom."

They started pleading. The lady in charge encouraged me to take the kittens, and the kids said that we could raise them together. Now I had three people pressuring me to take the kitten. A moment later, a family came up and took the other kitten. The twins were holding the black-and-white kitten. I stayed quiet. They held on to her until mass was over. All I could hear was that lady telling everyone that the kitten had found her home with the three of us. We went up to the front, and a blessing was prayed for the four of us. They immediately named her Sade. On the drive home, she slept on a blanket between the twins. Once we brought Sade home, Sassy became the chilled, dominant one. The family was growing.

A week after my sister's celebration, the twins called my mom while I was at work. They let her know that my second job was taking time away from them. I had no idea my mom had been called. She called me that week and asked if she could visit. While the twins were in school, I took a day trip to pick her up. The twins loved when my mom was in town; she spoiled them. The twins would tell my mom everything I did that was good and not so good, and my mom would then set me straight. Liam avoided coming home while she was in town. He'd wake up early to leave for work and come home right before bed. My mom would make comments about him coming home late. She told me that he had a family and should be home early to enjoy time with the three of us.

She would say, "No se ve bien." In English, that means, "It doesn't look right." That Sunday, my mom asked me which job I liked better: being a loan officer or working in retail. I explained that they both brought in income for the family. Working part-time as a loan officer provided extra money for vacations or savings. I told her that if I had to choose, it would be the retail job. She gave me a look.

Then she said, "Tomorrow you'll be quitting your part-time job as a loan officer. Your twins need you. I'm not asking; I'm telling you that you will do it for your family. I've been here for a few days, and there is not a connection here—just bodies walking around. You're trying your best to provide for your family, but slow down. Your twins miss and need you. They see you here, but you're doing homework or paperwork for a client loan. Enough is enough. You've had this job since 2005. You'll be quitting tomorrow, and all the extra time you gain will go to your twins. Love you, baby girl. This is best for you and your family. What the twins need is for you to spend more time with them."

I placed my head on her lap. She began to massage my scalp and play with my hair. I told her, "Thank you, Mom. I feel so bad that I didn't see it. It'll get better."

Tears rolled down my face. The next day, I gave my notice. Mom stayed with us for a couple of weeks, and it was nice coming home and seeing her there. On my days off, I would complete my homework before the twins came home from school. We immediately noticed the extra time I had for the family. I also noticed that Liam was hardly home; he had a new routine, and it didn't include me. My mom eventually went home. We missed her. She came on a mission and accomplished it; she was the voice of the twins. When the twins felt they weren't being heard, they'd call in the "big guns"—Mom!

The quality time brought us closer together. In the evenings, the twins weren't in their bedrooms; they were downstairs. We would watch movies, cook together, play pool, or just hang out. Before long, it was time for our family vacation to Destin, Florida. We were excited. Liam's parents would be meeting us there. Liam and I split the cost: I'd pay for the road trip food and drinks, while Liam would take care of the vehicle expenses. We split the cost for the hotel and the food expenses while there. We left our home around 4:00 a.m. on a Friday. The road trip was over twelve hours, and we arrived late that afternoon. His parents were already there. We checked into the Ramada Plaza Fort Walton Beach Resort.

The resort was located right on the beach, overlooking the water. It had a heated outdoor swimming pool, an outdoor hot tub, and a Polynesian grotto pool with a waterfall and a swim-up bar. The receptionist provided us with a map of the hotel and let us know that, with our wristbands, we were able to walk to the sister hotel next door to enjoy their amenities. The six of us started walking toward the room. When we got to the door, everyone placed their luggage inside. I assumed his parents' room wasn't ready, so they put their luggage in our room. Our room had two queen-size beds.

After enjoying a nice dinner, we all went back to the hotel and changed into our swimwear. It was time to relax by the pool. The beautiful grotto in the center of the pool looked similar to a cave. While laying out and enjoying a drink, I turned to Liam. I asked him, "What time will your parents' room be ready?"

He looked at me with an intense glare and said, "They are staying in our room. I paid for half of it. We'll sleep in one bed, my parents in the second, and the twins will sleep on the floor. They are kids; they'll be fine on the floor."

My heart dropped. I replied, "You failed to mention this to me during all of our planning. I also paid my half. They'll be sleeping in my spot, and I'll be on the floor."

He got upset and said, "The sleeping arrangements have been established, and that's it." Then he got up and walked away.

I chugged my beverage and looked out toward the twins. They were in the pool having so much fun. I had to excuse myself, so I walked toward the beach and called Olivia. I started venting my frustration and cried for a bit. I complained to her, "Why didn't Liam tell me? We could have paid for a room for his parents. Why are my twins stuck sleeping on the floor? I'm not letting Liam ruin our vacation."

Olivia tried her best to console me. After our conversation, I walked back to the bar to grab another beverage. Liam was back and had been looking for me; he had also brought me a drink. He turned to me and apologized.

He said, "I'm sorry. I should have told you about my parents sleeping in our room. Please understand that I didn't think you would be this upset."

Before I said a word, I chugged my second beverage. I then took a deep breath and said, "Don't keep any more secrets from me."

He promised he wouldn't. Liam leaned in for a kiss. We made up, but it didn't change the fact that I was still upset.

The next morning, Liam woke me up before sunrise. He asked if we could walk to the beach and enjoy the sunrise together. It was breathtaking. Destin beach had the whitest sand I had ever seen. The sky was a clear blue, it was low tide, and it was a bit chilly. Liam held me tight. We had a wonderful day.

That evening, Olivia called. She asked if I wanted to go to Las Vegas on Thursday and mentioned that it would be fun. I explained to her that I wouldn't have the money for two back-to-back vacations. She asked if I would go if I didn't have to worry about the money. I said I would.

The next few days were awesome. Liam and his parents spent the day together while the twins and I did our own sightseeing. We met up for dinner and relaxed at the pool that evening. At the pool, my daughter asked if we could wake up early to see the sunrise. I agreed. I asked my son if he wanted to join us, but he opted out.

We were leaving the next day after breakfast. The next morning, my daughter and I walked to the beach together. It was chillier that morning than it had been a day or two before when I was with Liam, so I brought a blanket for us. I held her while we waited for the sun to rise. I will always remember that moment.

That morning, we said our goodbyes. During our drive home, Olivia called and asked if I was still interested in going to Las Vegas. I told her again that I did not have the money to go. She explained that I could pay her back later. I told her I would think about it. During the drive, Liam was a bit quiet. Anytime I asked a question, he would give me a short response.

That evening, I called Olivia back and told her I would go. During one of the restroom stops, I called my mom to ask if she minded watching the twins for a few days so I could go on a girls' trip. She quickly responded that she could.

We arrived home very late that evening. While in bed that night, I turned toward Liam and told him that I was leaving for Las Vegas on Thursday for a girls' trip. His eyes opened wide.

He asked, "How are you going to pay for it? What luggage are you going to use? You can't borrow mine. You don't have enough money for a second vacation. Who's watching the twins? I'm not."

I took a deep breath. I explained that the girls were paying for my entire trip, including spending money. I then told him that I would be leaving in the morning to drop off the twins with my mom and that she would be watching the children. I further explained that I would be borrowing some of Olivia's luggage. I then asked him if he would take me to the airport for my flight to Vegas.

To that he snapped, "No! You can figure that out, too."

I turned to face the opposite direction. There was nothing else to say.

The next morning, I woke up early to wake the twins. They were already awake and had started repacking. I went downstairs to make breakfast. Liam was already there, and he asked me not to go to Las Vegas with the girls.

I replied, "It's been decided. My plane ticket has been purchased. I'll be picking up the ticket and luggage this evening."

And with that, Liam left the house. He was extremely upset. After breakfast, we made the drive to Mom's. After we arrived, I had lunch with the family and then headed back to the city. I actually drove straight to Olivia's to pick up the luggage and other things. We chatted for a bit. Olivia told me that the room would be free and that the only repayment they wanted was for the airfare and spending money.

I couldn't believe I was going to Las Vegas. I couldn't believe we were heading to Las Vegas. When I arrived home, Liam was waiting for me. He had cooked dinner for us. He asked me again not to go.

My reply was basically the same as it had been that morning: "My ticket has been purchased. Olivia gave me money to take a taxi in the morning. I'll be back on Sunday. They'll be driving me home."

He repeated his desire for me to stay home but then said, "I'll take you to and from the airport. There's no need to take a taxi or have your friends drive you home. Who's bringing the twins back to the city?"

I told him my sister was going to be visiting my mom and that she would drop them off at the house. I told him I would be back sometime after 6:00 p.m. on Sunday. After dinner, he watched me pack. We made love that evening, but the connection was completely off.

The next morning, Liam drove me to the airport. We said our goodbyes. I was looking forward to some girl time. The flight was smooth. The girls were on a different flight; they would arrive before me. I had been to Las Vegas several times before this trip. It was nice to be back. I took a taxi to the Bellagio Hotel & Casino. The receptionist had a key waiting for me. The view from the room was nice. I remember thinking, "Just a few days ago, the view was a beautiful beach. Today, my view is the grand hotels and casinos."

The girls were out poolside. I had had enough of the sun. I changed into some comfortable clothes. Before meeting up with everyone, I knelt, prayed, and cried. I praised God for everything. I was so grateful and thankful for God's continued blessings. That weekend, we drank, gambled, shopped, and enjoyed the nightlife. When I returned, Liam picked me up from the airport. He asked me about the trip.

I replied, "We had a great time."

Nodding, he responded, "Oh … you had a great time. Someone sounds very confident. You think you're a badass now that you've come back from a girls' trip."

I brushed off his comment. We were silent all the way home.

Meanwhile, my daughter had been researching magnet schools. She did not want to attend a traditional high school. A few weeks before spring break, she applied to a magnet school. The application included reference letters from teachers and staff, a report of satisfactory attendance, copies of report cards with a "B" average in all subjects, and an essay submission. It was stressful; not everyone was accepted to the school. We were thrilled when she received her acceptance letter to the Healthcare Magnet School. The school was for students who were interested in pursuing a career in the health professions. I realized that, for the next four years, the twins would be going to different schools. I was so proud of her for taking the initiative to change her future.

That Easter weekend, the twins and I drove back home to celebrate with the family. Again, Liam decided not to go. My mom asked how the twins liked the extra time with me. I told her that we were having fun and that they were looking forward to my graduation from college.

Liam and I had grown apart. I could see the writing on the wall and sensed a breakup was coming soon. Liam had been coming home late for the last few weeks. In my bedroom, there are sliding glass doors that lead to the backyard. Liam came home late one night and immediately jumped in the shower. I felt a nudge to check his wallet. Until then, I had never looked in his wallet without his permission, but I felt the need to check it without asking.

I opened the wallet and found a receipt from a nice restaurant I had never been to. I could see that he had dined with someone else. My heart sank. I felt the urge to check the envelope close to his wallet. I started shaking as I picked up the envelope and opened it. Tears began to roll down my cheeks. I was so overcome with emotion that I found it hard to breathe or move.

I soon discovered that Liam had been lying to me since the day we met. In the envelope, I found his W-2 tax forms. Liam consistently told me that he made 10% more than I did. He told me that he was on a strict budget and could not spare any additional dollars for our household. He also told me that if I needed any extra money, I would have to get a part-time job. I had believed him.

But the forms I held in my hand painted a very different picture. They told me that Liam earned more than twice the amount I earned in a year. They told me that he had been cheating me and lying to me from the very beginning of our relationship.

In that moment, I felt as though I had lost all faith in men. I thought, "Why did it happen again? My mom and everyone else were right about him. Why didn't I see it?" I was furious. A moment later, Liam finished his shower and emerged from the bathroom. He found me standing on the other side of the room, holding the restaurant receipt and the tax forms.

His jaw dropped.

He tried to explain, "I'm sorry, Reyna. The reason I didn't reveal my income is because I had a lot of debt to pay off. We went on one date. Nothing happened."

With tears streaming down my cheeks, I took a deep breath and said, "It's over. Get your shit out of the house. Leave right now."

He got dressed and then said, "I'll be back tomorrow, but I'll be staying until the end of the month. My half of the bills are paid until the end of the month."

Liam then walked out the front door, and I collapsed to the floor.

I cried for hours.

CHAPTER 8

THE UNEXPECTED

Liam came back to the house after work the next day. He couldn't even look at me. He jumped in the shower, got dressed, and left for the evening. My emotions were like a roller coaster of hurt, anger, frustration, betrayal, and broken trust. I was lying in bed facing the wall when he returned; a few moments later, he lay on the bed next to me.

After a moment of silence, he said, "I'm sorry, Reyna. Will you talk to me?"

I did not speak. Even though he was right next to me, I felt numb all over and alone. His routine remained the same for the next few days. I was so angry, and I cried every day. I recall that, one evening, I finally turned to talk to him.

I asked him, "Why did you hurt me? Why didn't you just leave before cheating on me? Why are you making it harder on me by staying in the house? Why are you creeping in and out? If you say you didn't cheat, why does everything you do display otherwise?"

He didn't answer any of my questions. He just started to cry, asking for a second chance.

To this, I replied, "It's over."

I turned away from him and fell asleep crying. During the last week before Liam moved out, he added some things to his daily routine. He normally showered, dressed, went out for the evening, and jumped into bed when he arrived home. Now, when he arrived in the evenings, he would remove his shoes and tiptoe to the shower. After he showered, he would quietly slide into bed. I'd just lie facing the wall, weeping. I had no energy to react or fight for us.

Liam moved out at the end of the month. A week later, he called to ask if he could pick up his remaining items. I recall that it was a Thursday when he stopped by the house. He walked in the door, and I gave him his things. He asked if we could chat. He held my hand and we kissed. That afternoon, Liam and I made love. I can't explain why. Before he left, he knelt in front of me and wept, again asking for a second chance. I kissed him and said, "No!" I was nice to him, but our relationship was over. There would be no second chance.

That evening, my colleagues and I met at a local restaurant called Kona Grill. It's an upscale casual spot where we regularly met for happy hour on Thursdays. After I arrived and parked, my phone rang. It was a colleague who reported, "I think your ex-boyfriend is here with some girl. He's wearing the mock turtleneck and sport coat you bought for him."

Boy, did my blood boil. I grabbed my things and swiftly walked into the restaurant. They were sitting at the bar. My chair and drinks were waiting for me. The girls pointed at Liam; it was him.

I thought, "What the fuck! That jerk! We just made love. Wow! How quickly we move on!" My colleague grabbed my hand and said, "Fuck him! Let's drink a shot to celebrate your breakup."

We took a shot, and I chugged my beverage. Liam was on the other side of the bar, facing away from us. The girl was standing in front of him, so I couldn't see her face. I excused myself, walked into the restroom, and started yelling at the top of my lungs. When I was done, I walked back out to rejoin my coworkers. The music was so loud that no one had heard me. When I reached my group, a second round of drinks was waiting for me. The girls and I decided to yell his name. We screamed, "LIAM!" He didn't even turn. Then I yelled, "LIAM!" The music had stopped for a split second when I screamed. He heard me and turned to face me, his face turning bright red. The girl he was with leaned over to look in our direction. Liam then gulped his beer and paid his check.

As they were walking out, my colleague told me not to look at them. I told her that I had to look at them as they left. When I looked, I saw that he had wrapped his arm around her. He held her tightly as they walked out together.

We continued to drink. As we drank, I began to think, 'I have been with Liam for over two years. Did I truly know him? Did I ignore the signs? Here we go again—another failed relationship.' I decided to focus on the twins and my goals. I convinced myself that this, too, shall pass and that God is good. I told myself that God showed me the kind of man he truly was: A CHEATER!

The next few months were extremely emotional. I turned my focus toward the twins, school, the gym, and work. My mom and Olivia were there for me during my healing. The twins didn't have much input regarding the breakup. My mom came to stay with us for a few weeks.

My son's outbursts had become more frequent. During his tantrums, I realized that he needed his father. I thought, 'Why wasn't I married?' He wanted his father to be part of his life. My son would call his father more often; he would tell me that if he lived with him, he'd do better in school and improve his attitude. He told me that his dad could do a better job of parenting him. I remembered how their father would tell me that he could be a better parent. He would say, "I would do a better job than you are now."

It seemed like nothing I said or did was enough. The techniques and counseling sessions weren't working. Since I had met Liam, the twins' father hadn't given me much grief. Now that Liam had moved out, their father began to give me attitude over the phone. I remember that I would just hang up on him when he started in on me.

The twins and I continued our normal routine. Priscilla continued to help me pick up the twins from school. Their school activities were coming to an end. This summer, the twins opted out of staying with their dad, and their father didn't fight it.

That summer, my routine didn't change: parenting, school, work, and the gym. In June of that summer, David's outbursts peaked. It was unbearable, but I was not about to give up on my son. I called my mom for advice.

She told me, "Mija, your son is seeking his father. His father is confirming he would care for him. You should give them what they want. Grant your son his request."

My heart sank. I tried to explain to her that he was my baby boy and that I didn't trust his father. I reasoned that because I was his mom, I should be able to parent him.

To this, my mother replied, "Mija, your son is a teenager. He needs his father. I've seen his outbursts. Let his father step in."

That weekend, we drove back home to visit Mom. While my son wasn't watching, I packed all his clothes in a duffel bag. It was breaking my heart, but my mom was right. I didn't know if I could actually go through with letting my son stay there on a permanent basis. On Sunday, we left my mom's house, and I told her that I couldn't leave him. She understood. Before the three of us started back for the city, we stopped by their father's house. My daughter stayed in the vehicle. My son and I walked inside to have a conversation with their dad. I pleaded with their father to help me when I called about his son. I asked for his help in calming him down. My son was standing next to me.

He then walked over, stood next to his father, and announced, "Dad could do a better job raising me."

His father agreed and said, "I'd do a way better job than you are doing now."

I took a deep breath and asked, "Prince, if you lived with your dad, you wouldn't have any more attitude and you'd listen?"

I then looked at their father and said, "You could raise our son without any problems?"

They looked at each other and said, "Yes, we would."

I excused myself from the room. I went to the car and grabbed the duffle bag from the trunk. I returned to the house and said, "Here you go. Your wishes have been granted. Prince, as of today, you'll live with your father. Matthew, he's your responsibility. Good luck to the two of you. Love you, son."

I then walked out and began to cry. I immediately called my mom. She calmed me down and said, "This is what they wanted. Remember that."

After a few hours had passed, my son called me and asked how I was and if I was coming back to pick him up.

I replied, "You'll be staying with your father. You both said you would be better together."

My son became furious and started yelling. "You left me. You abandoned me. What kind of mother would do that?"

It was heart-wrenching to hear those words come out of his mouth.

I finally answered, "Son, I didn't leave or abandon you. You kept telling me that you needed your father. He confirmed that he needs you, too. You're both getting what you want. Be careful what you ask for, because you both just got your request. Love you, Mijo."

The drive home was very difficult. Tears were rolling down my cheeks. All I could do was pray. The next few days and weeks were tough. My mom and the rest of the family watched my son; he spent a lot of time with my parents. Prince stayed at my parents' house and his father's. I called him every day. The conversations were short, but I heard his voice and he took my calls. Before we hung up, we'd both say, "I love you."

Their father would call me from time to time, yelling at me about the fact that he couldn't find my son. He would tell me that he had been calling and that my son wouldn't answer his phone. "Have him call me. Now!" then he'd hang up. I'd call my son, and he'd pick up on the first ring. I would inform him that his father was trying to reach him, that he was worried, and to please return his calls. To this, my son would say, "Okay. I'll call him."

I would then wait a few minutes, call his father back, and ask, "Did he call?" In reply, he would start yelling at me.

That summer, my son's girlfriend moved in with us for a short time. The house was quiet. It was different having two girls and two cats in the house, but not seeing my son was difficult. I kept praying for his conversion.

Soon, the twins would be entering high school as freshmen. It was nerve-wracking. My son would be staying with his father. He would begin his freshman year in my hometown; he would walk the same halls I did. My daughter would be attending a magnet school. The road of our lives up to this point had not been easy; it had been a roller coaster of bitter and sweet moments. I truly knew that God had His hands on everything we did. Placing my trust in Him every day helped me move forward. I trusted that my son would be home soon. This was not what I had envisioned for their high school years.

My son wasn't happy about beginning school without his friends. He understood that decisions were followed by consequences. My nephew, who was more like a brother to him, would be attending school with him. He was also like a son to me. My daughter was so happy to start school. On the first morning of the school year, she woke up early. She was nervous because she, too, would be meeting new friends, but she was ready for the challenge.

Dropping her off was a combination of nervousness and excitement all at once. I took the day off of work, just in case she needed me. My son had called both the night before and that morning before school; he was also feeling anxious and excited. I wished him all the best on her first day and asked him to call if he needed anything. Also, I asked him to call after he was home from school. I stayed near my phone all day, as I didn't want to miss a call.

As I arrived to pick up my daughter, I couldn't believe what I saw. Nearly all of the boys and girls who were waiting outside were reading a book. They were either sitting on a bench, sitting on the floor, leaning against the wall, or standing. My daughter loved to read; this school was perfect for her. When she got in the vehicle, she was grinning from ear to ear. She began telling me about her day and what was coming up on the school calendar. She planned to sign up for a few clubs, volunteer, and be part of academic competitions. She was ecstatic and couldn't wait for the next day. After we got home, my son called. He also had a fantastic day. He was happy for the change and looking forward to returning the next day. I breathed a sigh of relief. I remembered that their freshman year was extremely important to their future; it would be academically challenging, and it was a fresh start at a new school for both of them.

My son lived with his father for four months. During that time, my son got into some trouble. His father would leave for work each morning before my son left for school, so he would sleep in, skip classes, or not attend school at all. He had a lot of absences. By the time the school administrators contacted us, it was too late; he would have to attend alternative school.

My son also got in trouble with the law. As a result, he was ordered by a judge to perform community service. His dad and I were constantly yelling at each other over the phone. By the time my son had completed his hours of community service, I had seen and heard enough. In October, my son moved back home with me.

I immediately enrolled him in a new high school. Over time, I learned that his father had given him weed to smoke just to upset me. I told him that the only person he managed to hurt was our son. I was obviously furious about it, but what could I say? I knew that nothing I could say would make a bit of difference. The damage had been done. I had missed my son so much and was glad to have him back home.

I remember a sweet incident shortly after he came back home. One day, as I was leaving the house, my son stopped me. He let me know that he was now a freshman in high school and that he did not want me to call him by his nickname or kiss him on the cheek before school. I asked him why I couldn't, and he replied, "I'm grown up and don't want you to do that anymore."

I did not want to, but I agreed under one condition: no more checkbook. That meant no more money. At that, he smiled and said, "I was kidding, Mom. Call me whatever you want, whenever you want." Then he grabbed me and gave me a kiss on my cheek. I told him, "Keep the kisses coming." With that, I smiled and left the house. As I walked away, I thought, "That is what I thought. He's growing up, but I couldn't have my baby stop me from kissing or nurturing him."

That year, the twins' birthday fell on Thanksgiving. We celebrated their 15th birthday at the Embassy Suites Hotel, a short distance from my parents' home. We celebrated Thanksgiving, the twins', my niece's, and my sister's birthdays all together. Family and friends were also in attendance. We had Thanksgiving at my parents' house, and that afternoon, everyone joined us at the hotel. I had purchased the Thanksgiving turkey, ham, all the trimmings, and dessert from Bill Miller Bar-B-Q, a local restaurant chain. The festivities went on for hours.

The weekend was perfect. The kids saw their father but stayed away from him. Matthew was aware that Liam was no longer a part of my family, but I didn't need any drama. I was so grateful and thankful for my family's support during those months; I truly appreciated it. Everyone helped.

The annual holiday party at work was my thirteenth; during that time, I had not missed a single one. Everyone at work looked forward to the holiday party. That year, my twins were my dates. My son wanted to learn to tie a necktie. We had trifold brochures at work that provided step-by-step instructions for this task; also, he had Mom to teach him. Both of my kids learned to tie a half-Windsor knot. I thought, "From infants to 15-year-old teenagers…"

They inspired me to achieve my goals. Priscilla and her boyfriend also attended the party. We gathered together around the same table, having arrived at the same time. Upon entering the dining room, we saw a photographer set up on-site to take photos throughout the night. That evening, we took several photos together. We all wore red. The boys wore black suits with solid red ties. My daughter wore a red and black polka-dotted flared dress. Priscilla and I wore short, red silk dresses. We looked beautiful. We enjoyed the fine dining, fun party favors, and dancing. I introduced them to so many of my friends. I was so proud of the twins and how they interacted with everyone. We had a phenomenal time, and for the next few weeks, the holiday party was a central part of our conversations.

The holidays flew by that year. The twins decided to stay home with me and not spend the holiday break with their father. He agreed to that. During the break, they asked if they could enroll in driver's education courses. They wanted to earn their learner's permits and, later, their licenses.

After much research, I found a company that offered both classroom and behind-the-wheel instruction. It was a one-stop shop. After they completed the required hours to certify, the school offered the written exam and road test. If they successfully completed the program and passed their tests, they would earn their permits. At 16 years old, Texas residents can apply for a license. They were looking forward to registering for classes in the spring.

In the meantime, I would teach them how to drive. In my hometown, there was a community park with a rectangular parking lot. My nephew, the twins, and I decided to take an afternoon to take turns driving around the parking lot in the Ford Mustang. We practiced stopping, parking, parallel parking, and turning. Each one of the kids took turns driving around the lot. For me, it was nerve-wracking. The boys went first; they both had some experience driving and did very well.

My daughter didn't have that kind of previous experience. In fact, she couldn't see over the steering wheel, so we used a phone book for her to sit on. It worked, but I remember she was scared. She used both feet to drive, refusing to use one foot for both pedals. I felt like I had whiplash after her turn. She drove extremely slowly and braked with extreme force. She drove so slowly that we could have walked next to the car! She wouldn't have passed us.

We were patient with her. The boys were allowed to go twice around the parking lot before her next turn. We actually had a great time. I knew they would do well in their classes, though I knew my daughter needed extra practice. With her having no experience, the instructors would have their hands full.

A short time later, we were all back in school. This would be my last semester at the university. They were thrilled, and I was ecstatic. I couldn't believe that I would be earning my bachelor's degree and walking the stage in May. It would be a game-changer for the three of us; I would soon be working only one job, and all my free time would go to the twins. After eighteen years of attending college, I would finally be graduating. I would be the first person in my family to earn a bachelor's degree, and I was looking forward to new career opportunities.

Around that time, I remember receiving an unexpected call. It was from my mom. I always looked forward to chatting and catching up with her, but this call was different; she was not herself. Mom took the lead in the conversation.

She told me, "Mija, I called to let you know that your dad is dying."

My jaw dropped. I couldn't speak or move.

She continued, "He didn't tell me. While caressing his back one day, I noticed that there were blood clots… the same ones my sister had before she passed away from cancer. I asked your dad if he had cancer, and he said, 'Yes.' He told me that he has known for over three years but admitted to keeping it a secret. He went to the doctor and was diagnosed with Stage 4 cancer. The doctor recommended chemo, but he declined. He said that this is God's will and he didn't want anyone to worry; he just wanted to spend his remaining years loving and enjoying family and friends. He apologized and told me he was sorry, and that this was his penance. We cried together. Mija, I have to call the family. We'll see you soon. Love you, Mija."

My body felt numb. I sat on the floor and wept for hours. When the twins arrived home from school, they were having a great day. I didn't want to spoil it, but they had to know; they loved their grandpa. We sat around the kitchen table, and I told them what Mom had told me. I will never forget their reaction. They looked into my eyes and then bowed their heads in sadness as tears rolled down their faces. Immediately after our conversation, they asked when we planned on visiting. I told them we would be leaving after school that Friday. My son got up and walked upstairs; he was so angry. My daughter slowly walked upstairs. I gave them some time to get through the initial shock of the news.

Later that evening, I went upstairs to check on them. They were quiet. They had both already packed their bags and were ready to go on Friday. I went to work the next day and requested time off. I knew that requesting time off on weekends was discouraged, but this was definitely an exception.

My parents' love grew even stronger after the news. It was a huge blow to everyone, especially my mom. During this time, there was so much chaos among my siblings; emotions went through the roof. When we arrived at my parents' house, we ran inside. My dad opened his arms to hug us, and the three of us started crying. He reminded us that he wasn't dying today and that he loved us so much. We stayed near him the entire weekend, leaning on him while he caressed our hair. I could only wonder what he was thinking. He tried to remain calm, but I could see the fear in his eyes.

Before we left, we begged Mom to come stay with us for a few weeks to gather her thoughts and accept the inevitable. She agreed to come back with us in the next couple of weeks. My parents were having difficult conversations and needed time alone.

On one of our trips to my parents', my mom came back to the city with the three of us. She was emotionally exhausted and had lost weight. She had tried to hold it together for everyone, but she finally broke down. She wept for days. She was angry because Dad had never told her, but during this time, she began to accept what was happening.

We had some hard but important conversations. I explained to my mom that we needed to plan for his funeral; if we tried to plan after he passed, we would all be too emotional to really think through our decisions. She agreed with me. I gathered all the documents and information for Mom, and she made all the final decisions. We were glad that we planned in advance. There was some paperwork we needed that would take six weeks for us to receive, but we had a plan. It made Mom feel more at ease.

That Saturday morning when I woke, I saw that she was packed. She told me that she was ready to go back and take care of my father. Then she told me to take my time getting ready. We had breakfast, packed an overnight bag, and drove back home. It was a quiet drive.

When we arrived, Dad greeted us at the door. He was so excited to see Mom. We all hugged. My mom went into the kitchen to make us dinner. My dad was a smoker; he went outside to the backyard to smoke under a tree. There was a picnic table that he liked to sit on, and I went outside to join him.

We had a beautiful conversation. I asked him to tell me everything I didn't know about him. He smiled, placed his hand on my head, and scratched it. As he scratched, he said, "Mija, you know everything I wanted you to learn about me. I'll leave you with these three things to remember: First, take care of your mom for me. You're doing a good job; keep it up. Second, let your son try new things. Let him fail. It's okay; he'll get back up. Last, don't be too naïve."

I looked at him and said, "Dad, I'm not naïve."

He smiled at me and said, "Yes, you are."

We hugged and sat next to each other. I asked him, "Dad, is there anything else?"

Lighting another cigarette, he said, "You take after your mom. You're going to be fine."

That weekend, we left with our hearts full of Dad's love for us. We went home every weekend after that. The twins' father didn't bother me at all; he didn't even push to see the kids. He was aware of Dad's cancer.

On March 23, 2008, we celebrated Easter. Everyone was in good spirits. We were trying to create lasting memories with my dad. We joked and laughed with him about the fact that we would miss his burned barbecue. That year, the barbecue was perfect. After a few weeks, Dad took a turn for the worse. We were all emotionally spent, but we just pushed through for Mom. My professors were so understanding. My family would not be attending my graduation; as it should be, all the attention was focused on my dad.

The university was kind enough to let me borrow a cap and gown that belonged to an alumnus. I remember driving home to visit my parents. My dad was looking forward to taking a photo with me in my cap and gown. It took him eight hours to get ready; he didn't want anyone to help him shave. When he was ready, he called for me. My mom, the twins, and I had been waiting all day to take a photo with him. We gathered in the living room. Before he stood up, he said that he only had the energy to take one photo. I begged for two: one with the five of us, then a second photo with me and my parents. My mom and I held Dad to his feet. We were quick. After the photos, he slept for hours.

On May 10, 2008, I walked the graduation stage. I was 36 years old when I earned my Bachelor of Business Administration (BBA) with a concentration in management. I was so excited and proud of this huge accomplishment. To have the twins, my uncle, aunt, and friends attend the ceremony was emotional. My mom called me before the ceremony. On behalf of her and Dad, she congratulated me. She told me to enjoy the moment and that it was well deserved.

She told me that they would be there in spirit. I wish my parents and family would have been able to witness it. I had been attending college for the last 18 years; it had been an emotional rollercoaster. No one could ever take the degree and the knowledge I had gained.

||||||||||||||||

On May 22, 2008, my father passed away. We were devastated; a hole was left in our hearts. It was a beautiful ceremony. Mom and I read Dad's eulogy, and when we sat back down, a few of Dad's friends and family members walked up to say a few words.

A nun also came forward to speak. She gave her condolences to my mom and the family, then told us that Dad had volunteered at the church for the last decade. She explained that he was a great carpenter who had made many improvements and had repaired or completed many projects. She also mentioned that he drove the sisters to get groceries and to any appointments they had.

She shared that every Saturday, he went through a specific routine before he left the church: he would unbutton his shirt, rebutton it incorrectly, open a beer, and spill some on himself. She told us the sisters would ask him why he wouldn't tell his wife and family what he was doing for the church. Every time they asked, his answer was always the same: "It's no one's business. It's between God and me."

When she finished her story, everyone laughed. Mom and I turned and smiled at each other. Later, my mom recalled that when Dad would get home around 6:00 p.m. on Saturdays, she would smell beer on his clothes and always tell him to go shower before dinner.

We never knew that he volunteered.

CHAPTER 9

WORK-LIFE BALANCE

My father's passing left us overwhelmed with grief; it seemed like our world had been pulled out from under us. None of us were truly prepared—and no one could have been—for what happened to Dad. I found myself thinking, "How does one begin to put the pieces of a broken heart back together?" One of the emotions that overtook our family was anger, which resulted in a division between the siblings. Looking back on that time, I think we were all grieving in our own way. Our emotions were like roller coasters; we all experienced constant ups and downs.

We all realized that it was going to be a long road to accepting the fact that we had lost our father. Not having him around any longer was a profoundly sad thought and reality. My mom was our rock, but she was also in pain. That meant we all had to do our own "heavy lifting." I decided to take it one step and one day at a time. I knew the road would be difficult, and we all knew that, in time, we would heal, even if it didn't happen right away. We had to trust in God's journey for our lives.

During this time, we did our best to celebrate the successful freshman year the kids had in school. Also, I could finally say that I was a college graduate! I was very grateful for my mentor; without him, I would have struggled through college. After graduation, my advisor and instructors highly recommended that I pursue a Master's degree, but they suggested I first take a break from school to heal from my father's passing. I made it a point to remind myself to celebrate my accomplishment. After much thought, I decided how to do so. Since my mom and siblings weren't able to attend the initial celebration, I decided to celebrate by pursuing my graduate degree so that my family could attend the next graduation.

So, off I would go. The plan was to take a small break from school and then return to earn my Master's. From the time Mom gave us the news of my father's passing, our lives were a blur. We did our best to keep our heads up. My friends stood by my side. I remembered my dad sending me the mini boxing gloves and what they meant: when life knocks you down, get back up and fight. That was my plan. I made a promise to my dad, and I was going to keep it.

Around this time, the twins were enrolled in driver's education classes. They decided not to stay with their father for the summer, so when we went back to visit Mom, their father would come by to pick them up for only a few hours. It was difficult not seeing Dad when we walked through the front door. Over the years, I had grown used to seeing him in the living room, typically watching sports.

My son's behavioral troubles continued and actually worsened. It was frustrating to watch. He was already dealing with anger issues, and I truly believed his acting out was due to the loss of his grandfather. My son was closer to my dad than to his own father; my father mentored him as if he were his own son, supporting and encouraging all of his endeavors.

To complicate things, there was a huge "elephant in the room" regarding my relationship with my son. We had many difficult conversations that started with talking and ended in yelling. During these troubled talks, he would ask why I left him with his father. No matter what I said in response, it was never good enough for him. But I stood my ground. I reminded him that he and his father had believed I wasn't good enough to parent him and that they could do a better job without me. I told him I hoped his father could have made a positive impact on his behavior. I apologized for how everything unfolded, and I told him I loved him very much and would always be there for him.

Not being in school was nice; the twins and I had more time to do things together. We still enjoyed going to Barnes & Noble and loved going to the movie theater, visiting almost every week. I continued to exercise and enjoy my monthly massages; sometimes I was not motivated to keep up with them, but I pushed myself to go.

The kids and I had a lot of conversations regarding my dad's passing. They were close to their grandpa, and it was nice to hear about the experiences they had with my parents and cousins through the years. They were also looking forward to their sophomore year. I found myself wanting time to slow down because so many years had already passed, and I felt that I had missed so much of their lives.

Having graduated, I knew it was time to look for a new job. My current position had served its purpose, and it was time to move on. I was grateful for the many years I spent there. I started searching for job opportunities and applying to new organizations, reminding myself that it would be a long process and that I needed to be patient.

The twins were happy to have completed the ninth grade and to be entering the tenth. I found shopping for school supplies to be fun, and we took several trips to the mall. The most expensive items we purchased were my son's tennis shoes; each pair was costly. They were teenagers, and I learned that the price of apparel increases with age. We enjoyed several nice restaurants before or after our trips to the mall. By the end of each shopping day, we were exhausted, but the joy I saw on the twins' faces was worth the effort and expense. Having money set aside for things like this really helped, especially since I had not received any child support from Matthew for years. I had asked him to help with the expenses, and he did give me some money. I was grateful for any amount he provided, knowing it would support the twins and their needs.

Soon, they were both registered for sophomore classes. My son decided not to participate in any extracurricular activities, while my daughter registered for dual-credit courses, clubs, volunteering, and more. Her schedule was pretty packed, and I supported their decisions.

I also started looking for ways to volunteer during this period. My time as a Catechist volunteer teacher was ending; it had been a beautiful five years of learning, facilitating, and creating memories with students. During Mass, I continued to volunteer in the Eucharistic Ministry. I remember wanting to volunteer for hospice because of how the doctors, nurses, and staff did a fantastic job caring for my dad during his final days. I wanted to "pay it forward," as I thought it would be a great way to continue my journey of serving others.

I had no idea who to contact to begin volunteering. One day at work, a man came in to purchase a suit for a funeral. I offered my condolences, and he told me he would let the family know. He said, "I'm not related to the family, and I don't know any of their friends. I'm a hospice volunteer." It seemed like a strange response, but I was excited because I thought maybe he could introduce me to someone in a hospice organization.

I briefly shared with him that I wanted to volunteer. The man replied, "When I pick up my suit, I'll bring you a volunteer packet. Fill it out, mail it, and someone will contact you. You'll have to go through a background check."

He was true to his word. I completed the paperwork, submitted it, and waited for the call. Not long after, a lady from the hospice organization contacted me.

Everything checked out. They required volunteers to attend an eight-hour training class. After I completed the course, they handed me a folder containing my first patient's information. I was so nervous. She was 99 years old. When I arrived at her home, I looked up and noticed the name of the cross-street; it was the same street as my childhood address. I soon discovered that my patient's name was my mom's nickname, and her deceased husband's name was my dad's middle name. Furthermore, her last name was my mom's maiden name. It was hard to believe! In that moment, I knew that hospice was exactly what I should be doing with my extra time. When I told my mom, she was extremely proud of me. I volunteered for the next three years.

This year, the twins decided that they wanted their 16th birthday celebration at home with family and friends. Their father and I decided to throw the bash together. We agreed that during the party we would both be amicable with one another; however, when he passed me, he would whisper so no one could hear him harass me. When he did that, I quickly walked away and tried to avoid him throughout the evening. Just looking at him made my stomach turn into knots.

Both of our families drove into the city for the party. It was nice to see my mom and his mom reminiscing. I respected that his family supported the twins at all their special events, regardless of whether their father and I had been at odds all these years. The twins invited classmates to the party, and we had over 75 people attend. We had a DJ, catered food, cake, party favors, and other things. Everyone had a wonderful time; the sound of chatter and laughter warmed my heart. Naturally, I wished that my father were there, but we knew he was with us in spirit.

A few days later, we traveled home for Thanksgiving. It was a tough day. My mom was our rock, and her courage gave us the strength to move forward. After Dad's passing, Mom volunteered more at the church. We did our best to keep our spirits up, and each of us shared memorable moments of our dad. The food was always delicious because my siblings cooked. Since I was the baby of the family, they told me to relax. So, I thought, "Sure, I'll sit on the couch and watch football."

My mom came back to the city to stay with us for a few weeks. I had been applying for positions at several companies, but as of that time, I had not heard back from any of them. One day, one of my professors from the university walked into the store. He told me that he was truly impressed with my selling skills. He also informed me that there was a position at a community college that fit my skill set. That evening, I applied for the position.

A few weeks later, I received a call from the school asking me to interview for the position. I was immediately overwhelmed. My mom caressed my hair and reminded me that it was time for a change. We had been waiting a long time for a new opportunity. I prepared for the interview and was lucky to have mentors to help guide me. On the day of the interview, my mom and I prayed. The interview went well, and all that was left to do was wait for a call.

A couple of weeks later, I received a call for a second interview. Only two of the applicants were asked back, and I was one of them. This interview was with the dean of the school's workforce operations; it was very informal. I remember the last thing he asked me: "How is your family going to react when your schedule changes from working nights and weekends to weekdays, 8:00 a.m. to 5:00 p.m.?"

A grin broke over my face, and I told him that they would be happy and that I had been working weekends for over 14 years. I left thinking that this would be a true game-changer for our family. Before I left, he told me someone would be calling me after a decision was made. That call came a few days later—I was selected. I got the job! The caller informed me that the decision was still unofficial and that someone in Human Resources would be contacting me to do a background check and formally offer me the position. The caller also said that this may take a few months and to be patient with the process. The four of us were ecstatic. I was happy to be celebrating with the most important people in my life: my mom and the twins.

I didn't tell anyone at work; no one knew except my family and best friends. Somewhere along the line, I realized that this was the last year I would be attending the company holiday party. It was a bittersweet occasion. As always, it was a superb evening. The goodbyes to my colleagues who lived in different cities were more sentimental, as our time together would be ending soon. There were so many goodbyes. During the party, my mind flashed back to all of the past parties. Everyone reminded me that they were only a phone call away, but I had to be realistic. Even though I might try to hold onto a friendship, some friendships remain while others fizzle and fade. These people were in my life for a long season.

The holidays were difficult that year. Reminiscing about Dad was more like "crying festivities," though we would also laugh about the good times. The holidays were roller coasters by themselves.

Soon after, the twins were back in school. My daughter was hardly home, but my son had a lot of free time on his hands. As for me, it would be my last year working the retail "peak season." I was working nearly every day of the week, and it was getting old. I was grateful for all the managers who worked with my schedule so I could continue to attend school and support the children in their after-school activities. I had learned so much during my time at the store, but I was looking forward to continuing to expand my knowledge in the new position with the school.

When I was home, I cooked. I enjoyed cooking for the family. I started a new tradition for us on the Sundays I did not have to work: I opened the kitchen for breakfast "à la carte" requests. As long as I had the ingredients, they could order whatever they wanted. There were times that I cooked three or four different breakfast platters. The kids loved it. I told them that if they wanted to try something new, they would have to give me the recipe ahead of time; I would then purchase the ingredients and prepare it on the following Sunday. They asked if I could do this for all of our other meals, but I explained that it would be too difficult with my schedule and that one day a week was all I could handle for now.

In January of that year, I began my pursuit of a Master's degree. The university I attended offered a Master of Business Administration (MBA) program. It was offered in the same format as my undergraduate degree, so I was familiar with the process. It was nice to be back in school. This time, my goal was to remain a full-time student; there would be no part-time attendance. I didn't want earning this degree to take years.

To earn an MBA, the requirement was to take 12 three-credit courses for a total of 36 credit hours. The core courses were Managerial Accounting, Managerial Economics, Financial Management, Human Resource Management, Marketing Management, Business Research/Analysis, Quantitative Methods in Business, and a Capstone: Cases in Management Problems. We were instructed to choose two elective courses; I chose Information Technology and Organizational Development. I was ready for the challenge.

Meanwhile at work, my managers were making staff changes. Many employees had moved on from the company or had been promoted to new positions. There were now several open positions. About this time, the District Manager came into the store. We knew change was coming. One of the retail locations—one near my home—had an opening for an Assistant Manager. Since I was already working as an Assistant Manager, the District Manager pulled me aside. He was transferring me to that location, effective the next day.

The following day, I reported to my new store. I had worked there when I initially transferred from Corpus Christi. Every day, I walked into the store with a letter of resignation tucked in my front pocket. I wanted to be prepared to respond to the call I was expecting from the community college. Only a week had passed before I received that call. I was formally offered the job at the community college with a start date of February 23, 2009—only two weeks away. When the call ended, I walked straight to the back of the store where there was a computer. My hands were shaking. I logged onto the computer and submitted my resignation letter via email. Within a few minutes, the District Manager called me to confirm my resignation; apparently, he had already received the news. It all happened so quickly.

I was on "cloud nine." It was the uplifting news my family needed. As a family, we celebrated. I had two weeks to say goodbye to everyone, and we went out to celebrate friendships and new beginnings. There was laughter, tears, and many well wishes.

Before I knew it, February 23, 2009, was upon me. I remember walking onto the community college campus felt like a breath of fresh air. The campus was beautiful, and I sensed that my new beginning was here. There would be no more working evenings, weekends, or holidays; I was going to work a traditional business schedule and have holidays off. This was truly "work-life balance," which was something new to me. I was so grateful that all the work I had put into my degree had opened the door to a new career opportunity.

I purchased new business-casual clothes that I thought would be more fitting in my new workplace. I placed the bags in the closet and tucked them away. After I bought them, however, I decided not to wear them because I felt the cost was too high. The twins wondered why I had not worn the clothes yet.

One day, they pulled the bags of clothes out of the closet and asked me if they fit. They also asked what I thought about the new items. I told them that the clothes fit perfectly, the shirts fit well, and the dress slacks only needed to be hemmed. I explained that I did not like spending money on myself. They grabbed some scissors and began cutting the tags off the clothes, telling me that I deserved them. They told me that I worked hard and needed to treat myself. Then, they came and hugged me. It was a sweet gesture, and I knew they were right; I often forgot to put myself first.

After spring break that year, my son started his first job at a local fast-food restaurant. He was also beginning a new journey.

CHAPTER 10

THE TIDE IS TURNING

It had been nearly a year since my dad passed away. We were gathered for Easter weekend—another holiday without our beloved father. There was still much healing that needed to happen, as the family was still divided. Regardless of the division or the emotions, however, we gathered. My hospice training had given me a better understanding of the emotions everyone was experiencing; I could now see that everyone processed and healed in their own way and time. I remembered that, at the end of the day, we were family.

I found that coming together helped my family heal. My mom needed us, and we needed her. As far as the meal went, we all contributed by making side dishes while my sisters cooked the barbecue. The food was delicious. The kids had a blast during the Easter egg hunt, and we all joked, laughed, cried, and reminisced about past holidays with Dad. The twins spent half the day with their father and his family.

After the weekend trip, guilt and sadness began to creep into my thinking. I started reflecting on all the memorable moments I had missed with the twins. I had sacrificed so much time trying to meet goals that I believed would benefit the family, but I realized how short life is and that lost time cannot be regained. I understood that all I could do was take advantage of the time I had now and make new memories.

My son was enjoying his new job; he loved working and having his own money. We lived near his workplace, where he worked evenings and weekends.

Working filled his schedule, and he was really good at saving money. Both twins had their own bank accounts; I had them open these accounts to learn how to save and manage their funds.

I didn't want my daughter to work yet. She had a full schedule with school, so I told her that work wasn't an option and that I wanted her to focus on her studies. Only a few weeks remained before summer break began. I told her that if she needed anything, all she had to do was ask. During one of our "Straight Talk" conversations, the twins mentioned wanting braces. They explained why they needed them, and while I agreed, I explained that I couldn't afford them for both at once because my insurance only covered a portion of the cost. I told them that one could get braces now and the other would get them later. Our orthodontist provided payment plans, which made things a little easier for me financially.

My son and daughter talked it through, and my daughter decided to wait until I paid off her brother's braces. We scheduled my son's appointment for the first week of summer break. He was so excited. While he was with the orthodontist, I made payment arrangements. The balance was high, as expected, so I decided to pay half and make payments on the remainder. When we left the office, my son was thrilled about his braces and thanked me.

The twins decided to stay home for the summer. Their dad wasn't happy about that, but it was their decision, and I was not going to force them to go. However, we did visit my mom during that summer. Whenever we visited her, they spent time with their father.

As teenagers, they often wanted to be alone, and I had to push them to hang out with me. I guess they thought their mom wasn't "cool" anymore, or perhaps they just had different ideas of what cool was. I also realized they were simply trying to be more independent. No matter what I thought, I knew I sometimes crowded their space.

That summer was the first summer I didn't have to work late hours. We took advantage of the time and visited my sister and her family. It was nice to be able to relax and not worry about going to work on the weekend. We also had late movie nights at home and at the theater. We continued to enjoy Dave & Buster's, bowling, miniature golf, the beach, museums, and other activities. We had a good summer, and again, time flew.

The twins had been telling me for months that we should get a new vehicle. They kept complaining that they had no legroom in the Mustang, which was now ten years old. I loved my vehicle; there were no problems with it. I later figured out they had a reason for pushing me to get a new car: their plan was for me to give them mine. A new vehicle wasn't on my mind at the time, but I knew they had a point—legroom in the Mustang was an issue. The truth is, there was no legroom in the back seat.

So, I researched a replacement vehicle. I decided that I wanted a Sport Utility Vehicle (SUV). After doing the research, I got pre-qualified for a loan with my bank. My mom was visiting at the time, and she decided to stay at the house while we visited the local Lexus dealership. I had settled on wanting a used Lexus; I wasn't going to buy another brand-new vehicle.

We met a salesman, and he told me about a vehicle that had just been traded in. It was a one-owner vehicle with low mileage. It was drizzling that day, so he drove us to where the car was located on the lot. The twins and I took it for a spin. It was nice, but I needed to think it over. The salesman suggested that I take it home for the weekend while I made my decision. I hesitated, but the twins persisted and convinced me to go along with the idea. My son drove the Mustang, and we followed behind him. We had a nice weekend driving the Lexus. That Monday, I took it back to the dealership and dropped it off. I had to work out the numbers with the finance team, but that evening wasn't a good time to meet, so we ended up discussing the financial details over the phone.

The following Friday, the salesman brought the paperwork and the vehicle to my house. When we saw a gold Lexus pull into the driveway, we wondered whose vehicle it was. Then I watched as the salesman got out of the car. He came to the door, and when I greeted him, he asked, "Before we sign the paperwork, do you want to inspect your SUV?"

I didn't even recognize the vehicle. When I had driven it previously, the weather was bad and the car was dirty. Looking at it now, I thought, "Wow! Oh my God!" I couldn't believe that this was going to be our new vehicle. We were thrilled. We went inside and signed the paperwork. To show their appreciation, the managers gave me a wicker basket filled with goodies. It was beautiful. I was now the proud owner of a luxury SUV.

That Sunday, when it was time to head to church, the twins called me and asked where I was. I replied that I was in the vehicle waiting for them. They opened the garage door and saw me sitting in the Mustang while they were sitting in the SUV. They told me, "Mom, this is your vehicle. That's our Mustang. It's time you enjoy something new. We all deserve it." We laughed on the way to church. However, when I added the children as new drivers to the insurance policy, I experienced "sticker shock." Our insurance premium was more than the car payment!

The twins were entering their junior year of high school. As usual, we went shopping for the clothes they wanted and the supplies they needed. They both registered for school. Once again, my daughter was going to have a hectic schedule.

This year would be a bit more challenging for her, but she was ready for it. My son had been a "loner" at school the previous year, focusing only on his work. I hoped he would make new friends this year. The three of us were excited that they were one year closer to graduation. I had been attending school longer than they had, and school was exhausting. I could only imagine how they felt, having been in school since they were in pre-kindergarten.

The twins were used to my tradition of taking a photo of them on the first day of school. I had a photo album that included all these past memories. Every year, the first day of school was emotional for me; they had become more independent, and this year, they would be driving themselves to school. The twins had created a schedule to share the Mustang. There was a sense of joy I felt as I watched them pose for their pictures, though I could tell they were annoyed with me for making the same request every year. I was so proud of how beautiful and independent they were; words could not express the emotions I felt. I knew that one day I would have to let them go so they could begin their own journeys in life and make their own marks in the world.

My son made some new friends at school that year. They hung out every other weekend to play pool, watch movies, and just enjoy each other's company. I was so excited to see him bring home friends like he had in the past. After a few weeks of this routine, they started hanging out every weekend, and soon after, that expanded into the week. I remember asking my son why they were staying over during the week. He explained that his friends weren't getting along with their parents, so a short separation might help their relationships. I didn't mind, as long as everyone attended school. Apparently, their parents didn't mind, either.

So, we had gone from occasional weekends to nearly having teens move into the house. In the end, we had ten teenagers (eight boys and two girls) "move" in with us. Before any of this happened, I spoke to each set of parents. They were alright with them staying at our house. Even though there weren't enough beds for each of the kids, they didn't care; they were okay with it as long as they didn't have to go home. They slept on the floor in sleeping bags, racking out in the living room, the pool room, and the upstairs spare room. My son even gave up his bed for the girls. Every morning, they'd roll up their sleeping bags and neatly stack them in a corner.

In the meantime, I had no idea how I was going to afford to feed thirteen mouths. To save on food costs, I required them to get to school early to eat breakfast in the cafeteria, and I agreed to make dinner in the evenings for everyone. Beyond food concerns, I immediately put some ground rules in place. For example, once they arrived home, they had to sit and complete all their homework. I checked their work, and they were also required to show me their progress reports and report cards. Everyone had to pass; if their grades were below a C, they had to attend after-school tutoring. We also implemented "Straight Talk" with each of them. During their stay, we'd have one-on-one conversations where I made sure to spend time with each person. We discussed their concerns about going home and worked through their issues.

Additionally, the teenagers were required to go home once a month to spend a weekend with their parent(s). I sent them all home the same weekend, as they had to continue working on those relationships. I made it known to both the parents and the teenagers that this was only a temporary arrangement. I also insisted that holidays had to be spent with their families.

Along the way, I had the opportunity to mentor some of the parents. They explained that, often, they couldn't see eye-to-eye with their kids and just couldn't get along. I observed that they were able to oversee teams and manage people at work, but they couldn't manage or communicate with their own teenagers. They were thankful that I opened my home to them and told me that when their teenagers talked about my home, they were happy. I completely understood, but I reiterated that this was only a temporary arrangement. It was mentally exhausting for me; having ten extra kids was hectic.

Since they all shared the upstairs bathroom, they had created a schedule for taking turns getting ready for school. My daughter wasn't part of the rotation; she could go in and out when she wanted. She wasn't bothered by everyone living there because they didn't enter her bedroom; they gave her personal space. No one was allowed to use the master bathroom. A schedule was also created for washing clothes. On weekends, when it was time to do chores, it would take one hour to clean the upstairs and downstairs. Because there were so many of them, it was done pretty quickly, so I'd have them do extra chores outside. But that didn't take long, either.

During the week, they all had to get to bed early because they woke up so early to take turns in the bathroom. It all worked out. No one helped me with expenses, and I never asked. We went from a small family to a very large family in just a few months. Everyone in the house called me "Mom." They didn't have to, but they chose to. There was lots of laughter and love throughout the home. I loved it. It was hectic. When the teenagers were off to their families' homes, the twins and I bonded by doing activities together.

Having so many people in the home, I found that I definitely had to make time for myself. For my birthday, we celebrated with the twins and, in the evening, with my best friend, Olivia. It was nice to go out and have fun with adults. That year, the twins wanted to have a paintball party; they were turning 17 years old. Paintball is a game that involves players competing against each other. The object is to eliminate other players by hitting them with dye-filled gelatin capsules called paintballs that break upon impact. The twins were allowed to each invite 10 friends. They all met up at the house. My son's friends all wore black jogger tops and bottoms, while my daughter's friends all wore bright, colorful T-shirts and jeans. When all their friends arrived, the twins called me to the front lawn to meet everyone. On the right side of the lawn were my son and his friends; to the left were my daughter and her friends. No one had introduced themselves to each other. After meeting everyone, I called them all together in the middle of the lawn and said, "Today we are here to celebrate the twins' birthday and have fun. Before we head out, everyone is going to take a few minutes to meet each other's team. Shake hands and get to know everyone here. We'll be spending the afternoon together. We need everyone to come together."

With that, I turned and walked back inside the house. When I peeked through the front window, I saw that they were shaking hands. They were pairing up—one person in a bright shirt and another in a black jogger top. I just smiled. The twins called me after everyone had been introduced. We drove to the venue in separate vehicles.

When we arrived at the paintball park, I checked us in at the reservation desk. They were ready for us. There was a team of people getting the party ready with their gear. There were three teams that day: my son's team, my daughter's team, and the three of us (my son, my daughter, and myself). The rule was that no one except the twins could hit me. I was so excited to play. Our personal guide gave us the rules and explained the game. We played for a couple of hours. I'd bought some pizzas for everyone to enjoy after we finished. There were picnic tables on-site. It was nice to see everyone laughing and chatting about the experience. We were on such an adrenaline rush; we all had a blast.

A few days later, we drove back to Mom's and checked into an Embassy Suites. We checked in a day early in order to enjoy the amenities. We were ready to celebrate Thanksgiving with the family. On Thanksgiving morning, we arrived early to help my siblings with cooking and setting up. They tasked me with a few things; for the most part, they had me putting the final touches on the side dishes and desserts. It was nice to see everyone.

After the meal, the twins asked if I could drive them to their father's house. They then walked outside and waited in the SUV for me to drive them. The twins had recently obtained their licenses. They were in shock when I tossed the keys to them. I told them to take the SUV, that it was insured, and that they would be fine.

I told them to have fun. The expressions on their faces were priceless. I remember watching as they backed out of the driveway very slowly. I thought they might be thinking that I would stop them, but instead, I just waved goodbye.

In truth, I didn't want to see their father anymore; it was better this way. For my part, whenever I thought of him or saw him over the past few years, I would say to myself, "I forgive you, Matthew." I had never actually told him that because I wasn't ready to. I wanted to cut all ties with him. When the twins' father and I met over 23 years ago, we were tightly knit, but that connection was broken long ago. Now, my plan was to completely sever those ties, keeping a line of communication open only for the twins.

Graduation from my Master's program came quickly. I couldn't believe the day was finally here, and I was excited to walk across the stage. The best part was that my siblings, family, and friends would all be attending the ceremony and the after-party. In December 2009, I earned a Master of Arts degree in Business Administration, having managed to complete the course of study in just one year. As I walked across the stage, I could hear my family cheering and whistling for me. It melted my heart.

That evening, we continued the celebration at my home. Manny, Jeff, Olivia, colleagues, friends, family, and professors all attended. The teenagers in attendance wore black dress shirts, black slacks, and red ties. There was a valet who parked the guests' vehicles and served refreshments while my siblings served the food. The invitations had been sent out a few weeks before graduation and read: "It is with great pride that I, Reyna, announce my graduation from the university with a Master's Degree in Business Administration (MBA). Please help me celebrate this tremendous accomplishment by joining me at my graduation party."

Over a hundred people attended. I introduced my mom to everyone, though I wished my dad could have been there with us; I knew he would have been proud of me. Manny served as the DJ for the evening, the music was great, and we danced all night.

For my graduation gift to myself, a classmate and I traveled to Isla Mujeres in Mexico. We stayed at the Zoëtry Villa Rolandi in Cancun in a Junior Suite Superior Ocean Front, which featured a private furnished terrace and a hot tub. The ocean view from our room was breathtaking. We had a relaxing weekend enjoying the beach, excellent food, exploring, and smoking cigars. It was a wonderful way to celebrate. When we arrived back home, the twins and I packed for our own celebratory mini-vacation.

For Christmas that year, we flew to Fort Lauderdale, Florida. We stayed at the Hilton Fort Lauderdale Marina, where we shopped and enjoyed fine dining and the beach. We called our family on Christmas to say "hello" and let them know we were thinking of them. It was a cold winter Christmas back in Texas. When they asked what we were doing, I told them that the three of us were lying out on the beach and enjoying the sun. We had a great weekend. During both of these trips, I found time for reflection. I was proud of myself for the accomplishment of earning not one, but two degrees. I had managed to push through despite all the adversity. My primary motivation to succeed was my babies, who were now all grown up. My hope was that they would remember the hard work, dedication, and resilience I had modeled for them. The twins supported me throughout the journey and believed in me; I was very grateful for that. I thank God for His protection, direction, and strength.

My daughter had been asking for a puppy. After our trip, I surprised her with a Chihuahua. I worked with someone who had access to Chihuahua puppies and asked what I needed to do to purchase one. This co-worker had attended my graduation party, and I hadn't realized they were also "inspecting" our home. I guessed that for them to allow us to have a Chihuahua, the house had to pass their standards. My co-worker called during the holiday break and offered us the puppy, telling me our home would be perfect for her.

Shortly after that conversation, I asked my daughter if she would go with me to campus to pick something up from my colleague. She had no idea what was happening. When we arrived, we both got out of the vehicle, and they had the puppy bundled up. My daughter was so surprised! We thanked them, and she named the puppy Shai. She immediately fell in love with him; he was so adorable. From then on, everything was all about Shai.

Soon, my daughter was telling me about all the things we needed to buy for him. We stopped at my friend's residence to pick up supplies, including food. We had everything he needed, and my princess was thrilled. We were excited to be closing out the year and beginning a new chapter of our lives. Since my breakup with Marcus in 2000, I had not been able to pay off my credit card debt. It felt more like a boomerang card than a credit card; I would get close to paying it off, but then something would happen, and I would end up making more charges.

In January of the next year, I received an opportunity to teach as an adjunct professor. This extra job would give me the opportunity to sustain household expenses and pay off the credit card. I was so nervous, as I had never facilitated a college course. I asked a colleague who had been teaching the same course for many years to become my mentor, and he agreed. I decided to attend his night class as a student during the week. Using the content I learned from him, I would then tweak the curricula to fit my style of teaching.

My classes were scheduled for Saturday mornings. Before walking into the classroom, my stomach would get into knots. Once I got on stage, though, my nerves subsided. I was assigned two classes. I facilitated the Student Development Seminar in a classroom setting, where I conducted discussions on the essentials for achieving academic success. I led students in developing career and personal goals. I also designed strategies for completing assignments—with particular attention to meeting deadlines—and communicated time management techniques. After each class, there were always a few students who would stay behind to ask me questions about the lecture or their personal goals. Facilitating became a passion for me.

I don't remember exactly when, but around this time, someone recommended that I try my hand at teaching college classes online. I applied to do just that in February 2010 for the University of Phoenix Online. I interviewed and was selected to move forward as a faculty candidate. I began pre-training in April prior to facilitating a course. Their online instructor training was intense. My first online course began in July 2010. I was assigned to facilitate Foundations of Business. Topics included the evolution of business, analysis of economic systems, global considerations, the role of business ethics, and business forms. The additional income truly helped offset my costs.

Everyone in the household was attending class, passing their courses, creating goals for after graduation, and bonding with the family. The next steps involved moving out, but none of the teenagers were ready to go home. The hectic household became the new norm. At the end of the day, we all gathered in the kitchen to chat about our days. We had a small kitchen and dining room space, but we managed. Everyone had an opportunity to share. From the day we met, I watched these teenagers grow up; their experiences had shaped their lives. Our conversations were now different. I was blessed to have been a part of their journey. Many people had personal opinions as to why I should not have all these teenagers living with me, and I would listen to them. But at the end of the day, the decision was up to me.

In the meantime, I had applied for another face-to-face adjunct instructor position. The goal was still to pay off one more credit card. It was similar to the class I already taught on Saturdays; I was hired and started immediately. The professional development course was also in a classroom setting where I assisted students in establishing successful study skills. I led the students in prioritizing individual goals and emphasized the importance of meeting deadlines and completing assignments.

One of the assignments was the VARK model. VARK is a questionnaire that, once completed, suggests the learning style that best fits the student. In some cases, there could be more than one recommended learning style. There are four main styles: visual, auditory, reading/writing, and kinesthetic. The second assignment was the True Colors personality test. When the results of these tests were totaled, a student found that he or she fell into one or more personality types. The True Colors test is based on four types of personality identified by color: Orange (spontaneous), Blue (compassionate), Green (curious), and Gold (organized).

On a weekend when the teenagers were going home to visit their families, I presented both assignments. They all hesitated to participate, but they agreed to take the tests. I explained that there is always room to improve our communication skills; the results helped us understand each other and communicate more effectively. I sensed that the tide was finally turning slowly toward a new path for them. Things were looking up for our family, and that included our extended family.

But at times, we had setbacks. I remember on a particular Thursday, I was working on several projects. I had opened a blank Microsoft Word document and was about to work on a proposal for a client when I received a call from my son. After the call ended, I began to type on the blank document. I wrote: "*Today is May 27, 2010. As I sit here at work, tears roll down my cheeks. My heart is hurting, and I can't stop the pain. God, please come and hold me. I hate these moments. I want to be the best parent, and every time my son acts up, I blame myself. I know it's wrong, but maybe he is acting out because I have been working two jobs and going to school full-time. All the same, he is still acting out. I make excuses for him, but I know that his actions are his own. He is 17 years old and he knows right from wrong. Why do the tears keep falling down my cheeks? I know that one day this sadness will pass and my tears will dry up, but for now, the tears just keep falling as I continue to type.*"

As I typed, my colleagues would ask, "What is wrong?" My response was the same for all of them: "Nothing." They knew me as a happy-go-lucky person, and the truth was, most of the time I was. But there were "those days" that all parents endure.

I resolve to believe that God strengthens, directs, and protects us. I considered it an honor to parent my twins. I thanked God every day for my breath and theirs. God continued blessing us. The tears have stopped, and my heart feels lighter. Today was my day to begin healing my heart.

CHAPTER 11

CELEBRATION

The following summer, I sensed, was a new beginning for all of us. There had been much healing within my family in the previous few months. While our personalities were different, we just made things work. I was grateful for all the love and joy in our household.

Some of the teenagers who were living with us reunited with their parents. Parents and children alike were grateful that we had opened our home to them. For my part, I believed the honor was all mine. I remember asking the remaining teenagers to move back home for the summer; I thought it was time to hit the reset button on the situation. There was complete silence in the days following my announcement, and it felt weird not having everyone around the house, but we managed.

Meanwhile, my son was struggling through another round of emotional outbursts. I knew that the three of us needed time to come together, and my mother agreed. Again, the twins decided not to spend time with their father. My son spent most of the summer at work or staying with friends, so it was just my daughter at the house. We enjoyed going to Barnes & Noble, where we could read for hours. That was our Zen; we were able to lose ourselves in a book. She also spent time with her friends. The three of us also found time to meet up with my friend, Jeff. His kids were now teenagers, and it was always nice to see them.

As the summer came to an end, I realized that the twins would be entering their senior year of high school. I had to stop and let that sink in: SENIORS!

Woohoo! They would also be turning 18 years old. We were all ready for the next chapter of our lives.

As nice as that was, I also realized something else—the senior year traditions, and there would be two of everything: prom, senior portraits, class rings, birthday celebrations, yearbooks, graduation parties, and a graduation ceremony. I was so excited to plan all of their events.

As these milestones approached, the twins sat me down to have a "straight talk" conversation. They made two requests during the exchange: no large birthday party or graduation party. They wanted their celebrations to be intimate, including only their grandmother, their cousin, and the three of us. No one else. The rest of the family could join us for the graduation ceremony.

It felt like they had popped all my balloons. It was a hard pill to swallow. I wanted to shout their achievement from the rooftop, screaming, "WE DID IT! The three of us survived!"

But that is not how they saw it. I had to respect their wishes. After our conversation, I walked outside to take a few deep breaths, trying to wrap my head around what had just happened. My neighbor was outside, and we struck up a conversation. Naturally, I told him about the talk I just had with the twins.

After he listened to me explain, he replied, "You should be very proud of them. They are humble and don't need a large party to prove their accomplishments. They have nothing to prove to anyone. What they are saying is, 'Thank you. The most important people in our lives will be there celebrating our birthday and graduation.'"

I realized that he was right. I cried, then thanked him for his kind words. I walked back inside and hugged my babies.

Soon after that, the school year began. Of the ten "additions" to our family, only three of the boys returned for the school year. Everyone else stayed home with their families.

My daughter, once again, had a full schedule during the week as well as the weekends; she was part of an academic club that competed on weekends. My son worked almost every weekend, and the remaining boys either stayed with us on weekends or went back home.

After a couple of months of the same routine, I remember my daughter calling me while I was working one day. She mentioned that the boys were disrespecting my son, specifically telling me she had overheard them talking behind his back. So, she confronted them. She explained that her brother had opened their home to them, yet they were talking behind his back. She told them she didn't think that was cool and that she was going to tell her mom about it.

That evening, my daughter had more to say about what had happened. Afterward, I had a heart-to-heart talk with my son. I explained to him that their time in the house had ended; I told him I would not put up with them disrespecting him. I reminded him that we opened our doors because he wanted to help them, but regardless, I would not tolerate disrespect—not on my watch.

The next day, I had an individual conversation with each of the boys. At the end of each session, I informed them that they had one week to leave. Over the next couple of days, they moved out—apologizing for their behavior and thanking us for all we had done for them.

Around that time, my nephew graduated from high school and came to stay with us. We introduced him to Straight Talk. My mom also came to stay, and it was nice having them live with us. My son and nephew behaved more like brothers than cousins; they were inseparable and always out and about. My nephew was like a son to me—I called him "Mijo!"

It was always great to have my mom with us; she was our rock. While staying with us, she continued to encourage me to get massages. She was also concerned that I was working too many hours, but I loved what I did. It didn't feel like work to me because I had a passion for it. Also, I was still teaching at that time. My mom never held back what she was feeling, and I appreciated her honesty. Our moments together were priceless; I especially enjoyed when she hugged me and caressed my hair.

I had been dating on and off during that time, but when my mom came to live with us, I stopped. I wanted to spend every extra moment I had with my best friend.

We went back home to celebrate Mom's birthday with the family, and when the weekend was over, she came back with us. It turned out that she also needed a break from the family. We all loved going to the movie theater and going out to eat. It was nice waking up on weekends and having time to spend with everyone. The five of us celebrated the twins' 18th birthday at Osaka Steak & Sushi. Having Mom and my nephew there was perfect. The twins were right; we didn't need everyone else to celebrate occasions like this. We drove back home for Thanksgiving, and the twins drove to their father's to spend time with their family. My mom came back home with us afterward; we always loved having her stay.

In December of that year, in honor of Dad, I decided to donate my hair to Locks of Love. They are a nonprofit organization that provides custom-made hairpieces to people who have suffered hair loss due to medical conditions. At my previous job, there was a hairstylist my colleagues raved about. I asked about her, and someone passed along her phone number. I had kept her as a contact for many years. I decided to call Debra to schedule an appointment. Debra's salon was a home-based business; she had converted her garage into a salon.

When I called her, I mentioned that I wanted a transformation and that if anyone could pull it off, it was her. I had seen what she had done for others in the past. My hair was jet black and waist-length. The first thing she did at my appointment was braid my hair from the neck down to my waist. Then, she took a pair of scissors and asked if I was sure that I wanted to cut it.

I replied, "*Yes, let's do it.*"

She then cut and handed the braid to me. It was hard for me to believe that had just happened. Debra refused to let me peek in the mirror until she was finished. My long hair was now a very short shag style; my jet-black hair had morphed into three shades of blonde highlights. When I looked in the mirror, I was floored. I didn't recognize myself! However, I loved the new me. Debra had a beautiful gift for transforming people's hair.

During the holiday break, I received a letter from the high school. I learned that my son had been skipping school, and I had no idea. I realized that the only recent appointments he had been attending were his orthodontist visits. After his appointments, he had been coming back home, skipping the rest of the school day. Naturally, I was furious.

After the holiday break, we went to the school to talk to the staff. I asked what he could do to make up for the unexcused absences, as there were many to be addressed. I then discovered that the orthodontist's office had written him several excuses, but he hadn't submitted a single note to the attendance office personnel. During the meeting, my son reached into his backpack and produced the notes. With notes in hand, the staff member spoke to the principal, who accepted each one of the excuses. We were so thankful. What a scare! After all, only a certain number of absences per year were allowed, and my son was close to exceeding the limit. From that day forward, I felt obligated to call the attendance office after every dental appointment to confirm he had submitted his excuse slip. To their credit, they were very kind and understanding with me.

The next few months went by quickly. We prepared to commemorate the twins' amazing accomplishment, and all the graduation invitations were mailed to the family. The majority of our relatives informed us that they would be attending the two graduations and celebrations on two different days.

A few days before my daughter's graduation, her father was arrested for non-payment of child support. His family contacted me and asked if I could drop the charges so he could attend the graduations. I contacted the Office of the Attorney General, and the agent informed me that his arrest had nothing to do with my case; the non-payment was for another case on file. I contacted his mother and let her know what I had learned. The twins were extremely upset and disappointed that their father would not be able to attend their graduation ceremonies.

The five of us went to dinner before their graduation. I left work early to set up their table at the restaurant with balloons, gifts, and a cake. They didn't want a large celebration, but I would not deny myself the opportunity to express my joy and pride. Each of them selected a nice restaurant: my daughter chose an Italian restaurant, and my son chose a Japanese steakhouse.

When we walked into the Italian restaurant, my daughter pointed at the table I had set up and said, "I bet that's where we're sitting." My son knew exactly which table was ours. We all laughed and walked over. For their graduation gifts, my princess asked for a skydiving outing, and my prince asked for money.

We celebrated my daughter's graduation first. Before she graduated, she earned certifications in Microsoft Office PowerPoint, Excel, and Word. My son's graduation happened a few days later. The graduation ceremonies were emotional. As a family, we were full of excitement, joy, love, laughter, and pride. They looked so beautiful in their caps and gowns; they were all grown up.

My young adults were about to embark on adulthood. I remember them grinning in front of the mirror as they put on their caps and gowns. Of course, I became emotional. Most of our family attended the graduations: both grandmas, aunts, uncles, cousins, and friends. We cheered so loudly when their names were called. After each ceremony, I felt as if a huge weight had been lifted from my shoulders. The responsibility of a parent to see them through this journey was tough, but I did it; I now found myself the mother of two high school graduates.

I had also embarked on a new journey: I started my pursuit of a second graduate degree in Information Technology Management.

From infants to young adults, I had learned that parenting was no walk in the park. Our journey had been colorful (thrilling) and gray (uncertain). Our "roller coaster" had many elevated railways, steep inclines, and steep descents that carried us through sharp twists and turns. All of the twisting and turning had shaped us, and God was our hope and anchor.

I was grateful and thankful for the emotional support of my parents, family, and friends.

IF YOU TURN THE PAGE...

CHAPTER 12

FORGIVENESS

It is September 5, 2022.
This is my "Testimony to Forgiveness."

For many years, these are the questions I asked myself: "Why forgive him? Why is it important? What did I do to deserve such torment? How do you forgive someone who verbally and physically abused you? The observers can't unsee or unhear what they witnessed."

I'll never understand why the twins' father verbally and physically abused me. I didn't want to continue to be angry or have that anger affect my future relationships. Forgiving him was for myself. In order for me to heal, I needed to forgive. I didn't have to face him; I just needed to say the words out loud and accept that it was okay to be angry when I did. This is what I said out loud to myself:

"Time truly heals. I'm a testament to that. You were the person I loved and cared for from the depth of my soul. You were the someone I thought I might grow old with. You were my first love. I was the person who believed so much in us. My life hasn't been a walk in the park. I pushed through the fear, exhaustion, anxiety, procrastination, and sadness."

And, I finally said the words, "I forgive you." I had been repeating those words for years, but one day, I actually just let go.

I never spoke to the twins about it when it happened. But one day, now that they were old enough, I asked the twins to sit at the table for a "Straight Talk." I let them know that I truly forgave their father for everything.

After our conversation, I called their father. I said, "Hey, I'm calling to say that I forgive you." No other words came out of my mouth. He thanked me. After our call, I felt better. There was a release of all the emotions I had held for many years. However, a few days later, I felt a lingering unforgiveness in my heart. I thought, "Did I really forgive him? Nope."

He still owed a large amount of child support. I realized that if I truly wanted to break all ties and connections, I would have to forgive his debt, too. So, I had another conversation with the twins. I let them know that I had truly forgiven their father. I explained to them that there was a child support debt their father was required to pay by the Office of the Attorney General. I then told them that true forgiveness, in my case, meant releasing him from his debt. I told them that for me to have peace, I needed to forgive that debt.

How did I completely cut the severed rope that held us together? Well, I walked outside to call their father. I told him that I would be scheduling an appointment with the Office of the Attorney General to release him from his debt. He was shocked. He thanked me again.

On June 28, 2016, his debt was forgiven. It took two weeks to get it done. For me, no matter what anyone else thinks, it was never about the money. I did what was right for me. My goal was to create a lasting relationship between their father and the twins. As I write this, I can report that they have a good relationship.

Scriptures to Consider

"Daughter, your faith has saved you.
Go in peace and be healed of your affliction."
— Mark 5:34

"For I know the plans I have for you," declares the Lord,
"plans to prosper you and not to harm you,
plans to give you hope and a future."
— Jeremiah 29:11

"Our Father, who art in heaven, hallowed be thy name;
thy kingdom come; thy will be done on earth as it is in heaven.
Give us this day our daily bread; and forgive us our trespasses
as we forgive those who trespass against us; and lead us not into
temptation, but deliver us from evil. Amen."
— Matthew 6:9-13

"Then Peter came to Jesus and asked, 'Lord, how many times shall I forgive my brother or sister who sins against me? Up to seven times?' Jesus answered, 'I tell you, not seven times, but seventy-seven times.'"

— Matthew 18:21–22

"For if you forgive men their trespasses, your heavenly Father will also forgive you. But if you do not forgive men their trespasses, neither will your Father forgive yours."

— Matthew 6:14–15

"Be kind to one another, tenderhearted, forgiving one another, as God in Christ forgave you."

— Ephesians 4:32

Matthew's Testimony to Forgiveness (June 24, 2021)

"In May 2011, I was arrested because a warrant was issued for non-payment of child support. I served a year and a half in jail. I was an angry man. No one was above me. If you challenged me, I would fight back until you lost. At that time, I learned from a cellmate that my anger came from not being able to forgive myself. It took me six months, and with God's help, I forgave myself. My faith came back and I loved God again. I wrote letters to Reyna, my family, and friends asking for forgiveness. Also, I forgave them. I love you, Reyna, and always will."

REFERENCES

Mark 5:34 (NIV). Biblica, Inc., 2011. Bible Gateway.

Jeremiah 29:11 (NIV). Biblica, Inc., 2011. Bible Gateway.

Matthew 6:9-13 (NMB). Magnusson, R. D., 2016. Bible Gateway.

Matthew 6:14-15 (NKJV). Thomas Nelson, 1982. Bible Gateway.

Matthew 18:21-22 (NIV). Biblica, Inc., 2011. Bible Gateway.

Ephesians 4:32 (NRSVA). National Council of Churches, 1995. Bible Gateway.

THANK YOU

Thank you for the support and for walking this journey with me through these pages. As you close this book, please remember that you are God's masterpiece; you have the strength to persevere, the grace to trust the process, and the courage to embrace the new beginning that awaits you.

ABOUT THE AUTHOR

Raquel Perez has over 15 years of higher education experience, delivering innovative, high-quality, operational planning solutions across large organizations.

She holds two Master's degrees: Masters in Information Technology Management from Webster University, as well as a Master of Business Administration and a BBA in Management from the University of Incarnate Word.

Ms. Perez has been a facilitator at both the Community College and University level for over 18 years. Her strong commitment to uplifting others includes her community service as a Catechist Teacher, Youth Ministry advisor, Eucharistic Minister, and Hospice volunteer.

LET'S CONNECT

If you'd like to reach out with questions or to request copies in bulk for a group, please contact me at the email address below:

Raquel.Perez.Author@gmail.com

www.ingramcontent.com/pod-product-compliance
Lightning Source LLC
LaVergne TN
LVHW010611100826
845148LV00014B/2920
9798234019820